Going Solo - America's Best-Kept Retirement Secret for the Self-Employed

Going Solo - America's <u>Best-Kept</u> Retirement Secret for the Self-Employed

WHAT FINANCIAL INSTITUTIONS WON'T TELL YOU ABOUT SAVING FOR RETIREMENT

Adam Bergman, Esq.

ISBN: 1511614285
ISBN 13: 9781511614283
Library of Congress Control Number: 2015905508
CreateSpace Independent Publishing Platform
North Charleston, South Carolina
Cover Image Credit/Copyright Attribution: "Zurijeta/Shutterstock"

Table of Contents

Introduction

What Financial Institutions Won't Tell You about Saving for Retirement

THIS BOOK CAN MEAN THE difference between retiring rich and working for the rest of your life. Specifically, it is about saving for retirement using a type of retirement savings account called the Self-Employed 401(k), also known as the Solo 401(k) or Individual 401(k). This type of account was created by the Internal Revenue Service (IRS) to help:

(1) Self-employed people
(2) People who actively generate some portion of their total income through self-employment activities
(3) Small business owners with no full-time employees other than themselves and their spouses

If you fit into one of these three categories, then you should read this book. Why? The Solo 401(k) gives you significant advantages over a traditional IRA, SEP-IRA, and SIMPLE IRA. Compared to other retirement plans, the Solo 401(k) allows you to *save a lot more money* for retirement, it is *easy and cheap to administer*, and it provides you with a lot *more options and flexibility* for growing and leveraging your retirement savings, including the ability to invest in real estate and borrow money tax- and penalty-free.

It's difficult to determine exactly how many people in America qualify for the Solo 401(k). The Bureau of Labor Statistics states that there were around 14.4 million self-employed as of January 2014. But then there are also a lot of people who are partially self-employed yet fall in the category of working for a company or organization because they essentially have a "day job." The Freelancers Union claims that there are 42 million independent workers in the United States, or around a third of the overall workforce. The Census Bureau counts 20 million nonemployer businesses.[1]

Regardless, the percentage of our workforce who are small business owners, self-employed, or partially self-employed is significant and is growing as forces such as the Affordable Care Act make working independently more possible. For example, the number of self-employed workers surged by 370,000 in May 2015, according to the U.S. Labor Department's survey of households released Friday, June 5, 2015, and nearly one million workers have gone to work for themselves since just February 2015.[2] For people who fit this bill or think they might with a career change, the Solo 401(k) is the best retirement wealth-building tool available, and this book will show you why!

So Why Don't You Know about the Solo 401(k)?

This is a good question. If you haven't heard of the Solo 401(k) before or you don't know very much about it, you are not alone. Most people haven't, even though the option has been available since the 401(k) was created. In fact, many sophisticated and well-educated investors, including many tax attorneys and CPAs, are not familiar with the advantages of the Solo 401(k) and therefore overlook it as a superior means of growing and leveraging retirement savings. Those experts are often unaware that retirement assets can be invested outside of traditional financial markets, including in real estate, precious metals, and foreign currency, and via loans.

---

1 Justin Fox. "Where Are All the Self-Employed Workers, February 7, 2014. http://blogs.hbr.org/2014/02/where-are-all-the-self-employed-workers/

2 Steve Matthews. "The Do-It-Yourself Economy Just Hired 1 Million American Entrepreneurs, June 5, 2015. http://www.bloomberg.com/news/articles/2015-06-05/the-do-it-yourself-economy-just-hired-1-million-american-entrepreneurs

Are you surprised? I have a law degree and a master's degree in taxation, and have worked at several of the largest law firms in the world, and I only learned about these alternative investment options through research for a client. When I began to talk to colleagues about the features of a Solo 401(k), I discovered I was not alone in my ignorance. A prestigious tax lawyer and graduate of Yale Law School I worked with a few years ago, for instance, was incredulous when I told him about the Solo 401(k)'s full range of advantages. I showed him the language in the Internal Revenue Code (IRC) and the IRS publications that support it, and he was astonished to realize it was all true.

I advise tens of thousands of retirement account holders. A very significant percentage of them are eligible to adopt a Solo 401(k). When I tell them about its advantages, the most frequent questions I get are: Is this legal, and why haven't I heard about it before?

It is legal. The IRS created it and wrote it in the IRC, and the US Congress signed it into law. No worries there. But it is less widely known or understood for several interesting reasons.

The first reason lies in the name itself. The Solo 401(k) is not a term of art. In other words, it is not named as such in the IRC. A lot of tax professionals and others use the term "Solo 401(k)," and that is the name I like, but the Solo 401(k) is also occasionally known as an "Individual 401(k)," a "Self-Employed 401(k)," a "One-Participant 401(k)," a "Self-Directed 401(k)," or a "Uni 401(k)." Perhaps this creates a little confusion and uncertainty. Second, and more importantly, you may not have heard of the Solo 401(k) because of the way financial institutions that manage retirement savings accounts make their money.

There are around forty-seven million IRAs in this country. As of 2016, there are believed to be approximately fifty million people participating in 401(k) plans. The financial sector manages many trillions of dollars in retirement assets. That sector has no incentive to encourage you to manage your own retirement plan. Financial institutions like Vanguard, Schwab, Bank of America, and other major businesses make their money by holding your money and investing it in their financial products and services. They will offer you a Solo 401(k) plan for free. The only catch is that their version of the Solo 401(k) plan will restrict you to investment options that they, as your plan sponsor, already offer.

Typically, these include stocks, mutual funds, ETFs, money market accounts, and other financial instruments. Major financial institutions generally do not allow you to invest in real estate, foreign currency, precious metals, or other alternate assets, or to use your plan to make loans or even to make after-tax or Roth contributions to your plan. There's nothing nefarious about this. Financial institutions make money by selling you financial products. They do not make money when you invest in products they do not sell, such as real estate, or when you take money out of your account as a loan. Accordingly, they build their Solo 401(k) plans so that you can only do what profits them.

This can be great if you want someone to make your retirement investment decisions for you. But more and more people are questioning that wisdom. The year 2008 was a watershed year because so many lost money during the financial crisis. Indeed, it is believed that most retirees lost almost 40 percent of their retirement assets in under a year, and it has taken almost seven years to rebuild their accounts to where they were pre-2008 financial crisis. If you were about to retire in 2008, your lifestyle and plans took a serious hit. If you had years to go before retirement, it has probably taken you years to recover financially to the level of wealth you had prior to the crisis.

If there was a silver lining in that experience, it was the fact that more people are motivated now to be more active with their retirement assets. The people I work with often want to diversify their assets because they believe that leaving them in one form of investment such as stocks is too risky and not prudent. They also want to rely on their own expertise to grow their wealth in ways they understand. Many of them know more, for instance, about local real estate markets than they do about the senior management teams of global companies. So they want to invest some of their money in properties they understand and can manage rather than in stocks or funds they don't know much about or can only passively monitor. I can't blame them. Recently, I read an article that acknowledged that mutual funds, run by some of the most respected money managers in the world, perform no better than randomly chosen stocks.[3]

Knowing Your Options

There are different types of Solo 401(k) plans for all types of retirement planning and investment goals. These range from the free Solo 401(k) plans you get from a financial institution like Schwab, to custodian-directed Solo 401(k) plans that allow you to buy real estate and make other nontraditional investments through a custodian, to open-architecture self-directed Solo 401(k) plans that give you "checkbook control" and allow you to make your own investment decisions as the trustee of the plan through a local bank account. This book will help you understand which type of plan is best for you. If you are interested in more flexibility, independence, and control, it will show you how to do it all yourself.

Specifically, you will learn:

- Why the Solo 401(k) is the best-kept retirement secret in America, and how it differs from other retirement plans
- Whether you are eligible to participate in a Solo 401(k) plan
- How to adopt a Solo 401(k) plan
- What you can and can't do with your Solo 401(k)
- How you can make your own investments and leverage your assets to actively grow your retirement wealth and support your life and business goals

Grow Your Retirement Wealth!

The most important message of this book is also the most basic, but it's one that's worth closing this introduction with. As a self-employed person or

3 Jeff Sommer. Heads or Tails? Either Way, You Might Beat a Stock Picker. http://www.nytimes.com/2014/07/27/your-money/heads-or-tails-either-way-you-might-beat-a-stock-picker.html (July 26, 2014)

small business owner, you are swimming against the tide in the retirement savings world. Not only do you lack the support and matching contributions of an employer, but you also probably have investment and capital needs that an employed person does not worry about. In other words, it requires initiative on your part to start saving for your own retirement, even as the money you are putting away has a lot of competition in the form of other pressing financial needs. Saving for retirement as a self-employed individual or small business owner is critical if you are going to enjoy the benefits and fruits of a lifetime of hard work and intelligent decisions.

The good news—and it's very good news indeed—is that saving for retirement as a self-employed person or small business owner does not have to be painful or difficult. This book will show you how easy and rewarding it can be. In fact, the game is actually fixed in your favor if you take advantage of the Solo 401(k). You can save more money. You can do more with that money than you can with other retirement savings plans and apply more of your own expertise to the decisions you make. And you can even leverage that money, while still growing your retirement wealth, in ways that support your financial and business goals.

I'll show you how in this book. You just have to get started and stay committed to becoming a millionaire when you retire. Starting earlier is better. If you save just $10 a day through a Solo 401(k) plan starting when you are thirty-five years old and continue until you retire, and if you average an 8.5 percent return on your investment through that thirty-five year period, you will build up over $700,000 by the time you stop working. If you save $652 a month, or my current car payment with a latte a day thrown in, you will grow over $1.5 million dollars for retirement.

And if you don't, you can retire poor and find yourself completely reliant on your nonretirement savings and social assistance. Both paths are easy. One is a lot more appealing upon arrival.

Your Solo 401(k) may not even be your only retirement tool. But it can and should be a big part of your approach to building your retirement wealth. It's easy to get started. It's painless to do. And the power of financial freedom is within your grasp.

Let's get started.

CHAPTER 1

America's Best-Kept Retirement Secret

THE REAL SECRET IS THAT you can retire rich. And it's not that hard.

You've probably heard it said before, but if you put away a little money every year, you can end up with a financial future in retirement that is not just secure and comfortable but actually bountiful and exciting. You'll have the freedom to do things you've always wanted to do. Travel. Own a second home. Enjoy your hobby to the fullest. Indulge your grandchildren. Help pay for their education. Invest in an exciting idea. Loan money to a friend who needs it. Support a charity.

You can live in a manner that's meaningful to you.

It's within your grasp and power. It's not rocket science and it won't absorb or divert all of your energy and attention from what you do now. It just takes some knowledge and guidance, a few important decisions, and a little effort. A few dollars a day can generate a nest egg of close to a million dollars when you retire.

So Many Advantages

Before we dive into the intricacies of the Solo 401(k) plan, I want to highlight its primary advantages. This will help us stay focused on what is most important. You are reading this book because you want to understand what a Solo 401(k) plan can do for you—right now, over the course of your working life, when you retire, and even after you have passed on.

A Solo 401(k) is perfect for sole proprietors, small business owners, and independent contractors such as consultants. It is unique and very popular because it was designed by Congress and the IRS explicitly for small owner-only businesses—basically, any business with no employees other than the owner(s). That business can be established as a sole proprietorship, LLC, corporation, or partnership.

I've listed below some of the most important advantages. Don't worry if these terms and the others I am about to use are not completely familiar to you. I will explain them simply and fully in the chapters to come.

High Contribution Limits

While an IRA only allows a $5,500 contribution limit (with a $1,000 additional "catch-up" contribution for those over age fifty), the Solo 401(k) annual contribution limit is $54,000 for 2017, with an additional $6,000 catch-up contribution for those over fifty. In addition, if your spouse generates compensation from the business, he or she can also make high contributions to the plan.

Under the 2017 Solo 401(k) contribution rules, a plan participant under the age of fifty can make a maximum employee deferral contribution in the amount of $18,000. That amount can be made pretax, after-tax, or Roth. On the profit-sharing side, the business can make a 25 percent (20 percent in the case of a sole proprietorship or single-member LLC) profit-sharing contribution up to a combined maximum, including the employee deferral, of $54,000, an increase of $1,000 from 2017.

For plan participants over the age of fifty, an individual can make a maximum employee deferral contribution in the amount of $24,000. That amount can be made pretax, after-tax, or Roth. On the profit-sharing side, the business can make a 25 percent (20 percent in the case of a sole proprietorship or single-member LLC) profit-sharing contribution up to a combined maximum, including the employee deferral, of $60,000 for 2017.

A World of Investment Opportunities

Depending on the type of Solo 401(k) plan your business adopts, you could have the option to invest in almost any type of investment opportunity that you discover, including real estate (rentals, foreclosures, raw land, and tax liens), private businesses, precious metals, hard money, and peer-to-peer lending, as well as stock and mutual funds. Your only limit is your imagination. The income and gains from these investments will flow back into your Solo 401(k) plan without tax. Making an investment with your Solo 401(k) plan is as simple as writing a check. As trustee of the Solo 401(k) plan, you will have total control over your retirement assets to make real estate and other investments tax-free and without custodian consent.

Loan Feature

While an IRA offers no participant loan feature, if the Solo 401(k) plan your business adopts includes a loan option, then that Solo 401(k) allows participants to borrow up to $50,000 or 50 percent of their account value (whichever is less) for any purpose at a low interest rate (the lowest interest rate is Prime, which was 3.75 percent as of December 31, 2016). This offers a Solo 401(k) plan participant the ability to access up to $50,000 for use for any purpose, including paying personal debt or funding a business.

The Flexibility to Self-Direct Your Retirement Funds

With a Solo 401(k) plan, you can serve as trustee of the plan, giving you "checkbook control" over its funds. To this end, making an investment with your Solo 401(k) plan is as easy as writing a check. Another significant benefit of the Solo 401(k) plan is that it does not require the participant to hire a bank or trust company to serve as trustee. This flexibility allows the participant to serve in the trustee role. This means that all assets of the 401(k) trust are under the sole authority of the Solo 401(k) participant. A Solo 401(k) plan allows you to eliminate the expense and delays associated with an IRA custodian, enabling you to act quickly when the right investment opportunity presents itself. Also, because the

Solo 401(k) plan trust account can be opened at any local bank or credit union (Chase, Wells Fargo, or Citibank, for example), you will not be required to pay custodian fees for the account as you would in the case of an IRA.

Flexible Contribution Options

Contributions to a Solo 401(k) plan are completely discretionary. You always have the option to try to contribute as much as legally possible, but you also have the option of reducing or even suspending plan contributions if necessary. In other words, you have the ability to make contributions to your Solo 401(k) plan (up to an aggregate amount of $54,000 for 2017 if you are under the age of fifty), but you are not required to do so.

Roth-Type Contributions

With IRAs, those who earn high incomes are disallowed from contributing to a Roth IRA or converting their IRA to a Roth IRA. Depending on the type of Solo 401(k) plan your business adopts, your plan could contain a built-in Roth subaccount, which can be contributed to without any income restrictions. With a Roth Solo 401(k) subaccount, you can make Roth-type contributions and generate tax-free income and gains while having the ability to make significantly greater contributions than with a Roth IRA: up to $54,000 or $60,000 if over the age of fifty for 2017.

After-Tax Contributions

Generally, when an individual is over the age of 50, he or she is able to make employee deferrals in a pre-tax fund or Roth of up to $18,000 or $24,000. A profit sharing contribution can be made in pre-tax funds in the amount equal to 25% of compensation (20% in case of self-employment or a single member LLC), and both contributions cannot exceed $54,000 or $60,000 in the aggregate for 2017. An after-tax deferral, (neither Roth or pre-tax), is also an option that will allow a plan participant to make plan contributions up to $54,000 or $60,000 for 2017. For example, if a 40-year-old self-employed individual earns $100,000 in 2017, he or she would be able to make a maximum employee deferral contribution of $18,000 in pre-tax funds or Roth and make an after-tax contribution dollar-for dollar equal to $36,000. This is the difference between $54,000 (the maximum annual 401(k) contribution for 2017) and $18,000, the maximum employee deferral contributions limit. Those contributions can then be converted to a Roth. Whereas, if the individual made a profit sharing contribution versus an after-tax contribution, the employer profit sharing contribution would be limited to $20,000 ($100,000 multiplied by 20%) instead of a $36,000 after-tax contribution that can be converted to Roth. The employer profit sharing contribution would be made in pre-tax dollars providing the plan participant's business with a tax deduction, but the contribution amount would be less than an after-tax contribution. In other words, the advantage of making after-tax contributions versus a profit sharing contribution is that you can make a dollar for dollar contribution as opposed to a profit sharing contribution, which is based off a percentage of your compensation (20% or 25%). The reason for this is that after-tax contributions are not elective deferrals and therefore are not subject to the annual IRC Section 402(g) maximum deferral limit ($18,000 for 2017). However, they are subject to the annual IRC Section 415 limit ($54,000 for 2017; $60,000 for individuals age 50 or older eligible to make catch-up contributions of $6,000 for 2017). I will be discussing the differences between after-tax and Roth Solo 401(k) plan contributions in greater detail throughout the book.

Cost-Effective Administration

In general, the Solo 401(k) plan is easy to operate. There is generally no annual filing requirement unless your plan exceeds $250,000 in assets, in which case you will need to file a short information return with the IRS (Form 5500-EZ).

Offset the Cost of Your Plan with a Tax Deduction
By paying for your Solo 401(k) with business funds, you are eligible to claim a deduction for the cost of the plan, including annual maintenance fees. The deduction for the cost associated with the Solo 401(k) plan and ongoing maintenance will help reduce your business's income tax liability, which will in turn offset the cost of adopting a self-directed Solo 401(k) plan. The retirement tax professionals at the IRA Financial Group will help you take advantage of the available business tax deduction for adopting a Solo 401(k) plan.

No Tax on Nonrecourse Leverage for Real Estate Acquisition
When an IRA buys real estate that is leveraged with mortgage financing, it creates Unrelated Debt Financed Income (UDFI), a type of Unrelated Business Taxable Income (also known as UBTI, or UBIT) on which taxes must be paid. The UBTI tax is approximately 40 percent for 2016. But with a Solo 401(k) plan, you can use leverage without being subject to the UDFI rules and UBTI tax. This exemption provides significant tax advantages for using a Solo 401(k) plan versus an IRA to purchase real estate.

Retirement Saving Consolidation through Rollovers
A Solo 401(k) plan can accept rollovers of funds from another retirement savings vehicle, such as an IRA, a SEP, or a previous employer's 401(k) plan. Thus, you can directly roll over your IRA or qualified plan funds to your new 401(k) plan for investment or loan purposes. Note that only Roth IRA funds cannot be rolled into a Solo 401(k) plan.

Picture of Prosperity

So what's stopping you? Maybe you are self-employed and don't feel you have retirement options. If so, I think there's a strong chance, based on my experience working with thousands of people as a tax attorney and retirement savings account expert, that you may not know about or be aware of some of your best options for saving for retirement. This is not because you have made a mistake or committed an oversight, but because you are not a perfect match for the approach to building retirement savings that most adopt by default.

Here are some people that come to mind:

- A thirty-five-year-old contractor about to get married to a woman with two young children
- A doctor who works at a group practice but earns extra income interpreting lab results and injury claims for a business that his wife runs
- A widowed mother of two employed as a sports-league administrator who also makes a surprising amount of money selling crafts on eBay and Etsy
- A laid-off engineer turned real estate agent who keeps an eye open for foreclosed properties he can buy, refurbish, and rent
- An executive who has decided to step out of the corporate grind to leverage his experience and know-how as a life coach, while taking time to travel with his wife and still finance his grandkids' educations

When it comes to their work and interests, I have found that many Americans lead lives that are more creative, fascinating, and "outside the norm" than they probably realize. In my work, I meet people from every imaginable occupation: physicians and consultants, fashion photographers and engineers, corporate vice presidents and small business owners. Not only are these people absorbed in challenging jobs that keep them incredibly busy and take a lot of ingenuity to succeed in, but they also tend to be deeply involved in other areas of interest. They have hobbies that are more like second careers, or they own property, pool resources with friends and business partners, write books, build websites, tinker with ideas, or have investments that require a fair bit of attention. Along the way, they are trying to enjoy life and also save for the years when they will no longer want to or be able to work.

The people I have written this book for work very hard. They have been incredibly resilient in overcoming the challenges of a troubled economy and the stresses of an uncertain future. They are diligent about making good financial decisions: saving as much as possible, keeping expenses under control, minimizing debt, and putting money toward their mortgages, their children's college funds, and the charities that are meaningful to them. And they all feel that the "system" they live and work within does not quite fit or support their needs and dreams.

What do I mean by this? The people I am talking about may be dedicated to the company they are employed by or the field they work in, but they know that any security in a company or an industry is a thing of the past, and they are vigilant about considering options to maintain their lifestyle or simply survive if something goes wrong. Likewise, they are completely devoted to their country, and they understand the need and rationale for social security, some form of health-care system, and a basic level of taxation, but they have a sense that this cumbersome infrastructure supports other people in different circumstances better than themselves.

Finally, these people are also characterized by having made their own way in life in a manner that their parents probably never needed to. Their careers have not been marked by straight lines and clear paths. Though they may think of themselves as doctors, lawyers, business people, or teachers, these roles are not as cut-and-dry or as permanent as they used to be. To get where they are now, the people I work with have had to figure it out along the way, sometimes ending up in careers or work situations they never expected. Their big financial decisions have also been very complex and uncertain. There's no long-term security in just buying a house and gradually paying off a mortgage anymore; and other life expenses like college education can be an incredible burden. This leaves many people with a sense that they can't take chances or seize opportunities as much as they would like to.

Most of all, the people I am writing for have no faith that once they retire, their pensions and social security will adequately meet their needs. Nor are they sure that they will be able to save enough on their own to make up the difference.

While this can sound like a litany of complaints, the people I am talking about are not complainers. They have enjoyed the independence and creativity of a life without a predetermined career path. They appreciate the great opportunities that come with the challenges of our complex world. And they are optimistic, in spite of a near ten-year stretch of economic difficulty, that the future is bright. Indeed, they are excited about the things they will be able to do and enjoy for years to come, and believe they will somehow figure out a way to make it all work financially.

What they lack, I find, is a concrete and detailed understanding of how to make that happen. They know that there are tools available to them to save the money they are earning now for retirement later. They follow the rules and guidance that has been laid out for them, but they don't understand the big picture or the finer nuances as well as they would like. They have a sense that they are missing some vehicle or method for doing it better—a smarter way to accelerate their success and leverage all their hard work and accomplishments.

They are right.

How Much Have Americans Saved for Retirement?

Not enough, according to the best sources. According to Fidelity, the average 401(k) plan balance reached a new high of $91,300 in 2014 – up more than 30% from $69,100 in 2011, but insufficient to guarantee a work-free retirement. In addition, in 2011 the *Wall Street Journal* (*WSJ*)[4] said that the median household headed by a person age sixty to sixty-two has less

4 E.S. Browning. "Retiring Boomers Find 401(k) Plans Fall Short", Wall Street Journal, February 19, 2011.

than one quarter of what he or she needs to maintain a standard of living in retirement.

Furthermore, the *WSJ*, using data from the Center for Retirement Research at Boston College, calculated that such households had a median household income of $87,700 in 2009. If people need 85 percent of their income for retirement, this means they need to have $74,545 a year. Experts estimate that social security provides as much as 40 percent of preretirement income, or $35,080 per year. That leaves a gap of $39,465, and most 401(k) plans don't come close to making that up. According to the article, only 8 percent of households have the $636,673 in their 401(k) plans needed to generate that amount. Some families do have other sources of income, but you get the point.

Social security plans for solvency for the next seventy-five years, but according to the *New York Times*[5], it is currently solvent only until 2033 because of demographic pressures and the weak economy. And without reforms, it will pay only about 75 percent of promised benefits. Meanwhile, the nation is experiencing a retirement crisis. Less than half of households ages fifty-five to sixty-four have retirement savings, and of those, half have less than $120,000. Most retirees will be heavily reliant on social security, which currently pays on average $1,265 a month.

The majority of retirees with annual incomes up to $32,600 get two-thirds to all of their income from social security. Even at higher incomes (up to $57,960), social security is the single biggest source of retirement income, accounting for almost half. Only the top fifth of seniors, with incomes above $57,960, do not rely on social security as their largest source of income, and most of them are still working.

So what does all this tell us? Americans need to do a better job in proactively saving for retirement. The IRS has given us the tools. It's my hope that this book will show how easily the Solo 401(k) can be used to help secure a more financially stable retirement for the self-employed.

---

5 New York Times Editorial Board, "Social Security, Present and Future", New York Times, March 30, 2013

Beyond the IRA and 401(k)

Everyone has heard of a Traditional IRA (or Individual Retirement Account). This is the basic way that many Americans put aside a few thousand dollars of tax-deferred or after-tax income every year for their retirement. Many are also familiar with other variations of the IRA, such as the Roth IRA, SEP-IRA, SIMPLE IRA, Self-Directed IRA, and Rollover IRA. Don't worry if these terms and the others I am about to use are not completely familiar to you or if you are, like most people, somewhat hazy on the differences—I will explain them simply and fully in the chapters to come.

Similarly, most of us have signed up for a 401(k) plan at some point in our working years. This retirement savings vehicle is available to employees of companies that offer such a plan. The employee's contribution to their 401(k) amounts to some percentage of their total compensation and generally is deducted directly from their paycheck. That money is tax deferred or could be after-tax in some cases and is often matched by the employer, typically at a 3 percent rate in order to take advantage of the Safe Harbor 401(k) plan ERISA (Employee Retirement Income Security Act) rules.

As of 2015, there were approximately fifty million IRAs in the United States. As of 2012, approximately fifty-one million people participated in 401(k) plans. As of 2015, defined contribution plans hold $6.8 trillion, $4.7 trillion of which were in 401(k) plans. A lot of the people I work with have a mix of approaches in their retirement portfolio. They often have a Traditional IRA and a 401(k), and they or their spouse may also have a Roth, SIMPLE IRA, or some other variation. Together, these accounts represent their retirement savings.

Of course, there are limits to how much money can be put away in each of these defined contribution plans. Each plan also has features, eligibility requirements, rules, tax implications, and consequences that make it more or less attractive to a particular individual. Again, I will lay all this out clearly in subsequent chapters so that you have a full understanding and can simultaneously impress and overwhelm your friends at dinner parties. As I mentioned in the Introduction, it is extremely rare, however, that I meet anyone who has even heard of (let alone has a practical understanding of) another type of retirement savings plan, which I call the Solo 401(k).

As explained earlier, the Solo 401(k) is not a term of art and you will not find it named as such in the IRC. To confuse matters even more, there are a number of other terms commonly used by tax professionals to describe the same tool: Individual 401(k), One-Participant 401(k), Self-Employed 401(k), Self-Directed 401(k), and Uni 401(k). In fact, you can call it pretty much whatever you want, because it is not, as I mentioned, defined specifically in the IRC. I like the term "Solo" because it carries the sense of independence and self-reliance that I find characteristic of the people who are able to take advantage of it the most.

What makes the Solo 401(k) appealing to a certain type of person? There are actually three big reasons. First, the Solo 401(k) allows you to save *a lot* more money for retirement every year than a traditional IRA, SEP-IRA, or SIMPLE IRA (the most common retirement plans for the self-employed). Second, the Solo 401(k) allows you more flexibility for accessing your retirement savings and applying them to investments or other opportunities that you may find interesting or important. And third, the Solo 401(k) is a good match for people who are self-employed, who are business owners with no full-time employees, or who earn some portion of their income through self-employment.

In my experience, the number of people who are self-employed or partially self-employed is growing very quickly these days. In fact, a large number of Americans who have some sort of self-employment income are not even aware of it. I have also known many others who wish they could pursue a dream, hobby, or interest more passionately but are held back by worries that such an activity will detract from their efforts to earn as much as possible in their "day job." Knowing that self-employment income of any kind can be leveraged through a Solo 401(k) to build retirement savings faster often gives these people a greater sense of freedom and confidence to "go for it."

All Solo 401(k) Plans Are Not Created Equal

Most people believe that all Solo 401(k) plans, whether attained for free at a financial institution or provided by a specialized plan provider, are the same. But the nuances that differentiate the various plan options are important to understand. In general, there are three ways to establish and use a Solo 401(k) plan for retirement and investment purposes.

1. Financial Institution–Sponsored Solo Plan

This is the most common way to establish a Solo 401(k) plan. Most of the major financial institutions and US banks—such as Vanguard, Charles Schwab, E*Trade, Bank of America, and CIT—provide basic Solo 401(k) plan documents and investment opportunities, typically for no fee. The catch is that the Solo 401(k) plan documents you adopt are very basic and generally limit your options to making pretax employee deferrals and pretax profit-sharing contributions, while also limiting your 401(k) plan investment options to the financial product offering sold by that financial institution.

In essence, the plan will let you make basic pretax employee deferral and profit-sharing contributions but will generally restrict your investment options to stocks, mutual funds, ETFs, and other traditional financial products sold by the financial institution. In other words, this type of Solo 401(k) does not permit a loan feature, or the ability to make Roth (after-tax) contributions, or the option to make nontraditional investments, such as real estate and precious metals. The advantage of adopting a Solo 401(k) plan from a major financial institution or bank can be found in the price and simplicity of such a transaction.

2. Custodian-Directed Self-Directed Solo 401(k) Plan

This option generally offers Solo 401(k) plan participants the ability to make traditional investments, including stock, as well as IRS-approved nontraditional or alternate investments such as real estate, precious metals, private lending, and private business investments through a trust company. The custodian-directed self-directed Solo 401(k) plan option is generally attractive to retirement investors looking to make nontraditional investments with their Solo 401(k) plan while having a third party administer the plan.

These custodians or trust companies do not offer investment advice and are essentially in business to allow you to make IRS-approved nontraditional investments. Unlike a traditional financial institution such as Bank of America or Vanguard, which make money by selling financial products, these passive custodians and trust companies make their money by opening self-directed accounts and charging an annual fee. In some cases, the fees are based on account value and/or the number of transactions done in the account in a given year.

Most of the institutions that allow Solo 401(k) plans to make nontraditional investments are established as trust companies and simply let you use their plan documents and accounts to make the investments. Your Solo 401(k) plan assets are generally held at an FDIC institution associated with the trust company and all investments must go through the custodian, which is why it is referred to as a custodian-directed plan. In practice, this means that you need to go through the custodian and have the custodian send the funds.

In most cases, that custodian must also sign the necessary transaction documents to enable you to make a Solo 401(k) plan investment, including real estate. In some situations, you are permitted as trustee of the plan to sign the transaction documents, including the purchase agreement, but the issuing of check payments or wires for the purchase or for ongoing expenses, such as taxes or repairs, need to go through the custodian because the custodian controls the funds. The custodian-directed self-directed Solo 401(k) plan option has many attractive features, such as the ability to make nontraditional investments, but it also has some limitations, including annual fees and potential time delays that can result from having to go through the trust company to make transactions.

3. Open-Architecture Self-Directed Solo 401(k) Plan

The open architecture Solo 401(k) plan is quickly becoming the most popular self-directed option for the self-employed. The beauty of the open architecture Solo 401(k) plan is that it can generally be opened at most local banks and it allows the business owner to serve as trustee of the plan with total control over the investments made. Self-directed Solo 401(k) plans are generally provided by specialized plan provider companies, which are able to customize the plan based on the individual's retirement and investment goals. Most of the companies that offer self-directed open architecture Solo 401(k) plan documents are not typical financial institutions that sell financial products or house the Solo 401(k) plan account. These plan document provider companies essentially make money by selling the plan documents and offering advisory services regarding the features of the plan.

Major financial institutions generally do not include the self-directed features in their Solo 401(k) plan documents because that does not serve their financial interests. That has not stopped a number of specialized self-directed retirement facilitators from emerging as firms that specialize in helping to set up self-directed retirement solutions. This includes the self-directed Solo 401(k) plan, which has become more popular because of growing demand for the diversification of nontraditional investments, such as real estate.

The open-architecture self-directed Solo 401(k) plan has started to overtake the custodian-directed Solo 401(k) plan as the most popular self-directed Solo 401(k) plan option for a number of reasons:

- The plan can be opened at most local banks, which gives the plan participant more control and comfort than having the funds sit with a trustee in another state or at an unfamiliar bank.
- Once the documents have been purchased, there are typically very small annual compliance fees, since a Solo 401(k) plan has very little administrative requirements and generally none if the plan's assets are under $250,000.

- You will have "checkbook control," which means that as the trustee, you can make investments from your Solo 401(k) account by simply writing a check or executing a wire.
- You can also customize the plan documents to include all available options allowable by the IRS.

This book will help you decide which Solo 401(k) plan options best suit your needs.

Who's Eligible to Use a Solo 401(k)?

Let's look a little more closely at who is eligible to create a Solo 401(k), since that will determine whether you will be interested in digging deeper into the rules discussed in Chapter 3, or just contemplating the big picture to get a better sense of how your career, work, and retirement savings options might unfold someday.

There are two specific eligibility requirements for the Solo 401(k):

1. The presence of self-employment activity
2. The absence of full-time employees

As with anything drafted by the IRS, in between these dry declarations there is a world of variety and possibility.

Who is a self-employed person? The obvious answer is that she works for herself. Think of a self-employed contractor, an independent consultant, a primary care physician, or a freelance graphic designer. I have come to believe that the variety of ways a person can make a living are nearly limitless.

Notice that there is no stipulation that such a person has to own his or her own business or be incorporated in any way. Some people take the formal approach when they work independently by creating a corporation, LLC, or partnership, and some people don't, which means they have a sole proprietorship. In general, any person who is self-employed or performing some activity that generates self-employment income not through an entity is automatically treated as a sole proprietorship.

Regardless, the Solo 401(k) is still a fit so long as the person doesn't have any full-time employees, defined as people who work over a thousand hours for them annually. This means the independent contractor can still hire electricians, laborers, or architects to do a housing job, but can't employ such people full time. Or the graphic designer can pay an editor or a web designer or a videographer as an independent contractor, for example, but not as full-time employees.

However, the spouse of a small business owner is not counted as a full-time employee, even if the spouse's full-time income comes from the business. This is because spouses are not considered employees for ERISA purposes when it comes to determining 401(k) plan eligibility. Additionally, people under twenty-one are also not considered full-time employees, so you can feel free to put your children to work in the family business.

Finally, there's nothing in the eligibility requirements of the Solo 401(k) that stipulates how much of your income must come from self-employment activity. In other words, you do not have to be just a contractor, or a primary care physician, or a graphic designer. You can, in fact, be an endless variety of other things in addition. For instance, you can be a radio talk show host who also sells real estate, or a physician who works for a hospital and who also provides medical consultations for a local sports team. You might be a graphic designer for a major advertising firm who also does graphic design work on a freelance basis, or the manager of a flower shop who also sells antiques on eBay. Whatever portion of your income arises through self-employment activity can be used to build savings through a Solo 401(k). In essence, as long as there is the anticipation or expectation of earned income, the activity can be treated as a self-employment activity.

This is the real magic of the Solo 401(k). Rather than discouraging us from earning income in ways that are outside traditional lines, the Solo 401(k) allows us to leverage those interests and activities to save a significantly higher portion of our money for retirement and at the same time reduce a large percentage of the tax due on the income earned through the activity.

More Wealth-Building Power

How much more money can you save with a Solo 401(k)? As I mentioned before, *a lot* more. As of 2017, an IRA only allows a $5,500 annual contribution limit, with an additional $1,000 catch-up contribution for those over age fifty. In comparison, as of 2017, the Solo 401(k) plan allows for a contribution of $18,000 (or $24,000 if over the age of fifty), which can be close to 100 percent of the total compensation earned through self-employment income. If you earn more than that, you can increase your contribution amount up to 25 percent of your total self-employment compensation, or 20 percent in the case of a sole proprietorship, through employer profit-sharing contributions (this will be explained in greater detail in a later chapter).

So the total annual contribution limit for 2017 for a Solo 401(k), including both employee deferral and profit-sharing contributions, is $54,000, with an additional $6,000 catch-up contribution for those over fifty ($60,000). When a spouse participates in the same Solo 401(k) plan, he or she is also allowed to make separate and equal contributions. In 2017, this increased the total contribution to $108,000, or $120,000 if both spouses were over fifty and were able to max out their contributions for the plan.

There are always great tax advantages to saving for retirement, but this is especially so with a Solo 401(k). Not only are you reducing your immediate tax burden by making tax-deferred contributions to the plan, but also all the income and gains generated by your Solo 401(k) are generally directed back to your plan tax deferred (or tax-free in the case of an after-tax Roth account). In addition, because a Solo 401(k) is meant for self-employed persons, this essentially means your contributions come from the earnings of your self-employment business, which allow you to reduce the tax due on your self-employed income. Furthermore, you are eligible to claim an additional tax deduction for the cost of the plan, including its annual maintenance fees. In other words, the costs associated with the plan and its ongoing maintenance help reduce your income tax liability.

All of this means that you can build more wealth at a faster rate. The advantages of saving money for retirement are not as well understood as they should be. In particular, tax deferrals are wildly underappreciated.

The concept of tax deferral is premised on the notion that all income and gains generated by a pretax retirement account investment flow back into the retirement account tax-free. So instead of paying tax on the returns of a Solo 401(k) plan investment such as real estate, tax is paid only at a later date, leaving the investment to grow unhindered. For example, if a 401(k) plan participant invested $100,000 from a Solo 401(k) plan in 2016 and the account earned $10,000 in 2016, the investor would not owe tax on that $10,000 in 2016. Instead, the 401(k) plan participant would be required to pay the taxes when he or she withdraws the money from the 401(k) plan, which could be many years later. Assuming the 401(k) plan participant mentioned above is in a 33 percent federal income tax bracket, she avoided paying $3,333 in federal income taxes on the $10,000 earned on the 401(k) plan investment in 2016. That would have left $6,667 in the account. Instead, at an 8 percent annual return, those earnings actually go on to produce $533.36 in 2017, but would be over 40 percent more: $800 in total if we go back to the original account balance of $10,000. The beauty of tax deferral is that the deferral compounds each year.

Even more eye popping, take the example of Joe. Joe was thirty years old when he decided to start a Solo 401(k) plan and had a current retirement account balance of zero at that time. Assuming that Joe decides to make annual 401(k) contributions of just $3,500 each year until he reaches the retirement age of seventy and that he is able to generate an average annualized rate of return of 9 percent with a prevailing tax rate of 25 percent, then at age seventy Joe will have $1,289,022 of tax-deferred income in his 401(k) plan. In contrast, if that money had been invested outside of a retirement account as personal funds, the same assumptions produce just $699,475.

In other words, a Solo 40(k) plan allows Joe to accumulate an additional $589,547 of wealth. While Joe is not rich, he is able to put about $67 a week away for his retirement account every year. This small amount of money could turn into a million dollars plus for Joe by the time he retires. Now, imagine if Joe could put away $10,000 a year starting at age forty, with an average rate of return of just 7 percent. At age seventy, Joe would have over $1 million versus just over $730,000 in a taxable account. The numbers don't lie, and the Solo 401(k) plan can help the self-employed or small business owner build wealth fast while at the same time also benefitting from tax deductions and a reduction of taxable income.

Simplicity, Flexibility, and Independence

The Solo 401(k) is especially appealing for many people because of the amount of personal control and the range of options it offers. First, the contributions you make to the plan are completely up to you. You can contribute up to your limit every year, or you can reduce or even suspend contributions whenever necessary. For a person relying on self-employment income, this can be critical, since some years are certainly better than others in an up-and-down economy.

In addition, the Solo 401(k) is extremely simple to administer. There is no annual filing requirement when the plan has less than $250,000 in assets. If you grow your plan over that amount, you merely need to file IRS Form 5500-EZ (it really is easy), which is a short information return, and you are done.

The plan is also inexpensive to administer because you are not required to hire a bank or trust company to serve as trustee. Essentially, this puts you in the trustee role and plan administrator role, meaning that all the assets of your Solo 401(k) trust are under your sole authority. Also, depending on the type of Solo 401(k) plan you adopt, your plan would offer a range of investment opportunities, including real estate. And you would be able to use your retirement funds to make almost any type of investments without tax and without needing the consent of a custodian. This includes stocks, bonds, mutual funds, precious metals, and even real estate. As already mentioned, the income and gains generated by your Solo 401(k) assets can flow back to your plan tax-free.

You can even borrow up to $50,000 or 50 percent of the value of your account (whichever is less) for any purpose, including funding your business, launching or investing in a new business, paying off credit card debt, making personal mortgage payments, or loaning money to friends or family. The loan is tax-free and penalty-free. It must be repaid over a five-year period with payments that occur at least quarterly, but there are no penalties for early payment if you repay the loan before the five years is up. The interest rate you pay is up to you, though it must be set a reasonable rate, generally considered to be the Prime interest rate as per the *WSJ*.

As of beginning of 2017, for example, Prime was set at 3.75 percent, so the interest rate on your loan would have been a minimum of 3.75 percent. This is a very attractive rate compared to the interest charged for credit card debt and would rival anything you could get from your bank as a good customer. You are also permitted to set a higher interest rate, which is a nice way of directing additional funds to the plan in excess of your annual contribution limits.

How would this flexibility and range of options for retirement saving, as well as accessing and investing your funds suit your work, interests, and needs? To get a better picture, here are some stories of people whose situations you might recognize.

John, the Realtor

John is forty-five and lives in Dallas, Texas. He's had some ups and downs over the course of his working life that have affected his progress in saving for retirement. Still, he knows he has the intelligence and the will to make everything right. He starts by Googling for answers.

Until 2003, John worked for a global energy company. He was there for eleven great years, rising steadily up the ranks. Then he was let go when the group he was in got divested. This affected John's sense of job security. If a

Fortune 500 company was that unpredictable, what job was safe? Rather than go back to work with another big energy company, John decided to do something that gave him a little more independence while still providing some employment security. He became a real estate agent at a large national firm.

The market was hot for about five years, and John made terrific money, though he hardly saved any of it for retirement. Lacking a 401(k) plan, he simply didn't focus on putting money at the end of the year into an IRA. That didn't worry him too much until the housing crisis and recession slashed his commissions drastically. He struggled for the next few years just to get by. Ironically, he was more interested in saving during those down years, but he had barely enough money for essentials and nothing left over at the end of each year. Since then, however, the market has rebounded. John's very good at what he does, and he's now on pace for a record sales year.

Earning great money again has freed John to make better plans for the future. He checks his IRA statements one day and is confronted by the cold, hard truth: He hasn't saved nearly enough to retire the way he wants to. He knows he needs to accelerate his savings soon to build the kind of wealth he wants to have in the future.

But what's the best way to do that? He's earned extra money this year and believes the next few years will be good, too. He'd love to use as much of that income for retirement as possible, but he's frustrated by the contribution limit of $5,500 a year in a traditional IRA. After a few hours of Googling, John feels like he's found a much better answer in a Solo 401(k). He makes an appointment with a CPA and goes over the details.

Before they dive in, the CPA emphasizes to John how good a decision it is to save as much money as possible for retirement every year. By contributing to a plan on an annual basis, John can grow his retirement savings without being taxed on it. This will help reduce the extra burden he's facing now with his record sales year, and just as importantly, all the investment gains that John makes through his retirement savings plan will go back into his plan without being taxed. Through that tax deferral benefit and the power of compounding returns, John's retirement savings can grow a lot quicker going forward. It's not too late for him to make significant progress toward his goals.

The CPA agrees with John that a Solo 401(k) has some real advantages, and she asks some questions to determine how much of his income is available for such a plan. Although John works for a large national real estate company, it turns out that he is not actually an employee of that company, according to the rules of the IRC, because he earns 100 percent of his income as commission through a 1099 tax form. This means that he's legally considered an independent contractor. Commissions are treated as self-employment income, making them eligible for establishing a Solo 401(k). Moreover, since John doesn't employ any full-time people himself, he's a perfect candidate for a Solo 401(k).

When John and the CPA look closely at his income this year, they realize that he can put away $18,000 for 2017 through an employee deferral, plus 20 percent of his $120,000 salary, giving him approximately $40,000 for his Solo 401(k). This will be a great boost to his savings, but John's not sure he'll be able to manage putting aside $40,000 every year. What's more, he wants to do a variety of other things with his money than just save for retirement.

The CPA asks John how much of a contribution he'd like to try to put aside every year. John thinks that $18,000 is more reasonable on an annual basis, so the CPA does some back-of-the-envelope calculations to show John what $18,000 in annual contributions will do for him. If he starts with that amount now and saves it every year for the next thirty years at a conservative 8 percent annual rate of return, John will have close to $2.2 million available to him when he turns seventy-five. That's pretty good, and the news puts a smile on John's face.

The CPA then asks John what other things he would like to do with his money rather than devote it to a retirement plan. John answers that he doesn't know much about stocks, but he does know real estate. For that reason, he'd love to invest in some commercial real estate and maybe start a small business handling mortgages. The CPA points out that John can actually use the money in his Solo 401(k) to invest in all kinds of different ways. Specifically, he can put money into real estate through his retirement plan, and he can loan money to his own small business if he elects to take advantage of the Solo 401(k) loan option.

This flexibility is icing on the cake to John. Not only can he defer more taxable income with a Solo 401(k), he can save faster and allocate the money to investments that he understands well and that will help him further his interests and dreams. He leaves the CPA's office knowing he has work to do but a real purpose for doing it.

Mary, the IT Consultant

Mary is thirty-three and an IT consultant who lives in Sacramento, California. She got divorced three years ago, an ordeal that was very difficult in many ways, including financially. Since then, however, things have taken off. She started her own business providing IT support and software development to small and midsize corporations. She's already doing remarkably well and is looking to expand her services. She knows, however, that a big increase in her income will mean significantly higher taxes, and she's concerned about giving a lot of that money back to the government.

At an industry conference, she found herself in a class on that very subject and learned about various retirement vehicles, such as the SEP and SIMPLE IRAs, and something called a Solo 401(k). In the months after the event, she's read a lot more about these different options and thinks the Solo 401(k) might be perfect for her. She is, after all, already established as a single-member LLC and has no full-time employees. While that might change at some point down the road, right now she is eligible to adopt a Solo 401(k).

To Mary, the beauty of the Solo 401(k) is in the high contributions it allows, the tax breaks, and the power to use her savings to grow her business. Although she's quite young, she'll be able to put away $54,000 per year in 2017 ($60,000 if Mary was over the age of fifty) for retirement for the foreseeable future while also reducing her tax liability. What's more, she'll be able to borrow up to 50 percent of her account or $50,000, whichever is less, to finance her business. Mary attracts a lot of her customers through the Internet, but this requires paying for adWords on Google, Yahoo, and Bing. She'd like to invest in a higher-end search engine optimization service. Tapping her Solo 401(k) plan at a very favorable interest rate of just 3.25 percent is a lot more appealing than putting such charges on her credit card with its annual interest-rate charges of 14 to 18 percent.

Some of Mary's friends in the consulting world are sticking with SEP-IRAs because these plans are so familiar. But Mary believes that the advantages of the Solo 401(k) are really compelling. The SEP is just a pure profit-sharing plan, while the Solo 401(k) has an employee deferral feature that will allow Mary to increase her maximum contribution. Plus, the SEP also lacks the loan feature of the Solo 401(k), something Mary is looking forward to leveraging as an easy and flexible way to grow her business. Mary also loves the fact that she'll have "checkbook control" over her plan. She won't need to go to a bank or an institution to administer the plan—she can do it all herself and give herself a tax break for doing so.

Brian, the Engineer

Brian is fifty-five years old and lives in Springfield, Illinois. For almost thirty years, he worked at a midsize engineering company but was laid off in 2012 when the firm was bought by an overseas conglomerate. Although Brian is at the peak of his career, he's finding the job market extremely difficult for someone of his experience and salary expectations.

Brian has been incredibly frustrated by this until he realized that it's not the only path available to him. With his know-how and contacts, he could go out on his own. And because of ObamaCare, he no longer needs to rely on employer-based health insurance to cover his family. Anxious to get back into the game, he decides to start his own company and provide engineering consulting services to small businesses.

Brian speaks to his tax attorney about setting up the business and generating income as a self-employed person. The tax attorney advises him that an LLC is the way to go because of its limited liability protection and pass-through tax status. Almost immediately, Brian gets his first contract. His accountant tells him the time is right to set up a Solo 401(k) as a retirement vehicle. This will serve several different purposes: it will allow him to roll over his retirement funds from his previous employer, it will help him minimize his annual tax burden, and it will allow him to further his own investment strategy. You see, Brian has always done very well buying stocks, mutual funds, and precious metals, and he enjoys the sense of control this gives him.

After further discussions with his tax attorney, Brian learns something else that's appealing. It turns out that under the 401(k) plan rules, he can actually hire his wife to run his business, pay her a salary, and increase the contribution limits they can make to his Solo 401(k) up to $120,000 since both of them are over fifty for 2017.

Brian is a little worried about the complexity of making all this happen and the tax consequences of any mistakes, but Brian's attorney assures him that the administrative requirements are very simple. In fact, until his plan has more than $250,000, there are no filing requirements with the IRS. Once he surpasses $250,000, all that is required of him in terms of paperwork is IRS Form 5500-EZ, a two-page information request that he can complete himself without incurring any fees and submit to the IRS by July 31 each year.

Brian also asks his attorney about the possibility of converting $175,000 he had saved through his old firm's 401(k) plan to an after-tax (Roth) account. The attorney tells him that this recently became easier to do. In the past, you needed a triggering event such as turning fifty-nine years old to make a Roth conversion. Now, because of a change in law, the money can be converted as soon as it is rolled into a plan without a triggering event, though tax would still be due on the value of the conversion. Plus, if Brian makes employee deferrals or profit-sharing contributions on a yearly basis, these can also be converted into a Roth at any point without any vesting. This really excites Brian, since he's even more focused on gaining tax-free returns on his investments than he is on reducing his tax liability. He believes the market for precious metals is going to be very strong in the next few years and is eager to invest in it heavily.

So Brian elects to adopt a Solo 401(k) with a built-in Roth option, and he's excited about growing his assets through extra savings as well as investments that he directs and controls.

Amy, the Videographer with a Hobby

Amy is forty-eight and works full-time as a video coordinator for a TV station in Newark, New Jersey. She's very busy at her job, but on the side she has always enjoyed doing photography and videography for friends and friends of friends who ask her for help. Although she always considered this a hobby, in recent years her reputation has spread and she now has a fairly consistent business, which brings in about $30,000 a year.

Amy likes the extra money, but she doesn't really need it, so she decides to ask her investment advisor about options. The advisor has recently attended a seminar about retirement planning where he learned about the advantages of the Solo 401(k), and he thinks that might be just the ticket for Amy. She's eligible for a Solo 401(k) because she's been declaring her extra earnings every year as self-employment income on Schedule C of her 1040 income tax return. What's more, she operates that business as a sole proprietorship, has no full-time employees, and has been paying self-employment tax and federal and state income tax on the money.

Although Amy is employed full-time and contributes to her employer's 401(k) plan, it is completely acceptable for her to make employer profit-sharing contributions to a Solo 401(k) through her side business. In 2017, Amy maxed out and put $18,000 into her full-time employer plan, but she is also eligible to do a profit contribution equal to or up to 20 percent of the salary she earns from self-employment income: up to a limit of $54,000 for 2017, including the $18,000 she contributed to her full-time employer 401(k) plan. Since she earned $30,000 in 2017 from her side business, this enables her to defer another $6,000 or so into a Solo 401(k) plan to reduce her tax burden and further accelerate the growth of her retirement wealth.

Amy has another reason why the Solo 401(k) is attractive to her. She is interested in the ability it gives her to make nontraditional investments. She's part of a support network of young female entrepreneurs, and she thinks that many of these friends have great ideas and business plans. The problem, however, is that they are often turned down for loans from traditional banks. Amy loves the idea of helping to fund these start-ups through a private loan from her Solo 401(k). She'll be earning interest rates that are on par with average stock market gains in doing so, and she'll be helping out some talented and hardworking friends in the process. She knows that she could not tap her employer 401(k) for that purpose, so this feature of the Solo 401(k) is particularly exciting.

Helpful Knowledge

As you can see from these examples, a wide range of people are eligible to adopt a Solo 401(k). The basic appeal of that retirement vehicle over other options is clear: you can defer more taxes and reduce your tax liability while simultaneously building more retirement wealth with a Solo 401(k) than with any other retirement plan, except a defined benefit plan. The simplicity of the Solo 401(k) and its extra features make it even more attractive. Some people like the ability to grow their assets by investing it in real estate, stocks, precious metals, or other opportunities. Some appreciate being able to increase their retirement savings and tax deferral by involving a spouse in their self-employment business. Some welcome the chance to leverage their retirement funds by loaning money to their own business or to others at favorable interest rates. That flexibility can be very helpful today, when new challenges and new opportunities arise all the time.

The most important thing of all is to save. Too many people in America fail to adequately prepare themselves for their retirement future. As a result, too many struggle at a time in life when they should be able to enjoy the benefits of years of hard work. All of us can become millionaires by the time we retire. If we save as much as possible every year, our money will grow and grow. It's not hard and can be done with just a few dollars a day, but it does take foresight, discipline, and a little homework. The rewards in terms of quality of life, variety of opportunity, and flexibility of options ensure that such a decision will be one of the best investments you can ever make.

CHAPTER 2

A Brief History of Saving in America

Here's another secret: the government wants you to save for retirement. In fact, the government has made saving (and accumulating) a lot of money for retirement incredibly advantageous and enticing. For once, the game is rigged in your favor.

The rules of the game, however, and the path to "victory" are unclear. That's the reason why so many fail to win. Too many people do not even know what game is being played or how to take part in it.

So let's take a moment, in this short chapter, to understand how our retirement savings system has evolved into its current form and where the Solo 401(k) fits in. Later, we'll look at what kinds of opportunities are available to you as a result.

Evolution of Wealth Growing

The possibility of getting rich by saving is available to almost anyone today, but that wasn't always the case. Until a century ago, your best chance of retiring rich might have come from striking gold in Alaska or maybe building a railroad. Back then, most people didn't earn enough at their menial jobs to grow their wealth over time, and few over the age of sixty-five were able to retire. Most people kept working until they died or couldn't work anymore.

The first private pension plan in the United States was formed by the American Express company in 1875. Their goal was to encourage quality workers to stay with the company over the long term. This has been a theme in American business until quite recently, and it has suited the American culture and way of life quite well. In Europe, a tradition developed whereby the government takes a percentage of your salary and invests it for you, and then provides you with those benefits when you reach a certain age. This type of pension plan is often referred to as a public pension plan. In the United States, we've relied more on private enterprise to establish retirement pensions and on social security to serve as a safety net.

By the end of the 1800s, there were thirteen private pension plans in the United States, and the number continued to grow as many stalwart American firms established their own pension. In 1914, the IRC was amended to allow pensions paid to employees to become deductible like any business expense. This made it easier for corporations to establish and improve pensions for their employees.

In 1921, the IRS ruled that income from profit-sharing plans were exempt from the taxes an employee paid on his or her salary. In 1926, this exemption was extended to income from the employee's pension plan. Together, these provisions helped establish the foundation of a system in which businesses could align their long-term interests with employees, and employees could save more of their own money for retirement.

By the mid-1920s, as salaries improved people began to appreciate the possibility of growing their wealth even faster through investments in the stock market. Share prices climbed to unprecedented heights, and more ordinary people bought stocks than ever before. Housewives invested their rainy-day money. Shoeshine boys traded stock tips based on information they overheard while polishing the shoes of Wall Street investors. When the markets crashed on October 24, 1929, housewives, shoeshine boys, and Wall Street titans all shared the pain.

The Great Depression exposed a lot of Americans to poverty and hunger. It also gave rise in 1935 to social security, the safety net generated by payroll tax that has helped Americans stay above the poverty line after their retirement at age sixty-five. It should be noted that life expectancy was about sixty years then, so the system was not considered a financial burden to society the way it often is today. Even so, only about 6 percent of Americans were paying income tax and contributing to social security in 1939. The system truly was a massive redistribution of wealth from those who earned a lot of income to those who were less fortunate.

By 1940, 15 percent of private-sector workers in America were covered by a pension plan. America entered World War II in 1941. The next year, wages and salaries were frozen in order to keep inflation down. A year after that, however, a change was made to exempt that wage freeze from benefits like pension contributions and health insurance. Today's system of employer-based health insurance has its roots in this decision, as corporations sought alternative ways to attract and keep good workers. Such benefits were attractive to employees because individual income taxes were going up to help pay for the war. In other words, benefits became a means of earning more without paying additional taxes. Since almost 75 percent of workers were paying income tax by 1945 (a big shift from 1939), avoiding taxes by earning valued benefits was highly appealing to many people.

By 1950, about 25 percent of private-sector workers were covered by some private pension plan. Starting in 1956, a number of companies, particularly banks, added a new feature to their profit-sharing plans that came to be called a "cash or deferred arrangement," or CODA. Each year when employees were awarded a profit-sharing bonus, they were given the option to deposit some or all of that bonus into the plan instead of receiving it as cash. A CODA treated any amount the employee contributed to the plan as if it were an employer contribution, making it tax deferred.

By 1960, the number of private-sector workers covered by a private pension plan increased to 41 percent. Between the end of World War II and 1960, there was the rise of a sizable middle class: people with good jobs who could realize the American dream of owning their own homes. When President Kennedy was inaugurated in 1960, however, America had entered a tricky recession. Individual and corporate taxes were too high, and social security benefits were considered insufficient to keep the very poor going. Accordingly, Kennedy pushed a slew of bills through Congress to help the poor with benefits and help higher income earners keep and save more of their money.

One of those bills was Public Law 87–792, described as the "Self-Employed Individuals Tax Retirement Act of 1962," which gave self-employed people a tax deferral for income that they set aside in qualified pension plans. Until then, only people employed by companies with private pension plans could set aside tax deferred money for retirement. Now self-employed people could do the same.

Plans covering self-employed individuals were often called Keogh or H.R. 10 plans—after the principal sponsor, US Representative Eugene Keogh of New York—and its bill number in the House of Representatives. These plans were limited, however, and had difficult filing requirements, making them less attractive than the Solo 401(k) plan of today. Nevertheless, retirement saving mechanisms like the Keogh were recognized as a good thing. They encouraged people to save money, and they potentially lessened the burden on the government to provide for people after retirement.

In 1974, the Employee Retirement Income Security Act (ERISA) became law. ERISA was written to protect the assets of Americans so that the funds they placed in retirement plans during their working years would be available to them when they retired. ERISA sets minimum standards for pension plans in private industry to ensure fairness of application and compliance with rules. ERISA doesn't require any employer to establish a pension plan; it only requires that those that do so must meet certain standards.

IRAs were born when ERISA came into effect. IRAs were created to supplement retirement income and lessen the burden on social programs like social security. Congress wanted individuals not covered by a retirement plan at work to have an opportunity to save for retirement on their own in a tax-deferred account through a financial institution. An IRA is a trust or custodial account set up in the United States for the exclusive benefit of an individual or his or her beneficiaries. As with an employer's qualified pension plan, an IRA contribution is tax deductible and tax deferred until the funds are withdrawn at retirement.

At first, the annual amount that could be contributed was limited to $1500 of tax-deferred income, and IRAs were also restricted to people who otherwise couldn't contribute to qualified employment-based retirement plans. In 1981, these rules were relaxed so that anyone under age seventy and a half could contribute, and the amount was raised to $2000 plus an additional $250 for a nonworking spouse. In 1982, Congress adopted a unified system for all qualified plans, including those covering self-employed persons, believing that the tax incentives made available to retired employees "should not depend upon whether the employer is an incorporated or unincorporated enterprise."

What Is an IRA?

An individual retirement account, or IRA, is a tax-favored personal savings arrangement that allows you to set aside money for retirement. There are several different types of IRAs, which you can set up with a bank, insurance company, or other financial institution.

The original IRA is often referred to as a "Traditional IRA." You may be able to deduct some or all of your contributions to a Traditional IRA. For 2017, one can contribute up to $5500 annually, or $6500 if over the age of fifty. Distributions from a Traditional IRA are fully or partially taxable in the year of distribution. If you made only deductible contributions, distributions are fully taxable.

Distributions made prior to age fifty-nine and a half may be subject to a 10 percent additional tax. Unfortunately, you cannot keep retirement funds in your account indefinitely. You generally have to start taking withdrawals from your IRA or retirement plan account when you reach age seventy and a half. This is often referred to as a "required minimum distribution," or RMD. A Roth IRA does not require withdrawals until after the death of the owner.

Your RMD is the minimum amount you must withdraw from your account each year. You can withdraw more than the minimum required amount, and your withdrawals will be included in your taxable income except for any part that was taxed before (your basis) or that can be received tax-free (such as qualified distributions from designated Roth accounts).

Contributions to all types of IRAs can only be made from income that the IRS determines to be "earned." You do not have to work for someone else to have taxable earned income; you can also work for yourself. Compensation from either type of employment would be considered earned income, but the complete definition is a bit broader. According to the IRS, taxable earned income includes:

- Wages, salaries, and tips
- Union strike benefits
- Long-term disability benefits received prior to minimum retirement age
- Net earnings from self-employment

However, the following are examples of income that is *not* considered earned:

- Pay received for work while an inmate in a penal institution
- Interest and dividends
- Retirement income
- Social security
- Unemployment benefits
- Alimony
- Child support

What Is a Roth IRA?

In 1997, Congress, under the Taxpayer Relief Act, introduced the Roth IRA. This is like a traditional IRA but with a few attractive modifications. The big advantage of a Roth IRA is that if you qualify to make contributions, all distributions from the Roth IRA are tax-free—even the investment returns and appreciation—as long as the distributions meet certain requirements.

The rules for the Roth IRA are found in the IRC under Section 408A. Here are some of its characteristics and features:

- Contributions are not tax deductible.
- Unlike traditional IRAs, you may contribute to a Roth IRA for as long as you continue to have earned income.
- All Roth IRA contributions are made with after-tax dollars. This means that the amount of the contribution is treated as basis in the IRA.
- Earnings and gains are tax deferred and may be tax exempt. This means that all income and gains generated by a Roth IRA investment are not subject to income tax. As long as certain conditions are met and the distribution is a qualified distribution, the Roth IRA owner will never pay tax on any Roth distributions received. Essentially, if the Roth IRA account has been opened at least five years and the holder is over the age of fifty-nine and a half at the date of the distribution, there should be no tax on the entire Roth IRA distribution, including contributions, income, and appreciation.
- Unlike the Traditional IRA, there is no seventy and a half age limit on making contributions. Individuals of any age with compensation below a certain income threshold are eligible to contribute to a Roth IRA. The total amount you may contribute to a Roth IRA for 2017 cannot exceed the lesser of $5,500 ($6,500 if over the age of fifty) or 100 percent of compensation ($11,000 for married couples and $13,000 if over the age of fifty).
- The IRS has established income rules that govern who is eligible to make after-tax (Roth) IRA contributions. If your income exceeds a certain amount, you will not be allowed to contribute to a Roth IRA. For 2017, subject to adjustments each year, Single filers, Head of Household, or Married Filing Separately (and you did not live

with your spouse during the year) with modified adjusted gross income up to $133,000 can make a full contribution. Contributions are phased out starting at $118,000, and you cannot make a contribution if your adjusted gross income is in excess of $133,000.

Joint filers with modified adjusted gross income up to $196,000 can make a full contribution. Once again, this contribution is phased out starting at $186,000, and you cannot make a contribution if your adjusted gross income is in excess of $196,000.

The good news is that this income threshold requirement does not apply to a Solo 401(k) Plan Roth account.

The table is helpful in determining whether you are eligible to make Roth IRA contributions. You may ask, is there a way one can still make after-tax (Roth) IRA contributions even if one has exceeded the annual income level threshold? The answer is thankfully yes!

The Backdoor Roth IRA Contribution

The one way high earners can contribute to a Roth IRA is through the backdoor approach of converting a traditional IRA made with an after-tax fund, which has no income threshold, to a Roth IRA. Because the Traditional IRA contribution is made with after-tax funds, if you make the conversion immediately, it should be tax-free. You will only be required to pay taxes if the value of your investment increases between the time you make the initial after-tax contribution and the time you convert to a Roth IRA.

Note: If you maintain a Traditional IRA, the maximum contribution to your Roth IRA is reduced by any contributions made to your Traditional IRA.

How Do You Decide between a Traditional IRA and a Roth IRA?

There's no right or wrong answer. The decision generally depends on a variety of factors and circumstances.

If you are not eligible to take advantage of tax-deductible contributions to a Traditional IRA but qualify for after-tax contributions to a Roth IRA, then the Roth IRA is the better choice. Roth IRA contributions are made in after-tax dollars, while earnings are generally are not taxable.

If contributions to a Traditional IRA are tax deductible and you are also eligible to contribute to a Roth IRA, then:

- If you expect your retirement tax rate to be equal or higher than it is today, a Roth IRA could yield the greatest benefit.
- If you expect your retirement tax rate to be much lower than it is today, you may want to choose to make contributions to a Traditional IRA.
- If you expect your investment to generate strong returns, then a Roth IRA could be a better option.

Finally, if you are younger, the Roth IRA is more attractive because you will have more time to grow your retirement without paying any tax.

What Is a SEP-IRA?

A Simplified Employee Pension (SEP) plan provides business owners with a simplified method to contribute toward their employees' retirement as well as their own retirement savings. A SEP is essentially an employer-sponsored profit-sharing plan. Contributions are made to a retirement account or annuity setup for each plan participant: a SEP-IRA.

A SEP-IRA account is a Traditional IRA and follows the same investment, distribution, and rollover rules as Traditional IRAs. Employees must be included in the SEP plan if they have:

- Attained age 21
- Received at least $550 in compensation from your business for the year
- Worked for your business for at least three of the past five years

The 3-of-5 eligibility rule means you must include any employee in your plan who has worked for you in any three of the past five years as long as the employee has satisfied the other plan eligibility requirements. This is the most restrictive eligibility requirement allowable. You can choose to use less restrictive participation rules in your plan, such as allowing employees to participate immediately after they start work or after a shorter period of employment. If you use the 3-of-5 rule, you must count any work, no matter how little, in each of the prior five years. Use plan years (often the calendar year), not years based on the date the employee started working for you.

The contributions you make to each employee's SEP-IRA each year cannot exceed the lesser of:

- 25 percent of compensation; or
- $54,000 for 2017.

There are no catch-up contributions for a SEP-IRA as there are for a 401(k) plan. These limits apply to contributions you make for your employees to all defined contribution plans, which includes SEPs. Compensation up to $270,000 in 2017 of an employee's compensation may be considered. Also, contributions must be made in cash and you cannot contribute property.

What Is a SIMPLE IRA?

A SIMPLE (Savings Incentive Match Plan for Employees) IRA plan allows employees and employers to contribute to Traditional IRAs set up for employees. Employees may choose to make salary reduction contributions, and the employer is required to make either matching or nonelective contributions. Contributions are made to a retirement account or annuity set up for each employee: a SIMPLE IRA.

A SIMPLE IRA plan account is an IRA and follows the same investment, distribution, and rollover rules as traditional IRAs. Any employer (including self-employed individuals, tax-exempt organizations, and governmental entities) that had no more than a hundred employees with $5,000 or more in compensation during the preceding calendar year (the "100-employee limitation") can establish a SIMPLE IRA plan. You can set up a SIMPLE IRA plan effective on any date between January 1 and October 1 provided you (or any predecessor employer) didn't previously maintain a SIMPLE IRA plan. If you're a new employer that came into existence after October 1 of the year, you can establish the SIMPLE IRA plan as soon as administratively feasible after your business came into existence.

All employees who received at least $5,000 in compensation from you during any two preceding calendar years (whether or not consecutive) and who are reasonably expected to receive at least $5,000 in compensation during the calendar year are eligible to participate in the SIMPLE IRA plan for that calendar year. Each eligible employee may make a salary reduction contribution, and the employer must make either a matching contribution or nonelective contribution. An employee may defer up to $12,500 in 2017, subject to cost-of-living adjustments for later years. Employees age fifty or over can make a catch-up contribution of up to $3,000 in 2017, subject to cost-of-living adjustments for later years.

With respect to employer contributions, the employer is generally required to either:

- Match each employee's salary reduction contribution on a dollar-for-dollar basis up to 3 percent of the employee's compensation (not limited by the annual compensation limit); or
- Make nonelective contributions of 2 percent of the employee's compensation up to the annual limit of $270,000 for 2017, subject to cost-of-living adjustments in later years).

If you choose to make nonelective contributions, you must make them for all eligible employees whether or not they make salary-reduction contributions. With respect to the 3-percent match, you may elect to reduce the 3-percent matching contributions for a calendar year, but only if:

- The limit isn't reduced below 1 percent;
- The limit isn't reduced for more than two years out of the five-year period that ends with (and includes) the year for which the election is effective; and
- You notify employees of the reduced limit within a reasonable time before the 60-day election period during which employees can enter into salary reduction agreements.

Generally, the same tax results apply to distributions from a SIMPLE IRA as to distributions from a regular IRA.

The 401(k) Plan

The 401(k) that is so popular today was created practically by accident. It is a type of CODA, or cash or deferred arrangement. The name comes from the Revenue Act of 1978, which included section 401(k) allowing full-time employees to fund retirement accounts with pretax dollars matched by employer contributions. In 1980, a benefits consultant named Ted Benna spotted this provision and created a 401(k) plan program for his employer. He also asked the IRS to make some changes so that the plans could be more widely adopted. Within a year, a handful of large companies had adopted 401(k) plans for their employers.

According to the most recent statistics provided by the US Department of Labor, there are 638,390 defined contribution retirement plans in the United States, 513,000 of which are 401(k) plans, covering more than 88 million total participants (more than 73 million active)[6].

Unfortunately for self-employed people, 401(k) plans can only be established through an employer. As a result, until 2002 self-employed people typically relied on SEP or SIMPLE IRAs as their retirement vehicle of choice for good reason.

In 2001, however, Congress passed the Economic Growth and Tax Relief Reconciliation Act (EGTRRA) as part of the so-called "Bush tax

6 (DOL Employee Benefits Security Administration, *Private Pension Plan Bulletin: Abstract of 2011 Form 5500 Annual Reports*, June 2013)

cuts." This Act, which took effect in 2002, had a tremendous impact on retirement plans in general: increasing limits, making it easier to consolidate plans, and making the plans themselves more flexible, while also offering a catch-up provision for older workers. Most importantly for our purpose in this book, the Act provided people who were self-employed or who were small business owners with no employees the same advantages and benefits of a conventional employer 401(k) plan.

Before the EGTRRA Act, there was no compelling reason for an owner-only business to establish a Solo 401(k) plan. After all, the business owner could generally receive the same benefits by adopting a profit-sharing plan or a SEP-IRA. EGTRRA paved the way, however, for an owner-only business to put more money aside for retirement and to operate a more cost-effective retirement plan than a SEP or SIMPLE IRA.

Today, in 2017, the Solo 401(k), also known as the Individual 401(k) or Self-Employed 401(k) plan, allows an individual to maximize his or her contributions up to $54,000 ($60,000 if over the age of fifty) without burdening them with the administrative responsibilities of a conventional ERISA 401(k) qualified retirement plan. In addition, an individual participant can borrow up to $50,000, make Roth contributions, and have the "checkbook control" to make real estate and other investments without tax.

It's surprising that the Solo 401(k) plan is not more popular. The EGTRRA Act became law in 2002, and Solo 401(k) has incredible advantages over all other IRA accounts. And yet a large number of self-employed people still adopt the SEP-IRA over the Solo 401(k).

This book aims to change that.

Some Ins and Outs of the Solo 401(k) Plan

In a way, the Solo 401(k) was introduced to us in 1962, then greatly enhanced in 2002. The Keogh Plan or H.R. 10 Plan of 1962 was designated for self-employed business owners. But the rules for Keogh became cumbersome when the Tax Equity and Fiscal Responsibility Act (TEFRA) of 1982 removed the differences between corporate plans and Keogh plans for the self-employed, and mandated that they operate under the same rules. It wasn't until the Solo 401(k) plan emerged with EGTRRA in 2002 that self-employed individuals had an easy-to-administer and flexible retirement plan tailored to their needs.

Under prior law, employer profit-sharing and matching combinations were combined with the employee deferral when determining the maximum deduction limit of 25 percent of an employee's compensation. EGTRRA increased the deductible profit-sharing contribution limit from 15 percent to 25 percent of employee compensation and changed the application of deferrals so they are not counted against the employer's maximum contribution amount. EGTRRA also increased the annual contribution limit to 100 percent of a participant's compensation. It created a Roth contribution option as well and allowed participants to designate all or a portion of their employee deferrals as after-tax (Roth) contributions. Finally, EGTRRA also modified the IRC to enable a loan feature for unincorporated businesses, which prior to that only applied to ERISA 401(k) plans.

The administrative rules of the Solo 401(k) plan are also easier because they are not covered under Title I of ERISA. The goal of Title I was to protect the interests of participants and their beneficiaries in employee benefit plans. For example, ERISA requires that the sponsors of private employee benefit plans provide participants and beneficiaries with adequate information about their plans. It also ensures that the people who manage the plans must meet certain standards of conduct and provide reporting to the government and disclosure to the participants.

Since a Solo 401(k) plan does not allow any full-time employees other than owner(s) and their spouse(s), ERISA rules do not apply. After all, there are no nonowner employees to protect. The reasonable assumption is that the business owner and his or her spouse will take care of their own interests.

As I mentioned, despite all these advantages, some accountants and tax professionals still recommend SEP or SIMPLE IRAs for self-employed individuals or small business owners with no employees. The reason is that many CPAs believe that those plans are easier to administer and less costly, plus they just have more experience working with these types of plans. However, over the past several years more professionals are beginning to recognize the enormous retirement and investment benefits of a Solo 401(k).

The 401(k) Plan Documents

There are different types of Solo 401(k) plans. The basic plan is known as the master plan. This is generally drafted for several employers and offered by a plan sponsor, and it requires that each employer use one plan document and that all contributions be made into a single trust account. These plans are not very popular because they are not customized to meet individual needs.

A more customized plan, known as a "prototype," is the most popular type of Solo 401(k) plan offered by plan sponsors to employers. Unlike a master plan, a prototype enables each adopting employer to have a separate trust for the plan participant's contributions. There are two types of prototype plans. Standardized prototypes reduce complexity by limiting the plan to the most common features. It is the most popular type of prototype plan and includes such features as employee deferrals, profit sharing, Roth deferrals, and loan ability. This is usually sufficient for most people, but the nonstandardized prototype offers more flexibility and customization to satisfy the individual employer's needs.

There is also such a thing as an individual designed Solo 401(k) plan, drafted to meet the specific needs of the plan's sponsor or the adopting employer. There are extensive costs and filing fees, however, associated with establishing such a plan, and the IRS must formally approve the plan to ensure tax-exempt qualifications. These high costs generally deter most plan sponsors from using the individual designed Solo 401(k).

Most financial institutions offer standard prototype documents, which include basic benefits such as employee deferrals and profit-sharing contributions. However, there are Solo 401(k) plan providers in the marketplace that offer a type of open-architecture, self-directed prototype plan document. These include all the most popular features available to a Solo 401(k) plan, including employee deferrals, profit-sharing contributions, an after-tax (Roth) component, and a loan feature, including the ability to make traditional as well as nontraditional investments, such as real estate. There is really not much need to pay a tax attorney or CPA to draft an individual designed Solo 401(k) plan since there are prototype plan documents available that include all available IRS benefits.

To determine which type of Solo 401(k) plan is best for you, it is important to look at all the options the plan offers to make sure it satisfies your retirement planning, tax, and investment goals. Financial institutions in particular may not offer everything you want that makes a Solo 401(k) plan appealing. For example, a plan may require that you invest all your retirement savings in the plan into the stock market, or it may not offer a loan feature or allow you to make Roth-type contributions. Most people who are drawn to the Solo 401(k) plan are interested in serving as the trustee of their own plan, with "checkbook control" and the ability to make traditional and nontraditional investments without requiring the consent of some custodian at a financial institution.

Going Solo

America has always prided itself on its individualism and valued freedom, flexibility, and self-reliance. Yet the system of tax-deferred retirement saving in this country has short-changed self-employed people—the very people who comprise our ranks of entrepreneurs, small-business owners, freelancers, and the like—for a long time. With the Solo 401(k), those limitations have finally changed. The advantages of the individualized path are becoming stronger and more enticing.

It's expected that Americans will soon have around approximately $25 trillion in retirement savings within a few years. To get a piece of that pie, most financial institutions offer basic Solo 401(k) plan documents with very limited investment options and retirement-planning opportunities.

It's up to you to determine what features will give you the best options and take that course. This book will make those choices very clear and show you how to reach your goals.

CHAPTER 3

Are You Eligible to Use a Solo 401(k)?

CAN YOU TAKE ADVANTAGE OF the Solo 401(k)? We touched on the eligibility requirements briefly in Chapter 1. They are very simple, but I'll elaborate on them in this chapter so you have a full understanding of the parameters of this powerful retirement savings tool.

Basically, there are only two requirements:

1) The presence of self-employment activity
2) The absence of full-time employees

While not everyone can fulfill those requirements, the nuances are more forgiving than you might expect. Let's take a look at what the IRS really means.

SELF-EMPLOYMENT ACTIVITY

Are you fully or partially self-employed? For many people—especially those who have a second or third line of work—this is an ambiguous question, so we can try to answer it as unambiguously as possible. The first and foremost indication of self-employment activity is whether that work generates income. If you generate income from your self-employment activity, then you fulfill the first eligibility requirement for a Solo 401(k).

It doesn't have to be your main or only source of income, but it must be genuine income.

If all the work you do is for an employer, then you are not eligible. For example, you may be a lawyer at a large New York firm, or a general manager of a Ford factory, or a checkout clerk at Target, but you do not qualify if your work does not resemble self-employment activity. On the other hand, if that lawyer also consults for a court TV show, or the factory GM builds and sells go-carts, or the retail clerk also has a line of clothing he designs and sells, then it's more likely that person is eligible to adopt a Solo 401(k) plan.

Ultimately, the tax forms you file are indicative of whether your income is generated by self-employment activity or not. When you work for an employer, that employer must fill out a W-2 form on your behalf to report the wages, salary, or other forms of compensation that are paid to you and the any taxes withheld. In turn, you must report the income you have earned from an employer on the first page of your 1040 form. In contrast, someone who is self-employed or who has a single-member LLC must fill out Schedule C on their personal federal income tax return (IRS Form 1040) or IRS Form 1065. Also, in the case of a multiple-member LLC (partnership), they must report the income they have generated through self-employment activities.

On the other hand, if you are the sole owner of a C corporation or an S corporation, you would likely not need to file a Schedule C because you are generating a W-2 form for yourself. Nevertheless, you can still defer tax payments by contributing to a Solo 401(k) plan because that income is generated by self-employment activity.

It's important to note that even if your losses exceed your revenues because of the deductions you have made for your business, you may still be eligible for a Solo 401(k). You may or may not have any money to contribute to that Solo 401(k), but you may be eligible to adopt the plan anyway.

A key factor to consider is the type of income you receive. Someone who actively performs services or does something that earns self-employment income is considered eligible, in contrast to someone who earns passive income. For example, the investor who accrues interest on dividends or capital gains, the landlord who collects rental income, or the writer who receives royalties may not be considered eligible for that portion of his or her income because the income is not generated through activity.

Why is there a difference between active and passive income? It's all about the taxes. While you probably have to pay taxes on passive income, such as your alimony check or your lottery winnings, you're not subject to self-employment tax. Since a Solo 401(k) is set up to defer self-employment taxes, income that is not subject to self-employment tax cannot be used to contribute to the plan. In other words, since you don't pay self-employment tax on your capital gains, rental income, or royalties, you can't defer those taxes through a Solo 401(k) vehicle.

Self-Employed and the Self-Employment Tax

According to the IRS, you are self-employed if you are a sole proprietor (including an independent contractor), a partner in a partnership (including a member of a multi-member LLC), or are otherwise in business for yourself. (A sole proprietor also includes the member of a single-member LLC that is disregarded for federal income tax purposes and members of a qualified joint venture.) You usually must pay self-employment tax if you had net earnings from self-employment of $400 or more. Generally, the amount subject to self-employment tax is 92.35 percent of your net earnings from self-employment. Net earnings are calculated by subtracting ordinary and necessary trade or business expenses from the gross income you derived from your trade or business. You can be liable for paying self-employment tax even if you are currently receiving social security benefits.

The self-employment tax rate is a percentage set by law of your net earnings from self-employment. This rate consists of 12.4 percent for social security and 2.9 percent for Medicare taxes. The maximum amount of net earnings subject to the social security tax is set by law and changes annually. All of your net earnings are subject to the Medicare tax. Additional Medicare tax applies to self-employment income above a threshold amount received in taxable years beginning after December 31, 2012. The threshold amounts are $250,000 for a married individual filing a joint return, $125,000 for a married individual filing a separate return, and $200,000 for all others for 2016.

Net earnings from income tax are considered earned income. Earned income includes all the taxable income and wages from working either as an employee or from running or owning a business. It also includes certain other types of taxable income. Earned income includes:

- Wages, salaries, tips, and other taxable employee pay
- Net earnings from self-employment
- Union strike benefits
- Long-term disability benefits received prior to minimum retirement age

Self-Employment Income and Real Estate

In most cases, it is quite evident whether someone has self-employment income. Earning income through the performance of services or via a business is not hard to figure out. However, when it comes to rental real estate, the determination of whether the activity gives rise to self-employment activity and thus makes you eligible to establish and contribute to a Solo 401(k) plan, or whether it is passive rental income and not eligible, is generally based on the facts and circumstances. But it's also based on which tax schedule is filed on your individual federal income tax return (IRS Form 1040) -and how that reflects the rental activity.

Both Schedule C and Schedule E are used for reporting rental income. Rental income is reported to enable the IRS to assess taxes on the income. Rental income could be derived from many sources, including the rental of property and land, as well as personal property.

Typically, someone who is treating their rental income as self-employment or as business income subject to self-employment tax would report the income on the Schedule C of the IRS Form 1040.

The Schedule C is a form used for reporting income subject to self-employment taxes. Income not subject to self-employment tax is generally included on a Schedule E form. One of the more common reasons you may find yourself filling out a Schedule E is if you own real estate that you rent out to tenants. This also includes the rental income you receive when renting out space in the same home you reside in.

In most cases, if you are filing a Schedule E, it is because you are not treating the rental income as self-employment income. Accordingly, the IRS doesn't consider you self-employed, so you won't have to prepare a Schedule C. However, if you provide a range of services to tenants or manage your rental properties as your main business activity, then your participation in the rental may rise to the level of self-employment and require you to file a Schedule C rather than Schedule E. Hence, an individual who only has Schedule E income from real estate rental activities will generally not be eligible to adopt a Solo 401(k) plan, as the individual would not have any income subject to self-employment tax.

No Business Earnings: Is the Solo 401(k) Plan Still an Option?

What about someone who is working on a business or a project that hasn't generated any income yet? In general, where there's anticipation of self-employment income being generated that year (between January 1 and December 31), then that person is eligible to adopt a Solo 401(k) plan. In making that decision, a person needs to be honest with himself about the state or stage of his business plan.

Are you signing the lease on your store and planning to open the doors within a few months? Or are you only in the prototype stage for your invention, still need investment capital from friends and family, and can't reasonably expect to be generating any income for a few years? If so, you should probably hold off setting up your Solo 401(k) plan until your business idea is closer to becoming a reality.

Despite the emphasis on formal activity as an eligibility requirement, the IRS doesn't care how you legally establish your business. You do not need to generate self-employment activity through an LLC, C corporation, S corporation, or partnership. You can do so through a sole proprietorship, such as a freelancer, without any formal legal structure. The type of entity you do your business under is not relevant in this case. It could come into play for other matters involving your Solo 401(k), such as how much your profit-sharing contribution can amount to or when deferral contributions have to be made, but it doesn't impact the question of whether your income is generated by self-employment activity.

Here's what it all boils down to:

- Are you in business for yourself at some level?
- Do you expect to earn any type of income this year through the self-employment work you are engaged in?

If you're sitting on a beach, reading John Grisham novels, and supporting yourself through dividends, rent, alimony, payments from a successful class-action lawsuit, social security, and your pension, then you may be very content but you are not going to satisfy the IRS that you are earning income through self-employment activity. Similarly, if your business plan to create an app that will become more popular than Angry Birds is still in the hobby or idea stage and doesn't have a reasonable expectation of generating self-employment income for you this year, then you likely are not eligible. That doesn't mean you shouldn't be thinking about the advantages of a Solo 401(k) plan should your ideas become more real. In fact, the advantages might be so compelling that they actually give you the kick in the pants you need to get cracking!

Full-Time Employees

The second eligibility requirement is also easy to determine and has a few gray areas worth exploring. Do you have full-time employees working for you? If you do, then you are not eligible to establish a Solo 401(k) plan. If you lack full-time employees, you're home free and the Solo 401(k) plan is yours to adopt.

A full-time employee is defined as someone who works over 1,000 hours during the year, from January 1 to December 31. For context, someone who works 40 hours a week for 52 weeks accrues about 2,040 hours of work time. So a full-time employee can "seem" like someone working less than half time. According to the IRS and the Department of Labor, the person working for you is not considered to be a full-time employee only if that person works under 1,000 hours.

There are other types of employees who, for the purposes of the IRC, are not considered full time. These include people who are under twenty-one years old, union employees, and nonresident alien employees, meaning people who do not have a green card or valid visa to work.

When it comes to the Solo 401(k), why does the government even care whether you have full-time employees or not? This is because the Solo 401(k) is not subject to ERISA. In contrast, an employer of full-time employees is subject to ERISA. ERISA is a body of laws created in the 1970s to protect all employees from employers. This means that the employer has certain responsibilities to his or her employees. If that employer provides access to some sort of employer-based retirement plan, ERISA makes sure that all full-time employees are treated equally and no one is left out in the cold.

The big downside of ERISA is that it's complicated and costly to administer with burdensome reporting and record keeping requirements. For a big company, this is part of the cost of doing business. But for a freelancer, a solo consultant, or a small business, this sort of administration can be a real impediment. So the government decided to forego ERISA compliance for businesses with no full-time employees. Why no need for ERISA? Because a self-employed person is not going to take advantage of him- or herself. The IRS reasonably assumes that you will have your own best interests at heart.

This does bring up an interesting point, however. According to the Department of Labor Regulation 2510.3–3, spouses are not considered full-time employees. In other words, the government does not see the need to police your activities as an employer if your only employee is your spouse. It believes you will do what's right for your spouse and therefore ERISA rules need not and do not apply.

A similar line of thinking works for joint owners of an enterprise. If you have a partnership with two or more people, then those people cannot be considered employees for ERISA purposes, no matter how many hours they work. Therefore, if there are no other full-time employees involved, ERISA does not apply and you are eligible to establish a Solo 401(k) plan.

Who Is Eligible?

These two requirements, the presence of self-employment activity, and the absence of full-time employees fit the bill for a wide variety of people whom I encounter in my work, such as consultants, independent contractors, sole practitioners, doctors, lawyers, dentists, architects, and IT professionals. Often those people have part-time or even full-time jobs in which they are employed by a large corporation, school, hospital, non-profit group, and so on, yet they earn other income on the side. They find the Solo 401(k) a hugely advantageous way to save a lot of money for retirement.

Here are some examples of the kinds of people I encounter regularly.

Paging Dr. Jones

Dr. Jones is an OB/GYN in Tennessee who owns 25 percent of his practice, which employs fifty people. The medical practice has its own 401(k) plan; however, the costs of the plan have become too high, and the practice will need to be shut down.

Talking to his own accountant, Dr. Jones learns that when you move money out of a 401(k) plan, it generally goes into an IRA, unless you have another business with a 401(k) to roll the funds into. This is interesting to Dr. Jones because he also owns a small real estate firm with two properties and no full-time employees. Through that business, Dr. Jones maintains the properties, does improvements, finds tenants, and collects rental income.

The accountant considers this situation and determines that Dr. Jones's real estate business does provide services, since it devotes a lot of resources to managing the properties. She devises a plan whereby Dr. Jones will charge the real estate business a management fee, pay self-employment taxes on that fee, and treat the earned income as self-employment income. By accounting for that money on his Schedule C, Dr. Jones renders himself eligible to adopt a Solo 401(k) plan. This will allow Dr. Jones to move money from his medical 401(k) plan to his new Solo 401(k) plan tax-free, allowing him to make high annual contributions from the self-employment income earned by his real estate firm and to make nontraditional investments and loans.

Unfortunately for Dr. Jones, he can only contribute future funds from his real estate business and not from his medical practice. However, the great news is that he's not limited to $5,500 in annual contributions until he is fifty-five, as would be the case with a Traditional IRA. The Solo 401(k) plan gives him the opportunity to defer at least $54,000 annually for 2017 ($60,000 if over the age of fifty).

Dr. Jones prefers those options better than the alternative and decides to hire his wife into the real estate business to do accounting and bookkeeping. Now they can collectively double their contributions, since ERISA does not apply to a business in which a spouse works.

Connecting Chris

Chris is a self-employed IT consultant in Dallas, Texas. He provides database programming for a number of start-ups with his wife, Jodie, who is also a computer programmer. Together they have an LLC called IT Direct Technology, which is treated as a partnership for tax purposes.

Although they've been in operation for two years, this is the first year that Chris and Jodie have started making money. Their reputation has grown and they've attracted great clients. With that new source of income, they are beginning to think about the best way to save for retirement. Chris and Jodie are both thirty-two years old, and they feel like they are "late to the game" when it comes to retirement.

When Chris learns about the Solo 401(k) plan, he thinks it might provide the answer they need to save more money. Since he's self-employed, has no full-time employees, and his spouse is a partner in the business, he is fully eligible to establish a Solo 401(k) plan for his business. Then Chris and his wife can each defer up to $54,000 into the plan annually for 2017. They are also very excited about the prospect of being able to use the loan feature of the Solo 401(k) to grow their business in a few years by making some serious capital investments into IT.

Now they feel as though their small company can compete against bigger rivals while providing them with all the benefits of being employed.

Sylvia and Her Growing Baby

Sylvia is an accountant at a Fortune 50 company. She's been working for the same organization for twenty-five years and loves her work. She is also a great saver. She is fully vested in her 401(k) plan and maxes out every year.

Sylvia has another interest, however. She designs and makes baby clothes, and sells them online through various websites. Her business was going well until she was featured in a *New York Times* article, and that business suddenly boomed. In the past year, she has been getting orders from all over the world and has generated over $65,000 in pure profits.

Sylvia has no desire to quit her job, and she has the unusual problem of not knowing what to do with all the extra money she is making. But she is worried about the extra taxes she will have to pay as a result. She goes to her accountant to discuss how to reduce her tax burden.

Her accountant immediately suggests setting up a Solo 401(k) plan for her baby clothes business. Since she's already maxing out on her corporate 401(k), she won't be able to take advantage of the Solo 401(k) plan employee deferrals, but she can tap the employer profit-sharing component, which is comparable to a SEP-IRA. Since in this context Sylvia is self-employed, she will be able to put away roughly 20 percent of her net self-employment income. On profits of $65,000, this will amount to around a $13,000 reduction of her tax liability.

She's also drawn to the loan feature of the Solo 401(k). While a SEP does not have a loan feature, the Solo 401(k) does, and this will allow Sylvia to borrow 50 percent of her account value or $50,000, whichever is less, and use that loan for any purpose. Sylvia wants to tap her new Solo 401(k) retirement savings to grow her business without getting into credit card debt or borrowing from her older brother. The interest she must charge herself is very low: Prime interest rate as per the *Wall Street Journal*—which as of December 31, 2016 amounts to 3.75 percent. She'll be able to pay that money plus the interest back to her Solo 401(k) after using it to grow her business.

Finally, the accountant asks Sylvia if she would like to employ her husband in the business. She knows that Sylvia's husband is a semiretired computer programmer. If she does, Sylvia's husband, who is over fifty, will be able to defer $24,000 plus 20 percent of his compensation for an annual contribution maximum of $56,000 for 2017.

To Sylvia, this is a no-brainer. The Solo 401(k) is like a dream come true.

The "Controlled Group" Rules

Sometimes people still want to set up a Solo 401(k) even though their business has full-time employees. They wonder if they can set up a separate entity and draw income to it from the main business, then defer that income into a Solo 401(k).

Why would they want to do such a thing? For the simple reason that providing retirement benefits for employees costs a lot of money. Let's say, for example, you have fifty employees who are making, on average, $50,000 each. ERISA will require that you provide a 3 percent safe-harbor match for those employees, amounting to approximately $75,000 in total annually. The safe harbor contributions are deductible by the employer, but this could still become a significant business expense. In addition, you'll have to pay a record keeper to track and file everything the government requires. As a result, you may decide that it's too expensive or too burdensome to provide those retirement benefits to your employees.

On the other hand, you still want to save money for retirement for yourself. So what do you do? One lawyer I know decided to set up a separate LLC. He then had his law firm pay that LLC $100,000 per year so that he could defer it into his own Solo 401(k) plan tax-free. The IRS and the Department of Labor said, "Not so fast."

Basically, if you own 80 percent or more of a company that has employees, or if a lineal descendant does, and you also own a separate company that does or does not provide services to that first company, the IRS and the Department of Labor would likely consider you all part of one big company. This ensures that you will need to offer the same retirement benefits to everyone employed by either company. All of this falls under the "Controlled Group" rules set up by the IRS and the Department of Labor. Those rules were established specifically to protect employees from a business owner establishing a separate 401(k) plan for another business in order to avoid offering those employees the same benefits.

IRC Section 414 stipulates that a "Controlled Group" of corporations is any two or more corporations connected through stock ownership. They may be a parent-subsidiary group (when one member of the first corporations owns 80 percent of the other corporation), a brother-sister group (when five or fewer individuals own at least 80 percent of the stock of the corporations), or a combined group (which involves some combination of a parent-subsidiary and brother-sister group).

To determine whether someone is part of a "Controlled Group," the IRS takes into account the stock attribution rules. These are the rules by which shares or interest in the corporation are attributed. In general, you are also considered to be in control of those shares if the shares are in your spouse's name or your children's, grandchildren's, or parents' names.

The IRS does allow a company to be treated as a separate line of business if that entity has a valid business purpose and includes at least fifty employees. There are also restrictions on HCE (highly compensated employees) ratios in each separate business line, and the IRS must be notified of any request for approval.

Do all members of a "Controlled Group" have to participate in one plan? No. The members of a "Controlled Group" may each have a different plan. Similarly, two or more members of the "Controlled Group" may adopt a single plan. In either case, all employees of the "Controlled Group" must be taken into account for testing purposes.

For example, if one company is owned by a shareholder with greater than 80 percent and has no employees, but that same person also has ownership of over 80 percent in another company with full-time employees, a single plan may be adopted for both companies. However, the adopted plan must provide benefits to the eligible employees from the second company.

In other words, the rules are in place to restrict the owner(s) of a business with full-time employees from establishing a new company with no employees and adopting a Solo 401(k) plan that would exclude the full-time employees from the other company. The IRS and Department of Labor want to ensure that all eligible employees of a company that is part of a "Controlled Group" receives all available retirement benefits.

Here are some examples that illustrate the rules:

No, You Can't #1

Joe owns 90 percent of Company A that has three employees. Joe wants to adopt a qualified retirement plan but does not want to offer any benefits to his employees, so he decides to establish a new company that has no employees and adopt a Solo 401(k) plan through that new company. Before proceeding, Joe talks with a tax attorney about his idea. Joe's tax attorney quickly points out that since Joe would own more than 80 percent of Company A and the newly established company, both companies would be part of a "Controlled Group." This would prohibit Joe from establishing a plan for the new company without offering the employees from Company A the same plan benefits.

No, You Can't #2

Joe owns 45 percent of Company A and Joe's son, Mike, owns the remaining 55 percent interest. Company A has five full-time employees. Joe and Mike want to establish a 401(k) plan, so they make tax-deferred contributions, but they don't want to provide the employees with any plan benefits. Joe and Mike come up with the idea of forming a new company that will have no employees other than themselves in order to adopt a 401(k) plan through the new company. Joe talks this over with his tax attorney and learns that since Joe and Mike are father and son, under IRC Section 318 they will be treated as owning each other's shares, giving them each over 80 percent interest in Company A and triggering the "Controlled Group" rules. Hence, Joe and Mike would be limited from opening a 401(k) plan for the new business and not offering plan benefits to the employees from Company A. Joe and Mike could establish a plan for the new company, but the "Controlled Group" rules would require that the plan benefits be provided to all eligible employees from both companies.

Yes, You Can #1

Joe owns 78 percent of Company A, and Tim, his friend, owns the remaining 22 percent. Company A has twelve full-time employees and does not have a 401(k) Plan. Tim does some consulting on a part-time basis that has no relationship to Company A and wants to establish a new corporation for his consulting business and then to establish a Solo 401(k) plan through that new corporation. Tim asks his tax attorney whether he could adopt a Solo 401(k) plan for his new business without being required to offer benefits to the twelve full-time employees with Company A. Tim's tax attorney tells Tim that because he owns less than 80 percent of Company A and his consulting business does not provide services to Company A, new consulting company would not be part of a "Controlled Group" so he would not be required to offer 401(k) benefits from his new consulting company to the Company A employees.

No, You Can't #3

Joe and Tim each own 50 percent of Company A, which has four full-time employees. Company A currently offers its employees 401(k) plan benefits. Joe and Tim are each over the age of fifty-nine and a half, and are interested in using some of their retirement funds to purchase real estate. Unfortunately, Company A's retirement plan does not allow for nontraditional investments such as real estate. Joe and Tim decide to establish a new corporation, which they will each own 50 percent of and then have that new company adopt a new 401(k) plan. Before proceeding, Joe and Tim decide to speak with their tax attorney to make sure this strategy would work.

Joe and Tim's tax attorney advises them that since the new company will be owned by the both of them, just like Company A, the "Controlled Group" rules would be triggered since the same five or fewer individuals own at least 80 percent of the stock of the two corporations. Thus, Jim and Tim would not be able to adopt a new 401(k) plan without offering the same benefits to the employees from Company A.

To learn more about how "Controlled Group" rules apply, you'll need to consult a tax attorney, but the examples above should give you a pretty clear understanding of the basics.

The Solo 401(k) Plan and the SIMPLE: The Exclusive Plan Rules

Now let's consider a different set of restrictions that deal with limitations on adopting a Solo 401(k) plan. Basically, these rules prevent you from "double dipping" when it comes to tax deferments for retirement savings.

An employer establishing or maintaining a SIMPLE IRA plan is generally not able to maintain another retirement plan, including a Solo 401(k) plan. However, there are two exceptions to this exclusive plan rule. First, an employer may maintain a separate plan for union employees if those employees are excluded from the SIMPLE IRA. Second, in the case of a merger or acquisition, the employer may maintain both the SIMPLE IRA and another plan for the year the transaction takes place and for the following two calendar years.

The Exclusive Plan rule comes into effect when an individual who has recently established a SIMPLE IRA or has recently made contributions to a SIMPLE IRA wishes to establish a Solo 401(k) plan for that taxable year. Because that person had made SIMPLE IRA contributions already during the taxable year, a Solo 401(k) plan cannot be established because of the SIMPLE IRA Exclusive Plan rules. However, if the SIMPLE IRA plan was in existence during the year but no SIMPLE IRA contributions were made, then that person could adopt and contribute to a Solo 401(k) plan during the same year, though no SIMPLE IRA contributions can be made going forward. However, if the SIMPLE IRA was open for less than two years, SIMPLE IRA contributions will not be eligible to be rolled into a 401(k) plan.

Satisfying Requirements

Why are Solo 401(k) plan eligibility requirements so important to satisfy? It's all about ERISA. The government wanted to establish a plan for small businesses owners with no full-time employees and sole proprietors that would not be subject to the administrative burden, cost, and complexity of ERISA rules. But the government also wanted to ensure that the self-employed or small business owner with no full-time employees were offered the same advantages and benefits of an ERISA 401(k) plan.

The Solo 401(k) is so attractive in part because it is so incredibly simple to administer and does not require you to satisfy the complex ERISA nondiscrimination testing rules, such as the Top-Heavy Test. However, you are not able to adopt a Solo 401(k) plan if you have full-time employees, are in violation of the "Controlled Group" rules, or have an existing active SIMPLE IRA. To most people, that seems more than fair.

Now let's look at the nuts and bolts of adopting a Solo 401(k) plan.

CHAPTER 4

How to Adopt a Solo 401(k) Plan

So HOW DO YOU ADOPT a Solo 401(k)? The first answer is that you don't have to do it alone. Even though the Solo 401(k) is meant for individuals who want take a personal approach to retirement savings, this doesn't mean they need to create the plan themselves. You can, and probably should, consult a tax professional or tax attorney about the details to determine which features of the plan best suit your specific tax, retirement, and investment goals. And there's nothing wrong with getting that professional to create your paperwork for you also.

Just because you like the freedom of driving your car doesn't mean you need to know how to build one. On the other hand, you may actually want to build your car, or at least repair it, and it certainly doesn't hurt to know how the engine works or how to change a flat. In that spirit, let's go over the nuts and bolts of adopting a Solo 401(k) plan, and then you can decide how you want to go about adopting it later.

It May Be Personal, but It Is Also Business

First of all, you're actually setting up your plan for your business. Even though a Solo 401(k) plan is also called an Individual 401(k) plan, the plan is actually adopted by the employer or business. Unlike a traditional IRA and Roth IRA, which can be established by any individual with earned income, a Solo 401(k) plan is a retirement plan that *must* be adopted by the employer or business. Similar to a SEP-IRA and SIMPLE IRA, a Solo 401(k) plan must be established by the business for the benefit of the employee(s). In other words, an individual with no self-employment income via a business is not eligible to adopt or establish a Solo 401(k) plan. That individual may be eligible for an IRA or Roth IRA but would not be able to benefit from a 401(k) plan.

To see how it's done...

Let's Follow Fred

Fred's been working for a major consulting firm for most of his career, and he's now in his early forties. Early in his career, Fred found that the consulting firm helped him immensely. It got him started, taught him how to consult, brought him clients, and nudged him along. Now it's the other way round, and Fred is the one bringing in clients, developing new ideas, and teaching younger consultants the ropes. Overall, the firm has gone stale, and a series of missteps has hurt its reputation. Fred, and two of his colleagues, Rick and Denise, decide it's time to go out on their own. So the three, as equal partners, form a boutique firm called Blue Sky Consulting LLC, a newly established limited liability company.

There are a million things to do in order to launch the firm, but Fred and his partners want the foundation to be strong so they consider all the details. They want their firm to be small and have no desire to hire employees other than their spouses. One of the things they're worried about is how to retain the benefits they currently rely upon. They know they can now get healthcare through the Affordable Care Act, but they still want a retirement plan that's better than a traditional IRA. Fred suggests the Solo 401(k).

Fred has a lot of working life left and plenty of retirement money saved in his old corporate 401(k), but he's very ambitious to build his wealth quickly and he wants to pay as little tax on his earnings as possible. The Solo 401(k) has a ton of advantages and features that make it extremely appealing. Fred explains those to his partners, and they enthusiastically agree. They give Fred the green light to adopt a plan.

Which Option Is Best?

When it comes to deciding what type of Solo 401(k) plan is best for you and your business, it is important to look at all the options the plan provides to make sure it will satisfy your retirement planning, tax, and investment goals.

Most banks and financial institutions, such as Vanguard, Charles Schwab, and E*Trade offer Solo 401(k) plans and in some cases offer them for no fee. However, these Solo 401(k) plans only permit the plan participant to make limited investments, no alternative asset investments, and without benefiting from most of the available IRS-approved options such as the tax-free loan and Roth contributions. The reason behind this is quite simple. Financial institutions make money when they hold your funds and you buy their financial products, such as stocks and mutual funds, which generate fees for them. Most major financial institutions that offer Solo 401(k) plans restrict some of the plan features—such as alternative investments like real estate, the loan feature, and the after-tax (Roth) contribution option—to keep as much of your money in their hands, working for them.

If Fred and his partners' main retirement goals were to make pretax contributions and invest in stocks and related financial products, then a financial institution Solo 401(k) would be a great and very cost-effective option. However, if Fred and his partners were interested in having the ability to make traditional investments, such as stocks, as well as alternative assets like real estate, along with having the $50,000 loan feature and the ability to make (after-tax) Roth contributions, then they would need to seek out a plan provider company that offers a more self-directed open architecture Solo 401(k) plan.

Fred wanted to look at these options in more detail and did some research online about the Solo 401(k) plan options available for Blue Sky Consulting. Since the ability to make different types of investments, such as precious metals and real estate, and the loan feature were all important to Fred, Fred felt that the cookie-cutter financial institution Solo 401(k) plan documents would not work for him and his partners. He also liked the fact that a number of specialized Solo 401(k) plan provider companies offer tax advisory services that help with the adoption, establishment, and administration of the plan. This felt comforting and reassuring to him since the tax rules regarding qualified retirement plans can get tricky and complicated fast.

The Resolution

Before establishing a Solo 401(k) plan, Fred reviewed the LLC Operating Agreement and confirmed that all managers of the LLC would have to unanimously agree prior to the adoption of a retirement plan. In the case of a sole proprietorship or LLC, no formal corporate resolutions are required; however, Fred thought it would be a good idea to prepare a simple resolution that all the managers would sign. In contrast, an S corporation or C corporation must generally have a board resolution to adopt a plan. In addition, the individual establishing the Solo 401(k) on behalf of Blue Sky must be authorized to do so. In general, an officer(s) of the corporation or manager(s) of an LLC are the person(s) typically authorized to adopt the plan on behalf of the entity.

The path is similar in the case of a partnership or LLC. Documentation (generally the partnership or LLC Operating Agreement) must be followed when determining the mechanics involved for adopting a Solo 401(k) plan. For example, the partnership or LLC may require greater than 50 percent partner or member approval or even an unanimous approval, in some cases, before establishing a qualified retirement plan. Likewise, the partner or member/manager who establishes the plan must have the requisite authority to do so on behalf of the organization.

When Can You Adopt the Plan?

In general, a Solo 401(k) plan can be established at any time during the year. However, it must be established in the year in which the plan features are being utilized. In other words, an employer must adopt a Solo 401(k) in order for its participants(s) to be able to benefit from the plans features that year, including making contributions to the plan for the year of adoption. For example, if the Solo 401(k) plan was established on January 1,

2017, a plan participant would not be able to make contributions for the 2016 taxable year.

The Plan Documents

In Chapter 2, we touched on the difference between a master plan, which is the most basic approach; a prototype plan, which can be somewhat customized to an individual's preferences and needs; and an individual designed plan, which is highly customized but has extensive costs and filing fees.

Under a master plan, a single trust or custodial account is established as part of the plan for the joint use of all adopting employers. Under a prototype plan, a separate trust or custodial account is established for each employer. If the plan being adopted is a master or prototype, the documentation will consist of three main components: the basic plan document, the adoption agreement, and the plan summary description agreement.

Basic Plan Document

The basic plan document contains all of the nonelective provisions and rules governing the plan that are applicable to all adopting employers. It explains the terms and conditions under which the plan must operate in order to remain in compliance with regulatory requirements.

The Adoption Agreement

The adoption agreement contains the elective provisions that are included in the basic plan document. These are the choices the employer makes about how the plan will operate in terms of eligibility requirements, the vesting schedule, the loan feature, contributions, allocations, and so on. The adoption agreement is not the complete plan document, as it generally indicates only certain plan features that would be available to plan participants. The adoption agreement must generally be accompanied by a basic plan document, which provides in-depth details of how the plan should operate and the plan summary description document.

The employer should complete each provision in the adoption agreement, even if the employer is a sole proprietor with no employees. Once the employer signs the adoption agreement and the plan document, he or she should keep a copy and provide an executed copy to the plan document sponsor company. A copy of the basic plan document and adoption agreement does not have to be provided to each plan participant. If the plan is an individually designed plan or a volume submitter plan, the document will typically be self-contained. For example, there will likely be only one basic plan document, or at most there will be a basic plan document and an accompanying trust agreement.

For their purposes, Fred and his partners choose to go with a prototype plan because it allows a lot of flexibility but is not too costly or burdensome to administer. However, Fred's tax lawyer cautions him on one aspect. If Blue Sky Consulting adopts a preapproved prototype plan and then makes changes to the underlying plan document, the IRS may determine that they have actually adopted an individually designed plan, and the employer may not be able to rely on the IRS determination letter, which confirms the plan's legality. This depends on the changes that have been made and is subject to the amending rules of the individually designed plan.

How Do You Identify Your Plan?

In order to identify your plan to the IRS, a three-digit plan sequence number is used in annual reporting to the IRS. Your business determines the number, beginning with 001, for the first plan the business establishes. For example, if this is the fourth plan your business maintains or has maintained, the plan sequence number would be 004.

The Summary Plan Description (SPD)

A summary plan description (SPD) document is generally not required for a Solo 401(k) plan since the plan will typically only cover the owner and his or her spouse. Nevertheless, as Fred's tax attorney informs him, it is common practice to provide an SPD to each participant in a Solo 401(k) plan. The information must also be written in a way that the average plan participant can understand.

In the case of an ERISA 401(k) plan with employees, the adopting 401(k) employer must distribute the SPD to all eligible, common-law employees within 120 days of the plan's adoption. After the initial distribution of the SPD, the employer must distribute the document to new employees within 90 days after the employees become eligible to participate. The employer also must distribute the SPD to beneficiaries under the plan within 90 days after they begin receiving benefits.

Employers need only provide SPDs to the Department of Labor when requested. It is good practice for the plan provider or the attorney drafting the plan to provide an SPD to all plan participants as quickly as possible. With a Solo 401(k) plan, it is good practice to provide a copy SPD to all eligible plan participants.

The SPD is one of the Solo 401(k) plan's most important documents because it outlines in plain English all the relevant features of the 401(k) plan being adopted by the employer. In the case of a Solo 401(k) plan, it is not as important as an ERISA plan, because the owner of the business that adopted the plan is familiar with the available features of the plan that were selected to be made available. The SPD is a great resource for a Solo 401(k) plan participant who wants to better understand some of the available features of the plan without having to try to decipher the legalese contained in the plan documents.

In general, a SPD is a written summary of the provisions of an employee benefit plan that contains the terms of the plan and the benefits offered. The SPD must be written in plain language and be sufficiently accurate and comprehensive to reasonably apprise participants and beneficiaries of their rights and obligations under the plan.

The SPD typically details when an employee can begin to participate in the plan. It also describes the benefits provided by the plan, states when benefits become vested, and describes the remedies available if a claim for benefits is denied in whole or in part. If a plan is altered, participants must be informed, either through a revised SPD or in a separate document called a "summary of material modifications," both of which must also be given to plan participants without a fee. The SPD does not have to be filed with the Department of Labor, but it must be provided to the Department of Labor upon request.

EGTRRA Amendments

Fred's attorney also tells him that he will need to pay attention to updates in the EGTRRA and make good-faith efforts to amend the Blue Sky Solo 401(k) plan accordingly. The plan sponsor company will generally need to provide Blue Sky with the necessary documents to amend the plan documents as required by law.

Naming Your Solo 401(k) Plan: An IRS Surprise

Considering how big and complex the IRC is, it may be surprising to learn that there are no IRS rules or regulations that directly relate to how you should title or name your Solo 401(k) plan. In general, the common practice is to include some variation of the business name that adopted the plan with any of the following words or terms: 401(k) plan or 401(k), Solo 401(k), Individual 401(k) or IK plan, or Self-Employed 401(k).

For example, for ABC Corporation, the plan name could be the ABC Corporation Solo 401(k) plan, the ABC Corporation 401(k) plan, the ABC Corporation Individual 401(k) plan, the ABC Corporation Self-Employed 401(k) plan, or ABC Corporation IK plan. In other words, there is no right or wrong way to name your plan. It is a good idea from a banking and investment perspective, however, to have some reference to the fact that the account is associated with a tax-exempt retirement plan.

Trust Agreement

A 401(k) plan is essentially a trust. This is spelled out in IRC Section 401, which states that the plan's assets must be held in a trust. For this reason, the party responsible for the plan's investments is called a trustee.

Most plan documents incorporate the trust agreement and trust language into the basic plan document. However, it is not uncommon for a Solo 401(k) plan to have a separate individual trust agreement. The trust agreement contained in the basic plan document generally sets forth the responsibilities and duties of the trustee with respect to the Solo 401(k) plan.

So in the case of Blue Sky Consulting LLC, Fred checked the plan adoption agreement he received and saw that the prototype plan documents he was using stated that the trust provisions contained in the basic plan documents would apply to his plan. In other words, Fred's plan documents did not include a separate trust agreement, as all the relevant trust provisions were already contained in the plan document adopted by Blue Sky Consulting LLC, when Fred signed the adoption agreement.

Appointment of Trustee

The adoption agreement appoints the person who will serve as trustee of the Solo 401(k) plan. According to the IRS, a plan trustee is someone who has the exclusive authority and discretion to manage and control the plan assets. The plan trustee's job is to accept plan funds, manage them prudently, and distribute them to beneficiaries. A plan sponsor can either choose individual trustees—usually the owners or officers of the business—or a single institutional trustee, such as an affiliate of a bank, insurance company, or other financial institution.

In general, most Solo 401(k) plan documents allow the adopting employer to choose between two types of trustees (both of which are fiduciaries). First, there is a *discretionary trustee*, which is the most popular trustee option. It provides the trustee with exclusive authority and discretion over the management and control of plan assets. A discretionary trustee has fiduciary responsibility and liability for the selection, monitoring, and replacement of plan assets. Since the Solo 401(k) plan is generally adopted by a sole proprietorship or small business with no full-time employees, the business owner would typically serve as the trustee of the plan and should have no issue with performing all the discretionary trustee related responsibilities. In other words, a discretionary trustee has full power over all Solo 401(k) plan investments and plan-related activities, which is generally what the employer is seeking when adopting the plan.

In contrast, a *directed trustee* is a trustee who is subject to the direction of a named fiduciary who is not a trustee or an investment manager. A directed trustee has fiduciary responsibility and liability for taking direction for the selection, monitoring, and replacement of plan assets, and also has fiduciary responsibility and liability for monitoring the timing of deposits, transactions activity and accuracy, compliance with regulations under the Department of Labor and the IRS, and so on. In the case of a Solo 401(k) plan, it is extremely uncommon to have a trustee categorized as a directed trustee, since it runs in contrast to the main benefits of a Solo 401(k) plan, which is control over one's plan investments.

In some cases, a financial organization may be appointed as trustee of the plan, but typically the employer will choose the trustee. With a Solo 401(k) plan, the sole owner usually prefers to be the trustee of the plan. The reason for this is simple: the person who decides on a Solo 401(k) and adopts one almost always wants to be responsible for making the decisions about the plan's assets, as well as plan investment decisions.

Can a third-party serve as trustee of a Solo 401(k) plan? The answer is yes, but this is rarely done and entails a certain degree of risk. After all, would you want to put your retirement plan funds at the sole discretion of someone other than yourself? Even though the plan would be the owner of record on all such trustee investments, such a scenario could lead to fraud, bad decisions, and other negative outcomes.

Instead, in almost every case, the business owner or officer will serve as trustee of the plan. Fred and his partners have no interest in putting all plan investment authority and discretion in the hands of a third party, even though they know that all income, including losses and gains, would flow back to the plan.

Can a Plan Have More Than One Trustee?

In the case of a Solo 401(k) plan, more than one trustee can be appointed. Typically, with respect to a Solo 401(k) plan, this is done when there is more than one plan participant: for example, the business owner and spouse.

With Blue Sky Consulting, because there are three partners involved, the group decides to make Fred and Denise the cotrustees of the plan. Fred is the most knowledgeable of the plan and Denise is the most astute investor. In this case, both Fred and Denise will share the trustee powers as outlined by the basic plan document.

In most Solo 401(k) plans, the trustee has the authority to make decisions on behalf of the trust and is responsible for the day-to day operations of the trust, including but not limited to:

- Receiving plan contributions, and holding, investing, and reinvesting the funds as authorized
- Maintaining accurate records of contributions, investments, earnings, receipts, disbursements, withdrawals, and other transactions under the trust
- Making disbursements from the portion of the trust funds applicable to the respective participant or beneficiary

In addition, a standard basic plan document will provide a trustee of a Solo 401(k) plan certain powers, including the ability to:

- Purchase or subscribe for securities or other property and retain them in the Solo 401(k) plan trust
- Sell or exchange plan property as appropriate
- Engage in IRS-approved investments that are allowable under the plan document
- Consent, oppose, or participate in any plan reorganization, consolidation, merger, or other similar plan

- Consent, oppose, or participate in any contract, lease, mortgage, or purchase on behalf of the plan
- Accept and retain any securities or other property issued to the plan and to deposit such property where appropriate
- Agree to pay expenses or assessments levied with respect to any securities or other property so purchased or deposited by the plan
- Assign, renew, extend, or discharge any debt, mortgage, or other lien as may be deemed advisable
- Collect and receive any and all monies, securities, or other property due or owing or belonging to the plan
- Exercise personally or by general or limited power of attorney in connection with any plan matter
- Settle, compromise, or submit to arbitration, any claims, debts, or damages due or owing
- Borrow money from others for purposes of the plan or plan investment, upon such terms and conditions as the trustee may deem proper

What Is the Advantage of Having Two or More Solo 401(k) Plan Trustees?

When it comes to financial matters, people generally like to have control over how their financial assets are being managed. The same thought process applies to Solo 401(k) plan participants. Since the Solo 401(k) plan trustee is responsible for most of the day-day functions of the plan, it is typical for both plan participants, whether they are co-owners or husband and wife, to serve as trustee. On the other hand, serving as trustee is not a requirement. Particularly in the case of spouses, one spouse is usually appointed as trustee of the plan and that person deals with the day-to-day operations and activities of the plan while presumably making the bigger decisions together with the spouse.

There is one advantage, however, to having both spouses serve as trustees of the Solo 401(k) plan, especially if the business is a sole proprietorship. If one of the spouses should die, it is much better to have one remaining trustee of the plan in place because this allows for the easy transfer or rollover of the plan's assets into an IRA. Unfortunately, this happens more often than any of us would like, and nominating the other spouse as cotrustee can mitigate all the difficulties of dealing with the plan's assets. We don't worry about this when the plan's sponsor is a corporation because a corporation doesn't die. In the case of a sole proprietorship, once the owner of the business dies, the business dies with him or her and thus is not eligible to keep the Solo 401(k) open. When that happens, the plan is terminated and the assets are moved into an IRA in the name of the spouse, or the assets become an inherited IRA if the spouse is not a beneficiary.

When a spouse is not a cotrustee, this process becomes much more complex and can potentially involve probate and trust and estate matters. When a spouse is a cotrustee, he or she can take action on behalf of the plan and accomplish whatever is necessary to close the plan and move the plan assets into an IRA in an efficient manner.

One potential downside of having two trustees is that both trustees will generally have to sign all investment-related documents. This may nor may not be a big deal, but it is something that should be kept in mind when deciding who to appoint as trustee of your Solo 401(k) plan.

Since Blue Sky Consulting is an LLC, the business entity would only cease to exist if the LLC was dissolved. However, knowing that Fred and Denise are cotrustees makes any decisions that might need to be made in the event of either of their deaths much easier.

Beneficiary Designation

As part of establishing a Solo 401(k) plan, it is necessary to designate primary and contingent beneficiaries in the case of death of a plan participant.

The beneficiary will be the person or persons who will be the recipient of the deceased plan participant's Solo 401(k) assets.

In general, a spouse is almost always appointed as primary beneficiary of the other spouse's Solo 401(k) plan funds. This is so conventional that in common law property states, if you choose to elect a nonspouse as your primary beneficiary of your plan's assets, your spouse will have to sign and consent to the appointment of a nonspousal beneficiary. If the spouse elects to not be appointed as primary beneficiary of the plan account before the age of thirty-five, he or she must waive the election once again upon reaching the age of thirty-five.

By electing to have a spouse as beneficiary of the plan assets, all assets are transferred to the spouse tax-free and penalty-free upon the plan owner's death. This occurs by having the funds transferred from the plan to an IRA in the name of the spouse. The IRA will then become the spouse's IRA.

It is possible to elect more than one primary beneficiary. When doing so, it's important to select the percentages that determine the amount of plan proceeds distributed to each primary beneficiary.

For Blue Sky Consulting, Fred's wife is his sole beneficiary, and Denise's husband is her sole beneficiary. Rick, on the other hand, is in the middle of a divorce that has not been finalized. He is able to get his wife's consent to designate a nonspouse beneficiary and elects his four children as 25 percent beneficiaries each of his plans.

Are the Plan Proceeds from a 401(k) Plan Subject to Estate Taxes?

The answer is maybe. If the plan proceeds will be transferred to the spouse, there is generally no estate tax on the transfer due to the marital deduction. The marital deduction is straightforward. The estate executor totals the value of all assets owned by the deceased to arrive at the gross estate. From this sum, the value of all property left to the surviving spouse is subtracted.

The marital deduction is one of the major deductions in determining the taxable estate. There is no limit to the amount of the marital deduction. A married person easily can eliminate estate taxes by leaving the entire estate to his or her surviving spouse.

A spouse has the option either to roll inherited Solo 401(k) funds into his own individual retirement account with no tax liability at the time of the rollover, or to begin annual distributions based on his life expectancy, regardless of age. This allows the beneficiary to avoid the usual 10 percent early distribution penalty on funds withdrawn before he reaches age fifty-nine and a half. Only applicable income tax is due on distributions. It is important to remember to update the appointed primary beneficiary of your 401(k) plan in the case of his or her death.

If the 401(k) plan proceeds are left to a nonspouse (for example, a child, relative, or friend), then the amount of the plan transfer could be subject to estate taxes. In the case of Rick, upon his death the transfer of the 401(k) assets to his children could become subject to estate tax if his assets exceed a certain value.

For 2016, 401(k) account balances were not directly taxed at death. However, the plan participant's estate may be responsible for paying taxes if the assets exceed a certain value. In general, a 401(k) account may be subject to estate tax. Estates worth less than about $5.45 million are exempt from estate tax for the 2016 taxable year. Hence, if Rick's total estate on the date of his death is less than $5.45 million, his children would generally be able to receive the proceeds from his 401(k) plan without tax. Remember, because the 401(k) plan funds are being left to his kids and not his spouse, there would be no martial exemption from estate taxes, if applicable. Whereas, if Fred's estate was above that amount, an estate tax would be due.

Nonspouses cannot roll funds received from a 401(k) plan into their traditional IRA, but they can have the employer transfer the funds into an inherited IRA. This allows the assets to continue to grow tax deferred until the beneficiary reaches retirement age. A beneficiary can also take a distribution from the plan and pay tax on the amount as regular income.

There is no early withdrawal penalty if the distribution is taken from the deceased's plan. Once funds are rolled over into an inherited IRA, they are subject to regular IRA rules.

Does a Plan Beneficiary Receive All Plan Funds at Once?

In general, a married participant of a 401(k) plan is required by law to have the amount remaining in the plan paid to a spouse in a certain manner. So this would apply to Fred and Denise at Blue Sky. The manner of payment, often referred to as a "qualified preretirement survivor annuity," will provide the surviving spouse with a series of periodic payments over his or her life. The size of the periodic payments will largely depend on the amount remaining in the plan account.

The spouse may elect to waive the qualified preretirement survivor annuity election and elect instead to receive the funds in a lump sum that will be rolled over into another retirement account, assuming the plan has this option. Fred's wife Joan immediately does so; however, Denise's husband Alex thinks the periodic payment approach will suit his lifestyle and approach to money management better.

If the spouse elects to waive the qualified preretirement survivor annuity payment method before reaching the age of thirty-five, he or she must waive the election again once reaching the age of thirty-five.

Contingent Beneficiaries

After selecting the primary beneficiary of the 401(k) plan in the case of death, the individual plan participant then has the ability to select one or more contingent beneficiaries. The contingent beneficiary is the person who would receive the plan proceeds if the primary beneficiary is no longer alive.

You are able to elect more than one contingent beneficiary. If you do elect more than one though, you need to select the appropriate percentages that determine the amount of plan proceeds to be distributed to each beneficiary.

Fred chooses his children as his contingent beneficiaries in case Joan dies. Denise and Alex do not have children, so they choose Denise's sister, Laura, as their contingent beneficiary.

It is good practice to update your list of contingent beneficiaries every few years and especially in the case of the death of one of them.

Loan Documents

Under certain situations, if permitted by the plan adoption agreement, plan participants may be eligible to obtain loans of their vested plan balances, including rollover amounts, before the incidence of a distribution triggering event. Usually, using retirement funds would trigger a prohibited transaction, but Solo 401(k) plan loans represents a limited statutory exception to the prohibited-transaction rules[7].

In general, a 401(k) plan must follow two different sets of rules, one from the IRS and one from the Department of Labor, to allow for loans and to avoid tax and penalties. However, in the case of a Solo 401(k) plan, the IRS rules would apply. These rules are generally focused on the amount of assets available for the loan and the instances that could potentially trigger taxation.

The basic plan documents include all the loan documentation required to take a loan from your Solo 401(k) plan, including a loan application form, lending disclosure statement, and loan agreement. The process of completing a loan via a Solo 401(k) plan generally involves the plan participant completing these three forms. The plan participant is required

7 See IRC 4975(d)(1).

to sign the appropriate loan documents, and in addition, the plan participant's spouse must also sign the documents to give consent to the loan.

The plan administrator is also required to accept the loan application. For a Solo 401(k) plan, this is usually not an obstacle since the plan administrator is also typically the plan participant. If the plan administrator is not the plan participant, then the administrator should keep all loan documents.

A more detailed description of the loan process and features will be covered in Chapter 5. While no one at Blue Sky is ready to tap a loan from their vested plan balance, Fred is interested in doing so some years down the line to invest in some property he has his eye on.

Transfer Request Forms for Incoming Funds Transfers

The plan documents include a direct rollover form to assist you in transferring funds from your current trustee or custodian to the new Solo 401(k) plan. The purpose of the direct rollover request form is to notify the financial institution that is currently holding the retirement funds that the plan participant wishes to roll over your retirement funds to your new Solo 401(k) plan account. The direct rollover request form will inform the current retirement account custodian that the plan participant seeks to roll over his or her retirement funds to a 401(k) qualified retirement plan. This is important, because a rollover to a 401(k) plan is treated as a tax-free rollover and *not* a taxable distribution because the funds are going from one retirement account to another. Therefore, the direct rollover request form alerts the custodian that the funds will be rolled over tax-free and penalty-free to a 401(k) qualified retirement plan, as well as the name of the institution that will be receiving the funds.

Newly Assigned Employer Identification Number (EIN) from the IRS

An Employer Identification Number (EIN) is also referred to as a Federal Tax Identification Number. The EIN is generally used to identify a business entity or trust, such as a retirement plan. In general, a tax employer identification number (EIN) will be acquired on behalf of the plan. The EIN is used to allow the plan to open a bank account.

There is actually no formal requirement that an EIN be acquired for a Solo 401(k) plan since it is an owner-only plan. Many Solo 401(k) plan sponsors will use the plan participant's social security number or business EIN as the plan tax identification number. With Blue Sky Consulting, because there are three partners benefiting from the plan, Fred decides to acquire a separate EIN.

Does the Solo 401(k) Plan Trust Need an EIN?

A 401(k) plan is a trust, and under IRC Section 401, plan assets must be held in trust. There is no IRS or Department of Labor requirement that a separate trust be created in connection with the establishment of the plan. As a result, a separate trust is often not established as per the plan documents. This is the reason why, in such a case, no separate trust agreement is required to be included in the plan documents, and it is also why a separate EIN is not required to be acquired for the plan trust. Typically, an EIN would only be acquired for the plan itself. In the case of plan documents that include a separate trust agreement, some plan providers will suggest a separate EIN be acquired.

Process for Acquiring a Solo 401(k) Plan EIN

As mentioned, Fred and Denise decide that an EIN is best for Blue Sky's Solo 401(k) plan. An EIN can be acquired by completing an online questionnaire at the IRS website or by completing and sending in IRS Form SS-4 to an IRS representative. When securing an EIN for a Solo 401(k) plan, the IRS will require the following information:

- Name of adopting employer: Blue Sky Consulting
- Address and phone number of adopting employer: Baltimore, Maryland

- Name of trustee of plan: Fred Rankin and Denise Albolene
- Name of plan: Blue Sky Solo 401(k) Plan

IRS Determination Letter

The basic plan documents should include an IRS determination letter stating that this is a prototype plan that meets the requirements of a qualified plan. Most plan document sponsors request that the IRS review the plan document and issue a favorable determination letter on its qualified status in order to ensure that it complies with the IRC. Requesting a determination letter is not legally required, but many plan sponsors choose to do so.

Typically, the document sponsor company will be the party responsible for acquiring the plan IRS determination letter. In the case of a prototype document sponsor such as Fidelity, Vanguard, or IRA Financial Group, the document sponsor will provide the adopting employer with the plan documents and determination letter. It is good practice to keep a copy of the IRS determination letter along with executed copies of the plan documents.

Generally, if an employer adopts a standardized master or prototype plan, the employer may rely on the master or prototype document sponsor's favorable IRS opinion letter. The favorable opinion letter assures the employer that the plan documents have been preapproved by the IRS and that any subsequent tax disqualification of the plan will not be applied retroactively as long as the plan has been otherwise lawfully operated. The assurance that plans will not be retroactively disqualified is sometimes referred to as "guaranteed reliance." (Please see Appendix A for a sample copy).

In the case of a Solo 401(k) plan, most businesses adopt standardized master or prototype plans. As a result, these employers will not typically need to engage in any additional plan approval procedures. These employers ordinarily may rely on the IRS opinion letter granted to the document sponsor, but the notice to interested parties has no application to owner-only plans.

How Are the Solo 401(k) Plan Documents Updated?

A Solo 401(k) plan, which is considered a defined contribution plan, will need to be restated by no later than April 30, 2016, to incorporate the language and provisions from the Pension Protection Act (PPA) and various other required amendments that took effect between 2007 and 2011. This "PPA restatement" is named after the 2006 legislation passed by Congress, is generally considered the most important reform since ERISA, and will permanently incorporate the amendments that had been adopted from the previous EGTRRA amendments.

Approximately every six years, the IRS requires that plan documents be updated and resubmitted for review and approval. For individually designed plans, there is a five-year restatement cycle instead of a six-year cycle. The document plan sponsor will generally be the party responsible for making sure the plan documents are up-to-date and have been resubmitted for review and approval by the IRS.

The PPA restatement will incorporate the previous amendments for:

- Final 415 regulations
- Pension Protection Act (PPA)
- Heroes Earnings Assistance and Relief Tax Act (HEART)
- Worker, Retiree, and Employer Recovery Act (WRERA)
- Katrina Emergency Tax Relief Act of 2005 (KETRA)
- GULF Opportunity Zone Act of 2005 (GO Zone)

Other optional changes may be made by the document drafter at the same time.

A Solo 401(k) plan must adopt PPA provisions no later than *April 30, 2016*. This updated PPA document should be kept along with fully executed copies of all plan documents, amendments, and restatements made since the inception of the plan. If your plan is audited by the IRS or Department of Labor, they will ask to see signed plan documents and will review them to make sure they are up-to-date for all required remedial amendments.

Failure to restate the document before the deadline can result in disqualification of the plan and/or significant penalties. It is important that you act promptly to review the new document, update your plan sponsor regarding changes you would like to implement, and sign the adoption page and return it to Benefit Resources when you receive it.

Putting Paperwork Aside

This chapter has given you all the nuts and bolts you need to know to adopt a Solo 401(k) plan. Some people, reading these details, will find them clear and simple to follow. Others may feel daunted by the level of detail and the references to formal rules and codes. Either way, if you work with a plan sponsor document company or tax professional firm, they will take of all the details regarding your Solo 401(k) plan documents.

Compared to all other 401(k) plans the Solo 401(k) is incredibly simple and inexpensive to adopt and administer. But that doesn't mean you should hesitate to seek guidance and help. If you feel more comfortable with an expert, you should get professional help adopting your plan and drafting your documents. The end result is the same. You will still be able to leverage the power of the Solo 401(k) to your advantage in order to save far more money than you can through an IRA and gain plenty of other tools to achieve your career, life, and retirement goals in the process.

To that end, let's put the boring paperwork aside for now and look more closely at the exciting features of the Solo 401(k). After all, this is the real reason you're reading this book.

CHAPTER 5

The Features of the Solo 401(k) Plan

WHAT MAKES THE SOLO 401(K) the most attractive retirement plan for the self-employed? In a nutshell, the Solo 401(k) plan is so appealing because it has a very high annual contribution limit and the most flexibility in terms of retirement plan options. It is also easy and inexpensive to administer.

In this chapter, we're going to define the Solo 401(k)'s contribution limits and parameters, explore the range of options available to Solo 401(k) plan investors, and compare the Solo 401(k) plan to other retirement plans. If you are not yet sold on the Solo 401(k), the many exciting tax, retirement, and investment benefits should help turn you into a big fan.

How Much Can You Save?

When you make a contribution to a Solo 401(k) plan, you are putting a portion of your self-employment or W-2 income into your retirement savings plan. In this way, you avoid paying tax on that income in exchange for also putting off any personal immediate use of those funds.

As a Solo 401(k) participant, because you are essentially self-employed, you can contribute to your plan as an employee and as employer. This means that your total annual Solo 401(k) plan contribution consists of two parts:

1. Employee salary deferral contribution
2. Employer nonelective or profit-sharing contribution

In contrast, a SEP-IRA is purely an employer profit-sharing plan.

Before EGTRRA became effective in 2002, there was no incentive for an owner-only business to establish a 401(k) plan because that owner could generally receive the same tax benefits by adopting a SEP-IRA. EGTRRA cleared the way for an owner-only business to defer more money into a retirement plan and to operate a more cost-effective, less complex type of plan. One of the ways that EGTRRA made the Solo 401(k) more popular was by adding the employee deferral feature found in a traditional multiple-employee 401(k) plan. Remember, you can never defer more into a plan than you earn.

IRC 402(g) Employee Deferral Limit

The 401(k) plan employee deferral limits can be found under IRC Section 402(g). Section 402(g) employee deferral limit is a per employee limit. This means that if you are eligible to participate in multiple 401(k) plans, you can't make employee deferrals to another plan once you (the employee) have reached the employee deferral limit of $18,000 (or $24,000 if you are over the age of fifty) for 2017.

Employee deferrals may be made in pretax or after-tax (Roth) dollars. When made in pretax form, employee deferrals are not subject to federal income tax but are still subject to the Federal Insurance Contribution Act (FICA) and Federal Unemployment Tax Act (FUTA) tax withholding. Employee deferrals also may not exceed the annual deferral limit under 402(g).

After-tax (Roth) employee deferral contributions may also be made if the Solo 401(k) plan allows them. The Roth contributions are elective deferrals but should be in a separate 401(k) plan bank account so that the plan administrator can keep track of the pretax and after-tax (Roth) contributions. The aggregate amount of pretax and after-tax (Roth) IRA employee deferral contributions may not exceed the IRC 402(g) limit, which is $18,000 (or $24,000 if the plan participant is over the age of fifty) for 2017.

As an example, Joe works for ABC Corporation and elects to defer the maximum amount of $18,000. If Joe had self-employment income in a separate business and had a Solo 401(k) plan, he would not be able to make employee deferrals to his Solo 401(k) plan because he already reached the employee deferral 402(g) limit from the ABC Corporation 401(k) plan.

Employer Profit-Sharing Contributions

IRC 404 limits employer profit-sharing contributions or nonelective employer contributions to 25 percent of your self-employment compensation, or up to 20 percent when you are a sole proprietor or a Schedule C taxpayer. As the name suggests, employer profit-sharing contributions are contributions made by the employer and not the employee. In other words, while employee deferrals are made by the employee or plan participant, employer profit-sharing contributions are nonelective and made by the employer.

Employee deferrals come from the plan participant's salary and are not calculated when considering the maximum employer profit-sharing contribution, since employer profit-sharing contributions come from the employer or business. Solo 401(k) plan employer profit-sharing contributions are 100 percent discretionary, where the business owner can decide from year to year whether to make profit-sharing contributions.

Are Profit-Sharing Contributions Based on the Company's Profits?

I get this question a lot. The term "employer profit-sharing contributions" suggests that these contributions are made by the employer and are based on the profits of the employer. This is not exactly accurate. While contributions are made by the employer and are 100 percent discretionary, the amount of the contribution is a percentage based on the employee's salary or self-employment income amount.

I want to expand on this concept, since it often confuses people. Although the contribution is coming from the employer, it is not based on the profits of the business but wholly based on the employee's W-2 salary of self-employment income amount. Clearly, the business needs to have some working capital or profits available to actually make the contribution, but the amount of the contribution is not based on the percentage of profits of the employer.

For example, if a business was established as a C corporation and had $100,000 of profits but the owner received a W-2 salary of just $30,000, the employer profit-sharing contribution percentage would be based on the W-2 amount of $30,000 and *not* the profits of the C corporation. So if the employer wanted to make employer profit-sharing contributions, the maximum would be 25 percent of the salary or W-2 amount of $30,000 and not the profits of the business.

Remember that for employee deferrals and employer profit-sharing contributions, everything is based off the salary/W-2 or self-employment income amount. So if Ben, who is forty years old, earned $80,000 in salary from his S corporation and the business showed profits of $800,000, Ben's employee deferral and the company's employer profit-sharing contribution figure would be based on his salary amount of $80,000 and not the company's profit. Accordingly, in 2017 Ben would be able to defer $18,000 as an employee deferral and the S corporation can make a 25 percent employer profit-sharing contribution equal to 25 percent of his $80,000 salary for a total of $38,000.

A detailed discussion on calculating the maximum employee deferral and employer profit-sharing contribution amounts will be addressed later in this chapter.

415 Solo 401(k) Plan Contribution Limit

The IRC 415 limit specifies the maximum amount that you can contribute to a 401(k) plan in a given year. According to IRC 415, the maximum amount that may be allocated to a Solo 401(k) plan for 2017 is 100 percent of compensation, up to a maximum statutory amount of $54,000, or $60,000 if over the age of fifty.

In total, this means that for 2017 you can contribute a maximum of $54,000 or $60,000 if you are over age fifty to a Solo 401(k) plan. If your spouse also participates in your Solo 401(k) plan and earns compensation from your business, he or she is allowed to make separate and equal contributions, which increases your combined annual total contribution to $108,000 for 2017, or $120,000 if you are both over age fifty. Remember, your spouse is not treated as an employee for ERISA purposes, and you are allowed to include your spouse in your plan, so long as he or she is an employee of your business, without triggering the ERISA 401(k) plan rules.

Unlike the employee deferral limit, which is a per-employee limit, the IRC Section 415 employer profit-sharing contribution amount is a per-plan limit. This means that you can receive employer profit-sharing contributions from multiple plans that push you (as the employee) over the annual maximum limit, which for 2017 is $54,000, or $60,000 if over the age of fifty. This brings into play some very interesting retirement planning opportunities.

It's important to note that Solo 401(k) contributions are flexible. In other words, your employee salary deferral and employee profit-sharing deferral are both optional, and you can change the amount you contribute at any time. So if your business is booming one year, you may wish to contribute to your allowable limit. However, if your business is less profitable or you have other needs for the money in another year, you can contribute less. In sum, you can change the amounts you contribute for any reason.

There is no rule that you have to make contributions to a Solo 401(k) plan. In other words, you are under no obligations to make any contributions to your plan. Of course, it is in your interest from a long-term retirement standpoint to save as much as you can in your plan, but you are not required to do so by the plan. That being said, it is good practice to make an employee deferral or profit-sharing contribution to the Solo 401(k) plan at least once every couple of years. Otherwise, if no contributions are made to the plan for a number of consecutive years, the IRS could argue that the plan is no longer active and, hence, no longer valid.

What Is Deemed to be Compensation for Solo 401(k) Plan Contribution Purposes?

As we touched on in Chapter 3, the definition of compensation for someone who is self-employed is based on the type of business that is adopting the plan. In the case of a business formed as a C or S corporation, the business owner will generally receive a salary via a Form W-2. In the case of a sole proprietorship or single-member LLC, the owner's compensation is typically based on the net earnings of the self-employment business, which is reported on Schedule C of the IRS Form 1040 (the US Individual Income Tax Return).

In the case of a partnership or multiple-member LLC, IRS Form K-1 (which lists partner's share of income, deduction, credits, and so on) will identify whether the income is compensation or not. The Form K-1 will also indicate whether the income allocated to the member's K1 is remuneration for services performed (i.e., guaranteed payments), which is treated as compensation, or business or investment returns, which is typically not compensation.

Forms of Income Considered Compensation for Solo 401(k) Plan Purposes

The definition of compensation is crucial for determining whether the income you have generated is eligible to be contributed to a Solo 401(k) plan. According to the IRS, compensation for plan allocations is the pay a participant received from you for personal services for a year. The IRS generally defines "compensation" as including all the following payments:

1. Wages and salaries
2. Fees for professional services
3. Other amounts received (cash or noncash) for personal services actually rendered by an employee, including, but not limited to, the following items:
    a. Commissions and tips
    b. Fringe benefits
    c. Bonuses

For a self-employed individual, compensation means earned income that is net earnings from self-employment. For self-employed individuals or an owner of a single-member LLC, for Solo 401(k) plan purposes, self-employment means gross income from your trade or business (provided your personal services are a material income-producing factor) minus allowable business deductions. For C or S corporations, compensation is defined as your W-2 amount. In the case of a partnership of multiple-member LLC, net earnings include a partner's distributive share of partnership income or loss (other than separately stated items, such as capital gains and losses). Guaranteed payments to limited partners are net earnings from self-employment if they are paid for services to or for the partnership

How to Calculate Your Employee Deferral Limits

When it comes to the employee salary deferral portion of your Solo 401(k), the rules governing your contribution limit are simple. You can contribute almost 100 percent of your self-employment earnings up to a maximum of $18,000, or $24,000 if you are over age fifty for 2017.

For example, Jen is forty-two years old and is a sole proprietor. She earned $15,000 in self-employment income as a consultant in 2015, which she reports on a Schedule C.

- Net earnings (before qualified plan deduction): $15,000
- Calculate 1402(a)(12)deduction: $13,852.50
- Calculate Medicare and FICA: $2,119.43
- Half of self-employment tax: $1,059.72
- Self-employment income: $13,940.28

Therefore, Jen would be able to defer up to $13,852.50 into the Solo 401(k) plan if she elected to do so. Now let's assume that Jen earned $20,000 in 2015 and reported it on her Schedule C.

- Net earnings (before qualified plan deduction): $20,000
- Calculate 1402(a)(12)deduction: $18,470

- Calculate Medicare and FICA: $2,825.91
- Half of self-employment tax: $1,412.96
- Self-employment income: $18,587.05

In this case, because Jen's self-employment income amount is above the $18,000 limit, she would only be able to defer the maximum employee deferral amount for 2015, which is $18,000. However, if Jen was over the age of fifty, then she would be able to defer the entire amount of self-employment income earned because the maximum contribution limit would be $24,000 ($18,000 plus a $6000 catch-up for being over the age of fifty).

How to Calculate Your Employer Profit-Sharing Maximum Contribution Amount

The limit of your employer profit-sharing contribution, on the other hand, depends on how your business is taxed and is dictated by IRC Section 401(a)(3). If you are taxed as a C corporation or S corporation and you receive a W-2, then the amount of your employer contribution is limited to 25 percent of the compensation paid. This means, in general, that a profit-sharing contribution up to 25 percent of W-2 earnings can be contributed. In other words, in the case of a corporation, the employer profit-sharing contribution must be based on the compensation paid by the company identified on the IRS Form W-2 rather than the overall profits earned by the company. Your contribution is effectively limited by how much you pay yourself in salary on a W-2.

If you are taxed as a multiple-member LLC or partnership, then you can contribute up to 25 percent of the business's overall self-employment earnings for your employee profit-sharing deferral. In other words, your 25 percent employer contribution limit is based on your K-1 income attributable to self-employment earnings. This means it does not necessarily include the overall income of your business if some of that income is attributable to passive investments that are not considered self-employment earnings.

If you are taxed as a single-member LLC or Schedule C sole proprietorship, then the amount of your employer profit-sharing contribution is limited to 25 percent of your business's income that is subject to self-employment tax. To figure this out, you must do an additional calculation starting with your earned income to determine your maximum contribution. In effect, this brings the maximum contribution of 25 percent down to 20 percent of your earned income. (A step-by-step worksheet for this calculation can be found in IRS Publication 560, page 23, a copy can be found in Appendix A) But, in general, your compensation is considered to be your net earnings from your self-employment. This definition takes into account: (1) your deduction for half of your self-employment tax, and (2) your deduction for contributions on your behalf to the plan.

Employee Deferral Contributions and Profit-Sharing Rules for 2015

	Maximum Employee Deferral Amount if Under 50 Years Old for 2015	Maximum Employee Deferral Amount if Over 50 Years Old for 2015	Maximum Employer Profit-Sharing Contribution Amount for 2015	Total Aggregate Contribution Amount if Under 50 Years Old for 2015	Total Aggregate Contribution Amount, Including Employee Deferral/Profit-Sharing Contribution If Over 50 Years Old for 2015
Sole Proprietorship	$18,000 of self-employment income amount after applicable FICA and self-employment tax deducted (Schedule C)	$24,000 of self-employment income amount after applicable FICA and self-employment tax deducted (Schedule C)	20 percent of net earnings	20 percent of net earnings	$59,000
Single-Member LLC	$18,000 of self-employment income amount after applicable FICA and self-employment tax deducted (Schedule C)	$24,000 of self-employment income amount after applicable FICA and self-employment tax deducted (Schedule C)	20 percent of net earnings	20 percent of net earnings	$59,000
Multiple-Member LLC	$18,000 based off W-2 or guaranteed payment amount of IRS Form 1065 (Schedule K-1)	$24,000 based off W-2 or guaranteed payment amount of IRS Form 1065 (Schedule K-1)	25 percent of compensation	25 percent of compensation	$59,000
C Corporation	$18,000 based off W-2	$24,000 based off W-2	25 percent of compensation	25 percent of compensation	$59,000
S Corporation	$18,000 based off W-2	$24,000 based off W-2	25 percent of compensation	25 percent of compensation	$59,000

Here are some examples to explain how these different scenarios play out:

Joe and Green Garden Inc.

Joe is thirty-six and owns his own garden supply company, Green Garden. Business is good, and he earned $100,000 in compensation from Green Garden in 2016. For his employee salary deferral, Joe can contribute $18,000 to his Solo 401(k). In addition, for his employee profit-sharing contribution, he can contribute 20 percent of his self-employment income amount, net any self-employment tax.

- Net earnings (before qualified plan deduction): $100,000
- Calculate 1402(a)(12)deduction: $92,350
- Calculate Medicare and FICA: $14,129.55
- Half of self-employment tax: $7,064.78
- Self-employment income: $92,935.23

Since Joe's self-employment income amount is above the $18,000 limit, he would only be able to defer the maximum employee deferral amount for 2016, which is $18,000. Joe's maximum profit-sharing contribution amount would be $18,587.05, equal to 20 percent of $92,935.23, his self-employment income amount, for a total annual maximum 401(k) contribution of approximately $36,587 including the deferral contribution of $18,000.

Cathy and Straight Lines

Cathy is fifty-five and works as a freelance graphic designer, where she made $40,000 in 2016. For tax purposes, she is considered a sole proprietor of her business. In this case, she can defer $18,000 for her employee salary deferral and 20 percent of the net self-employment income she earns from her business, after paying self-employment tax.

- Net earnings (before qualified plan deduction): $40,000
- Calculate 1402(a)(12)deduction: $36,940
- Calculate Medicare and FICA: $5,651.82
- Half of self-employment tax: $2,825.91
- Self-employment income: $37,174.09

Since Cathy's self-employment income amount is above the $24,000 limit, she would only be able to defer the maximum employee deferral amount for 2016, which is $24,000 since she is over the age of fifty ($18,000 plus a $6,000 catch-up contribution amount). Cathy's maximum profit-sharing contribution amount would be $7,434.82, equal to 20 percent of $37,174.09, her self-employment income amount, for a total maximum annual 401(k) contribution of approximately $31,434.82, including the employee deferral contribution amount of $24,000.

Mark and Home Care LLC

Mark is forty-four and a nurse who has a home-care contract with his local hospital. For insurance reasons, he formed his own business, Home Care LLC. In 2016, he earned $80,000 in this work. This means he can defer a maximum of $18,000 (for employee salary deferral) plus 20 percent of his self-employment income amount, minus any self-employment taxes paid.

- Net earnings (before qualified plan deduction): $80,000
- Calculate 1402(a)(12)deduction: $73,880
- Calculate Medicare and FICA: $11,303.64
- Half of self-employment tax: $5,651.82
- Self-employment income: $74,348.18

Since Mark's self-employment income amount is above the $18,000 limit, he would only be able to defer the maximum employee deferral amount for 2016, which is $18,000. Mark's maximum profit-sharing contribution amount would be $14,869.64, equal to 20 percent of $74,348.18, his self-employment income amount, for a total maximum annual 401(k) contribution of approximately $32,869.64, including the deferral contribution of $18,000.

Patricia and Invest Well Inc.

Patricia, who is fifty-five, has her own investment business, Invest Well Inc., an S corporation. In 2016, she earned $30,000 in compensation from her corporation, which was reported on an IRS Form W-2. Patricia was able to make an employee deferral contribution of $24,000, plus a 25 percent employer profit-sharing contribution based on her W-2 compensation amount.

- Maximum profit-sharing contribution: $7,500
- Maximum 401(k) contribution: $18,000
- Maximum 401(k) catch-up: $6,000
- Maximum contribution: $30,000

Since Patricia's self-employment income amount is above the $24,000 limit, she would only be able to defer the maximum employee deferral amount for 2016, which is $24,000 since she is over the age of fifty. Patricia's maximum profit-sharing contribution amount would be $7,500, equal to 25 percent of her $30,000 W-2 income amount. However, because her employee deferral amount of $24,000 plus the profit-sharing contribution amount exceeds her W-2 salary, Patricia is only able to defer $30,000. This is because you are not permitted to defer more than you earn from your business.

Joe and Kim, and Family Video Inc.

Joe and Kim are both thirty-five and married. Joe is the sole owner of the C corporation Family Video Inc., an online service that produces family videos from digital photographs. Kim is Family Video Inc.'s only employee and serves as producer, editor, and web designer. In 2017, Joe and Kim each made $250,000 from Family Video Inc. Since Joe and Kim are married, the plan will not become subject to the ERISA tax rules and Kim and Joe will be treated as separate employees for purposes of calculating their maximum annual plan deferral contribution amounts.

Joe:

- Maximum profit-sharing contribution: $54,000
- Maximum 401(k) contribution: $18,000
- Maximum contribution: $54,000

Kim:

- Maximum profit-sharing contribution: $54,000
- Maximum 401(k) contribution: $18,000
- Maximum contribution: $54,000

Since Joe and Kim's W-2 income amount is so high, they will easily be able to max-out on both their employee deferral ($18,000) and employer profit-sharing contribution amount. This will allow them to make their full annual 401(k) plan contributions of $54,000 each, or $108,000 in total for both spouses for 2017.

How to Make 401(k) Plan Contributions of $100,000 or More in a Year

It's not widely known, but under certain circumstances an individual who is employed by an employer with a 401(k) plan and also has self-employment income could make 401(k) plan contributions of up to $108,000, or $120,000 if over the age of fifty for 2017. This means that in some special circumstances, an individual who has a full-time job *and* is able to make employee deferrals *and* receives employer profit-sharing contributions from his or her full-time employer *and* at the same time has significant self-employment income from separate businesses, can make annual 401(k) plan contributions in excess of $100,000.

Getting interested? This is how it works.

Remember that, according to Section 402(g), the employee deferral limit is a per-employee limit. This means that if you are eligible to participate in multiple 401(k) plans, as soon as you (the employee) reach the employee deferral limit of $18,000 (or $24,000 if over the age of fifty) for 2017, you are not able to make employee deferrals to another plan. However, unlike the employee deferral limit, which is a *per-employee* limit, the IRC Section 415 employer profit-sharing contribution amount is a *per-plan* limit. So you can receive employer profit-sharing contributions from multiple 401(k) plans, which push you as the employee over the annual maximum limit ($54,000, or $60,000 if over the age of fifty in 2017). This brings some very interesting retirement-planning opportunities into play.

Let's take the example of Jim the software engineer. Jim is forty and employed by a public company that has a 401(k) plan, but he also has a successful consulting business that he does in his free time. Jim sets up a Solo 401(k) plan for his consulting business. Jim is a high-income earner and had no problem contributing the maximum amount to his employer's 401(k) plan for 2017, which was $18,000. Jim's consulting business also had a great year and is flush with extra cash that Jim doesn't really need to use to maintain his current lifestyle, so he would also like to contribute the maximum amount to his Solo 401(k) plan associated with his consulting business.

Jim consulted with his tax advisor and was told that he would not be able to make further elective deferrals to his Solo 401(k) plan because he has already contributed his personal maximum, $18,000 (IRC 402(g) limit) to his full-time employer plan for the public company for 2017. But Jim has enough earned income from his self-employment business to contribute the overall maximum contribution amount for the year: $54,000 for 2017, if permitted. Jim's tax advisor tells him that only the IRC 402(g) employee deferral is employee-based, but the IRC 415 employer profit-sharing contribution limit is plan-based and not limited to what he receives in another plan from another nonrelated employer. Jim's tax advisor confirms that Jim would not be able to make an employee deferral contribution to his consulting business Solo 401(k) plan, but he *could* make a nonelective employer profit-sharing contribution of $54,000 to his Solo 401(k) plan so long as he has sufficient income from the business for 2017.

Jim's tax advisor confirms that the IRC 415 employer profit-sharing contribution limit is not reduced by the elective deferrals under his employer's plan because the limit on employer profit-sharing contributions applies to each 401(k) plan separately. Of course, Jim is told that he would have to earn enough income to reach the maximum employer profit-sharing contribution amount of $54,000. Jim wants to go through the figures with his tax advisor in greater detail and calculates that he earned $300,000 from his self-employment consulting business in 2017. Naturally, he's keen on maxing out his potential Solo 401(k) plan contributions for the year.

Jim's tax advisor runs the same numbers and tells him that he will be able to make a profit-sharing contribution of $54,000, which is 20 percent of Jim's $300,000, or $60,000 for 2017. Since $60,000 is greater than the 2017 maximum Solo 401(k) plan contribution limit of $54,000, Jim is only able to defer $54,000 from his consulting Solo 401(k) plan for the year because he is not allowed to defer more than he earns in income for the year. Jim then does some quick calculations in his head and realizes that he is able to defer $18,000 to his full-time employer 401(k) plan and $54,000 to his Solo 401(k) plan in the form of employer profit sharing contributions, giving him $71,000 for the year.

Now let's assume that Joe makes an employee deferral, or $18,000, and his public company employer makes a profit-sharing contribution of $10,000, giving Jim a $28,000 401(k) plan contribution for the year. Let's also assume that Joe earns $200,000 from his part-time consulting business during the year. Jim will be able to make an employer contribution equal to 20 percent of his $200,000 self-employment income amount, or $40,000. Remember that the employer profit-sharing contribution percentage works out to 20 percent if you are self-employed. So even though Jim contributed $28,000 to his full-time employer 401(k) plan, IRC 415 rules allow Jim to still make employer profit-sharing contributions up to $54,000 for 2017 to his Solo 401(k) plan because the employer profit-sharing contribution limits are plan-based and not individual-based like the IRC 402(g) employee deferral limits. Therefore, Jim is able to make 401(k) plan contributions of $28,000 to his full-time job's 401(k) plan and another $40,000 employer profit-sharing contribution to his consulting Solo 401(k) plan, allowing him to surpass the $53,000 amount and contribute $68,000 for the year.

Though many people are unaware of this, the IRC 415 employer contribution rules allow you to make 401(k) plan contributions of up to $108,000 if under fifty (and $120,000 if over the age of fifty) for 2017 so long as you are lucky enough to receive employer profit-sharing contributions from an employer, in addition to employee deferrals, and also earn enough income from an unrelated self-employment business to make high employer profit-sharing contributions. As we will see shortly, these contributions can be pretax, after-tax, or Roth, allowing for some really exciting tax-planning opportunities.

What Is the Deadline for Making Solo 401(k) Contributions?

The deadline for making Solo 401(k) plan contributions is typically dependent on the type of entity that has adopted the Solo 401(k) plan as well as the type of contribution: employee deferral versus Profit-sharing contribution.

Sole Proprietorship

Employee Deferral: In the case of a sole proprietorship, a business owner under the age of fifty may make employee deferral contributions up to $18,000 for 2017 and an employee over the age of fifty may make a $6,000 annual catch-up contribution for an annual deferral contribution imitation of $24,000. An employee must elect to make the employee deferral contribution by December 31 of the year. However, the employee deferral contribution can be made up until the tax-filing deadline. The employee deferral contribution can be made using pretax and/or after-tax (Roth) funds.

Employer Profit-Sharing Contribution: The sole proprietorship business may make annual profit-sharing contributions for the business owner and spouse annually. IRC 401(a)(3) states that the amount of employer contributions is limited to 25 percent of the entity's income subject to self-employment tax. Schedule C sole proprietors must do an added calculation starting with earned income to determine their maximum contribution, which in effect brings the maximum 25 percent of compensation limit down to 20 percent of earned income. A step-by-step worksheet for this calculation can be found in IRS Publication 560. In general, compensation is your net earnings from self-employment. This definition takes into account both of the following items: (i) the deduction for one-half of your self-employment tax, and (ii) the deduction for contributions on your behalf to the plan. The profit-sharing contribution must be made by the business's tax-filing deadline (April 15).

Single-Member LLC

Employee Deferral: In the case of a single-member LLC, the single-member-LLC owner under the age of fifty may make employee deferral contributions up to $18,000 for 2017 and an employee over the age of fifty may make a $6,000 annual catch-up contribution for an annual deferral contribution limitation of $24,000. The single-member-LLC owner must elect to make the employee deferral contribution by December 31 of the year. However, the employee deferral contribution can be made up until the tax-filing deadline. The employee deferral contribution can be made using pretax and/or after-tax (Roth) funds.

Employer Profit Sharing Contribution: The single- member LLC business may make annual profit-sharing contributions for the business owner and spouse annually. The IRC states that the amount of employer contributions is limited to 25 percent of the entity's income subject to self-employment tax. Schedule C single-member-LLC owners must do an added calculation starting with earned income to determine their maximum contribution, which in effect brings the maximum 25 percent of compensation limit down to 20 percent of earned income. In general, compensation is your net earnings from self-employment. This definition takes into account both of the following items: (i) the deduction for one-half of your self-employment tax, and (ii) the deduction for contributions on your behalf to the plan. Profit-sharing contributions must be funded by the business's tax-filing deadline (April 15).

Multiple-Member LLC

Employee Deferral: In the case of a multiple-member LLC, multiple-member-LLC owners under the age of age fifty may make employee deferral contributions up to $18,000 for 2017 and an employee over the age of fifty may make a $6,000 annual catch-up contribution for an annual deferral contribution limitation of $24,000. The multiple-member-LLC owners must elect to make the employee deferral contribution by December 31 of the year. However, the employee deferral contribution can be made up until the tax-filing deadline. The employee deferral contribution can be made using pretax, after-tax, or Roth funds.

Employer Profit-Sharing Contribution: The multiple-member LLC business may make annual profit-sharing contributions for the business owners annually. IRC Section 401(a)(3) states that the amount of employer profit-sharing contributions is limited to 25 percent of the entity's income subject to self-employment tax. Profit-sharing contributions must be funded by the business's tax-filing deadline.

C Corporations and S Corporations

Employee Deferral

An employee of a corporation will receive a W-2. When it comes to making employee deferral contributions, the employee must make the deferral contribution during the year. The timing of the deferral contribution will typically depend on the business. In the case of a corporation that uses a payroll company, the employee deferral will typically be deducted from the employee's paycheck. If the company does not use a payroll system, the employee can elect to make deferral contributions at any time during the year. Once the election is made, the Department of Labor safe harbor is that the funds are deposited into the Solo 401(k) plan account within seven days. The employee making the employee contribution should make sure that he or she has earned enough compensation during the pay period to cover the employee contribution. For example, if the employee wishes to make an employee deferral contribution of $18,000 on December 30, the employee will need to be sure that he or she has earned sufficient compensation during the pay period to cover that deferral contribution. The employee deferral contribution can be made using pretax and/or after-tax (Roth) funds.

Employer Profit Sharing Contributions: The corporation may make profit-sharing contributions for the corporation's owner(s)/employee(s) annually. IRC Section 404 states that the amount of employer profit-sharing contributions is limited to 25 percent of the entity's income subject to self-employment tax. Profit-sharing contributions must be funded by the business's tax-filing deadline.

The Solo 401(k) Plan Roth Component

As I mentioned, before EGTRRA became effective in 2002, there was no compelling reason for an owner-only business to establish a Solo 401(k) plan because the business owner could generally receive the same benefits by adopting a SEP-IRA. One of the most important rules set forth in EGTRRA was the creation of the designated Roth contribution option for 401(k) and 403(b) plans. This provision allows plan participants to designate all or a portion of their employee deferrals as after-tax (Roth) contributions.

Some people mistakenly believe that there is a pretax or regular Solo 401(k) plan and a Roth Solo 401(k) plan (after-tax). This is not true. The

Roth feature is just a component of a Solo 401(k) plan that can be included or not, based on the decision of the employer. The availability of the Roth component is typically designated in the plan adoption agreement.

Roth deferral contributions should generally be made to a separate designated account under the plan. This can be done by simply creating a new bank or brokerage account under the plan name and plan EIN, if applicable. The reason for establishing a new account for Roth 401(k) plan contributions is so the plan administrator can keep track of and maintain an accounting of the pretax and after-tax contributions and asset values. This becomes especially important in the case of rollovers or distributions.

The designated Roth 401(k) elective deferral contributions follows the same rules as a pretax 401(k) plan deferral. However, unlike a pretax deferral, your Roth 401(k) employee deferral is included in your gross income in the year you make the contribution. The tax treatment of a Roth employee deferral is much like a Roth IRA.

Unlike a Roth IRA, there are no income restrictions with your 401(k) Roth contribution option as long as your plan offers this feature. Like employee deferrals, Roth employee deferrals and a pretax employee deferral together may not exceed the IRC 402(g) limit, which was $18,000 for 2017. Roth employee deferrals and the allocated earnings must be separately account for under a 401(k) plan.

Your Roth contributions are invested in your retirement plan account, the same as any pretax contributions you make. But your Roth money is tracked separately than your pretax money and will appear as a separate item on your retirement plan statements. You can still contribute to a Roth IRA even after maximizing your Roth 401(k) deferral as long as you can satisfy the Roth IRA contribution rules.

Many people want to know what the benefits of making Roth 401(k) contributions are, since they are after-tax and do not allow you to defer paying taxes when you contribute them to your Solo 401(k) plan.

Making a pretax Solo 401(k) plan contribution will give you an immediate tax deduction that can reduce your federal income tax, but it will require you to pay tax and a 10 percent early distribution penalty if you are under fifty-nine and a half, and withdraw the pretax funds in the form of a distribution. (Note: Applicable FICA and self-employment taxes would still be applied to the compensation amount prior to the tax-deductible contribution.)

In contrast, in the case of an after-tax (Roth) Solo 401(k) plan contribution, no immediate tax deduction would be available. But as long as certain age and holding requirements are met, all contribution amounts, income, and appreciation from the Roth account would come out of the 401(k) plan tax-free and penalty-free. Roth contributions are subject to federal income tax *before* the money is contributed to your account. This is unlike a Traditional IRA or any pretax 401(k) employee contributions, which are made to your account without federal income taxes being deducted. So you defer federal taxes on your before-tax contributions (and any investment earnings) to a later date when you withdraw the funds in the form of a taxable distribution.

Like traditional contributions made to your retirement plan, your Roth contributions grow without tax until retirement. Unlike before-tax contributions, however, your Roth money can be withdrawn without paying additional federal income tax as long as you meet certain requirements (i.e., qualified Roth distribution). Indeed, you can live off your income and gains from the Roth portion of your Solo 401(k) without ever paying additional tax.

To qualify for federally tax-free withdrawals of your Roth contributions (and any related investment earnings), there are certain tax law requirements:

- Generally, you wait must wait at least five years after January 1 of the year you make your first Roth contribution to the 401(k) plan before taking a withdrawal.
- Your withdrawals must begin after you have reached age fifty-nine and a half, or if you have died or have become disabled.

Should You Make Roth or Pretax Contributions?

Often tax professionals and financial advisors are asked whether it makes sense to make a Roth after-tax contribution or a pretax contribution. The upside with Roth contributions is that your Roth withdrawals in retirement (including any earnings and gains on those contributions) are completely tax-free if you meet those requirements listed above.

When deciding whether you should make Roth contributions, before-tax contributions, or a combination of the two, here are some important considerations:

If you feel your tax rate in retirement will be higher than it is today, Roth contributions may make sense for you. However, if you expect your tax rate to be lower in retirement than during your working years, you may benefit more from making before-tax contributions and paying taxes when you withdraw your money. It is hard to imagine, but we are currently in a historically low tax-rate environment. For most of the century, including some boom times, top-bracket income tax rates were much higher than they are today. In fact, during the 1950s and early 1960s, the top bracket income tax rate was over 90 percent. In light of our growing deficit, social security shortfall, and heavy government spending, it is not far off to suggest that income tax rates will be higher when you retire then they are now. That being said, no one knows what will happen tomorrow when it comes to Congress and taxes, and especially not in twenty or thirty years, so an educated guess is all one can muster.

How confident are you in your expected returns? If you are very confident that your investments and/or cash flow from your investments are relatively secure and will grow over time, a Roth account would make sense. Bear in mind that many people felt that Enron, Lehman Brothers, and Bear Stearns were safe investments and suitable for Roth funds, and we all know how those companies turned out. In general, Roth 401(k) investments seem to work well with real estate income-producing investments as well as dividend-growth investments where the cash flows are generally perceived as stable.

The farther away your retirement, the greater opportunity for tax-free growth and the more potential you have for tax-free gains. Basically, if you will not be retiring in the near future, Roth contributions may make a good deal of sense, since your account has more time to potentially grow in value. This may make the tax advantages of Roth contributions even more important to you—although Roth dollars can benefit retirement savers of all ages.

Important Considerations in Determining Whether to Make Pretax or After-Tax (Roth) Contributions to a Solo 401(k) Plan

	Pre-tax Contribution	After-Tax (Roth) Contribution
Your age	Getting older potentially reduces the attractiveness of a Roth.	The younger you are, the more Roth offers greater advantages.
Need for Current Income Tax Deduction	The greater the need, the greater benefit for a pretax contribution.	The less the need, the more attractive the Roth contribution becomes.
Future Tax Rates	The belief that tax rates will be lower when you retire increase the attractiveness of the pretax contribution.	The belief that future tax rates will be higher increase the attractiveness of a Roth.
Investment Confidence	The less confident you are in the stock market or your 401(k) plan investmen options, the more attractive the pretax account will be ,because at least you will benefit from a current tax deduction.	The more confident you are in your investment returns and their growth over the years, the more attractive the Roth account becomes because all future appreciation will be tax-free.

What Is the Advantage of a Roth Contribution?

In order to get a better handle on the potential advantages of making Roth contributions, it is helpful to run several possible scenarios:

- Starting balance: $0
- Annual contribution: $17,500
- Current age: 30

- Age of retirement: 65
- Expected rate of return: 9.77 percent
- Marginal tax rate: 25 percent
- Total amount of contributions: $612,500

At age sixty-five with a Roth 401(k) plan, the individual would have $4,733,705 tax-free. Whereas if a pretax 401(k) plan was used, the amount of the account at age sixty-five would be valued at $3,550.279.

Now assume that the individual wanted to retire at age of seventy:

- Starting balance: $0
- Annual contribution: $18,000
- Current age: 30
- Age of retirement: 70
- Expected rate of return: 9.77 percent
- Marginal tax rate: 25 percent
- Total amount of contributions: $720,000

At age seventy with a Roth 401(k) plan, the individual would have $7,874,958 tax-free. Whereas if a pretax 401(k) plan was used, the amount of the account at age seventy would be valued at $6,922.392.

- Starting balance: $0
- Annual contribution: $18,000
- Current age: 30
- Age of retirement: 65
- Expected rate of return: 8 percent
- Marginal tax rate: 25 percent
- Total amount of contributions: $630,000

At age sixty with a Roth 401(k) plan, the individual would have $3,234.530 tax-free. Whereas if a pretax 401(k) plan was used, the amount of the account at age sixty-five would be valued at $2,943.507.

Now assume the individual wanted to retire at the age of seventy:

- Starting balance: $0
- Annual contribution: $18,000
- Current age: 30
- Age of retirement: 70
- Expected rate of return: 8 percent
- Marginal tax rate: 25 percent
- Total amount of contributions: $720,000

At age seventy with a Roth 401(k) plan, the individual would have $4,862,706 tax-free. Whereas if a pretax 401(k) plan was used, the amount of the account at age seventy would be valued at $4,365.891.

- Starting balance: $0
- Annual contribution: $18,000
- Current age: 40
- Age of retirement: 65
- Expected rate of return: 9.77 percent
- Marginal tax rate: 25 percent
- Total amount of contributions: $450,000

At age sixty-five with a Roth 401(k) plan, the individual would have $1,799,367 tax-free. Whereas if a pretax 401(k) plan was used, the amount of the account at age sixty-five would be valued at $1,659.603.

- Starting balance: $0
- Annual contribution: $18,000
- Current age: 40
- Age of retirement: 65
- Expected rate of return: 8 percent
- Marginal tax rate: 25 percent
- Total amount of contributions: $450,000.

At age sixty-five with a Roth 401(k) plan, the individual would have $1,372,259 tax-free. Whereas if a pretax 401(k) plan was used, the amount of the account at age sixty-five would be valued at $1,284.037.

- Starting balance: $0
- Annual contribution: $18,000
- Current age: 40
- Age of retirement: 60
- Expected rate of return: 8 percent
- Marginal tax rate: 25 percent
- Total amount of contributions: $360,000

At age seventy with a Roth 401(k) plan, the individual would have $2,126,420 tax-free. Whereas if a pretax 401(k) plan was used, the amount of the account at age seventy would be valued at $1,594.815.

The examples above show the enormous retirement benefits to making after-tax (Roth) contributions starting at a young age and on a consistent basis. That being said, there is certainly nothing wrong with having several million dollars in a pretax retirement account, although if your federal and state income tax rate was at 50 percent when you retired, that million-dollar-plus retirement account would still be nice but definitely not as nice as being able to live off the money tax-free and without ever having to pay tax on the money again.

Taking this a step further, one can argue that with a 50 percent tax rate, having $1 million in a Roth 401(k) plan is like having $1.5 million in a pretax account. Numbers never lie—the hard part is turning down your CPA who is pushing for you to make the pretax contribution so it reduces your current income tax and also makes him or her look better in your eyes. You need to think long term by focusing on the advantages of tapping a tax-free account when you retire, especially if taxes are higher than they are now.

How Do You Report the Employee and Profit Sharing Contributions on Your Tax Return?

Making an employee deferral or profit-sharing contribution to a Solo 401(k) plan is only half the battle. In order to get a tax deduction (in the case of a pretax contribution) or to notify the IRS (in the case of an after-tax [Roth] contribution) you must report the type and amount of the contribution on your individual tax return (IRS Form 1040) as well as on the entity tax return, if applicable.

Sole Proprietorship and Single-Member LLC

In the case of a sole proprietorship or LLC owned by one owner, Solo 401(k) plan employee deferral contributions and employer profit-sharing contributions would be reported on line 18 of IRS Form 1040. In the case of a Roth Solo 401(k) employee deferral contribution, the word "Roth" should be included next to the amount of the contribution, indicating that the contribution is after-tax. In order for the sole proprietor or owner of the single-member LLC to not receive double benefits from the employer contribution, the employer contribution is not made on the IRS Form 1040, Schedule C.

Multiple-Member LLC or Partnership

In the case of an LLC owned by two or more persons or a partnership, employee deferrals would be reported on line 18 of IRS Form 1040. In the case of a Roth Solo 401(k) employee deferral contribution, the word "Roth" should be included next to the amount of the contribution indicating that the contribution is after-tax. With respect to employer profit-sharing contributions, the LLC or partnership would include the total amount of profit-sharing contributions on line 18 of IRS Form 1065 (US Return of Partnership Income) and then indicate the partner's profit-sharing contribution on IRS Form 1065, K-1, line 13, Code R. Because a partnership is a pass-through entity for tax purposes, the individual partner would then include that amount on IRS Form 1040, line 18.

C Corporation

In the case of a C corporation, employee deferrals would be reported on line 18 of IRS Form 1040. In the case of a Roth Solo 401(k) employee deferral contribution, the word "Roth" should be included next to the amount of the contribution indicating that the contribution is after-tax. With respect to employer profit-sharing contributions, the corporation would indicate the amount of the partner's profit-sharing contribution on IRS Form 1120 (US Corporation Income Tax Return), line 23. Since a C corporation is not a pass-through entity, the individual plan participant would not report the employer profit-sharing contribution on his or her IRS Form 1040.

S Corporation

In the case of an S Corporation, employee deferrals would be reported on line 18 of IRS Form 1040. In the case of a Roth Solo 401(k) employee deferral contribution, the word "Roth" should be included next to the amount of the contribution, indicating that the contribution is after-tax. With respect to employer profit-sharing contributions, the corporation would indicate the amount of the partner's profit-sharing contribution on IRS Form 1120S, line 17, but the individual would not need to report the employer contribution amount on line 18 of the IRS Form 1040.

After-Tax Vs. Roth Contributions

In the case of an IRA, most people know that IRA contributions can be made in pre-tax, after-tax, or Roth. However, it is not widely known that a Solo 401(k) plan can allow you to make after-tax (non-deductible) plan contributions based off your income on a dollar for dollar basis. A contribution to a pre-tax 401(k) plan is a tax-deductible contribution; however, it is subject to tax when distributed and penalty if under the age of fifty-nine and half. Unlike pre-tax elective contributions, a Roth 401(k) plan contribution is an after-tax contribution that is currently includible in gross income but generally tax-free when distributed, assuming the individual is over the age of fifty-nine and half and the Roth 401(k) plan account has been opened at least five years. Whereas, when after-tax plan contributions are made from an employee's compensation (other than Roth contributions), then an employee must include it as income on his or her tax return, but any income generated from the after-tax contribution would be subject to the pre-tax contribution distribution rules. Hence, unlike a Roth 401(k) plan, which generated tax-free income and gains for a qualified distribution, an after tax 401(k) account which is not converted to Roth would not receive the same tax-free treatment on any income or gains generated as the Roth 401(k) (the after-tax contributions would be distributed tax-free).

Making an after-tax contribution to a Solo 401(k) plan does not reduce your taxable income, but taxes are deferred on any earnings that the after-tax money makes. In other words, no deduction is given for the after-tax contribution, but unlike a Roth 401(k), any income or gain is still subject to tax. Not the best situation and certainly not as tax-efficient as a Roth 401(k).

A recent IRS ruling has made it easier to convert those after-tax contributions directly to a Roth IRA when you retire or leave your company. Under the new rules, you can rollover your pretax contributions and any earnings into a traditional IRA, while putting the after-tax contributions into a separate Roth IRA, where the money can then grow tax-free. Earlier, plan participants had to jump through a series of steps to achieve that result because IRS rules on the subject were uncertain. But in 2014, the IRS issued a clarifying notice, known as 2014-54, which greatly simplified the situation. Notice 2014-54 clarified this rule and allowed the pretax and after-tax funds that were distributed from a plan on a pro rata basis to be separated once a distribution is made. Allocating after-tax contributions is only possible when the entire account (including both pretax and after-tax amounts) is rolled over. If only part of it is rolled over, the pro rata rules still apply. The IRS notice is also only applicable to after-tax contributions to employer plans; it doesn't apply to IRAs. The pretax funds can be rolled into a Traditional IRA, whereas the after-tax dollars can be converted into a Roth IRA. The Notice made it much easier for individuals to roll their after-tax funds into a Roth IRA and benefit from all the advantages of a Roth IRA.

Prior to the notice, it was very hard to move after-tax contributions to a Roth and that left the individual with after-tax funds, which didn't provide them a tax-deductible contribution and would not provide them with tax-free income or gains, an unsatisfying and unfriendly tax proposition. So after Notice 2014-54, after-tax contributions to a 401(k) or Solo 401(k) plan can be rolled into a Roth IRA and can then reap the benefits of being a Roth IRA. For example, if a 40-year-old self-employed individual earns $100,000 in 2017, he or she would be able to make a maximum employee deferral contribution of $18,000 in pretax funds or Roth, and make an after-tax contribution dollar-for-dollar equal to $35,000. Alternatively, the individual could make a full after-tax contribution of $54,000, or $60,000 if over the age of fifty-nine and a half. This is the difference between $54,000 (the maximum annual 401(k) contribution for 2017) and $18,000, the maximum employee deferral contributions limit. Those contributions can then be converted to a Roth. The advantage of making after-tax contributions versus a profit-sharing contribution is that you can make a dollar-for-dollar contribution as opposed to a profit-sharing contribution, which is based on a percentage of your compensation (20 percent or 25 percent). If a profit-sharing contribution is made instead of an after-tax contribution, the individual would only be able to make a $20,000 contribution (20 percent of $100,000 of income), giving him or her an annual contribution of just $38,000 versus $54,000 if employee deferrals were combined with after-tax contributions. In other words, after-tax contributions are not elective deferrals and therefore are not subject to the annual IRC Section 402(g) maximum deferral limit ($18,000 for 2017). However, they are subject to the annual IRC Section 415 limit ($54,000 for 2017; $60,000 for individuals age 50 or older eligible to make catch-up contributions of $6,000). Hence, if an individual is under the age fifty and earns $54,000 from self-employment income, that individual would be able to make after-tax contributions to the Solo 401(k) plan in the amount of $54,000, dollar-for-dollar and then do an immediate conversion to Roth. Whereas, if the individual made an employee deferral contribution she would be limited to $18,000 and then a 20% employer profit sharing contribution providing her just $28,800, versus $54,000 if she made after-tax contributions.

So why aren't after-tax contributions more popular? One of the reasons is that not all Solo 401(k) plans allow for after-tax contributions. In addition, many tax advisors are unaware of the power of making non-deductible contributions especially since Notice 2014-54 was only recently published. If you are interested in making after-tax contributions to a Solo 401(k) plan, you should check the 401(k) plan documents to confirm that the plan allows for non-deductible contributions.

Easy Administration

The Solo 401(k) is also appealing to individuals because it is easy to operate. Generally, there is no annual filing requirement unless your Solo 401(k) plan exceeds $250,000 in assets as of December 31 of the previous tax year. This is the case if the assets in your Solo 401(k) meet the requirement alone or if your assets exceed $250,000 when they are combined with any other qualified retirement plan that you or your spouse have more than 80 percent ownership over.

If your retirement assets do exceed $250,000, you will need to file a short information return with the IRS (Form 5500-EZ). This is due on July 31 and is filed in paper form. It must be filed by you (the plan owner) and your spouse. IRS Form 5500-EZ is your mechanism for reporting to the IRS the fair market value of the assets held by your Solo 401(k) plan.

That's it. One form. To view a copy of IRS Form 5500-EZ please see Appendix B.

Investment Opportunities: Unlocking a World of Investment Potential

According to the Investment Company Institute, a national association of US investment companies, as of December 31, 2014, 401(k) plans and other defined contribution plans held an estimated $6.8 trillion in assets and represented approximately 28 percent of the $24.7 trillion US retirement market. These plans include employer-sponsored retirement plans, individual retirement accounts (IRAs), and annuities, and the assets include mutual funds, closed-end funds, exchange-traded funds (ETFs) and unit investment trusts (UITs). In comparison, n comparison, 401(k) assets were $2.2 trillion and represented 16 percent of the U.S. retirement market in 2004.[8]

In 2011, 51 million American workers were active 401(k) participants. Since almost all 401(k) plans and IRAs are set -up with traditional financial institutions, such as Fidelity, Vanguard, and Mass Mutual, the investment opportunities offered to the millions of retirement holders are almost always equity-based investments, such as stock, mutual funds, and ETFs. There is really no financial incentive to offer 401(k) plans or IRA account holders the ability to make investments in which the financial institution holding the account does not make any money.

For example, if you have $150,000 in an IRA account at a major financial institution and own a number of mutual funds, the financial institution will typically earn fees from facilitating these investments. If, however, you took your $150,000 and bought precious metals or real estate, the financial institution will no longer have use of those funds and will not have the ability to generate any more fees on them.

8 **Investment Company Institute (ICI), http://www.ici.org/policy/retirement/plan/401k/faqs_401k, Frequently Asked Questions About 401(k) Plans**

This is why nontraditional investments with retirement funds are not overly publicized through mainstream media sources. It's no surprise. Why would a major financial institution spend millions of dollars on a TV, radio, or online media campaign to educate the public that the IRS allows nontraditional investments? Accordingly, most Americans are not aware that the IRS allows retirement accounts to be invested in all sorts of different investment products, such as precious metals, real estate, private notes, loans, businesses, tax liens, currencies, options, and much, much more.

If the 2008 financial crisis had any positive impact, it is that many Americans started asking about alternative investment options for their retirement accounts. It is believed that the financial crisis cost retirees almost 40 percent of their retirement assets, and many are still trying to get back to where they were prior to the crisis. The sudden and steep stock market fall, coupled with the lack of faith in Wall Street and the global financial markets, caused many Americans to seek a more balanced and diversified retirement portfolio. With this came a sharp increase in the number of Americans looking at a self-directed IRA or self-directed Solo 401(k) plan as the vehicle for attaining a level of account diversification.

Alternative investments such as real estate have always been permitted in IRAs. It even says so right on the IRS website. Yet few people seemed to know about this option until recently. The nontraditional and self-directed retirement market was relatively small prior to 2008. Early adopters heard about the nontraditional asset option and took advantage of it to buy real estate and other nontraditional assets. This small group of retirees were on the cutting edge of investment options and largely did not have an impact on the larger retirement investment community.

The crossover began after the 2008 financial crisis. Many times a day I hear from people throughout the country—young, old, rich, middle class, educated, even attorneys and CPAs—asking me whether they can buy real estate with retirement money. Then they ask, "Is this really legal?" This is followed by, "How come I've never heard about this?" I have talked to tens of thousands of retirement account holders and am always amazed by how many people still don't believe that they can buy real estate or secure other nontraditional assets with retirement money.

People who are drawn to the Solo 401(k) generally love the flexibility and opportunity it offers for using retirement funds for a wide range of investments. Depending on the plan documents your business has adopted, you can use your Solo 401(k) assets to make almost any type of traditional or nontraditional investment on your own. Specifically, with an "open architecture" self-directed Solo 401(k) plan, you benefit from:

High Contributions

Like all Solo 401(k) plans, for 2017 a self-directed Solo 401(k) plan will allow a participant to make annual contributions of up to $54,000 with an additional $6,000 catch-up contribution for those over age fifty. The high contribution feature is one of the reasons a Solo 401(k) plan is the most popular retirement vehicle for the self-employed.

Tax- and Penalty-Free Loans

Unfortunately not all Solo 401(k) plans offer the loan feature as a 401(k) plan option. Remember, the employer or plan document sponsor determines whether the loan feature will or will not be included the Solo 401(k) plan. The plan adoption agreement is the document that indicates whether the loan feature is included as a plan option. Most Solo 401(k) plans offered by traditional financial institutions such as Vanguard or Bank of America do not offer the loan plan feature because the level of administration needed to keep track of the loan and the diminished money available to invest with the financial institution make it unappealing.

On the other hand, most self-directed plan document sponsor companies that work with self-directed Solo 401(k) plans typically offer the loan feature in their plan documents. The Solo 401(k) loan feature allows plan participants to borrow up to $50,000 or 50 percent of their account value (whichever is less) for any purpose, including paying credit card bills, mortgage payments, or anything else. The loan has to be paid back over a five-year period at least quarterly at a minimum Prime interest rate (you have the option of selecting a higher interest rate). The Solo 401(k) plan loan feature will be discussed in greater detail in this chapter.

In-Plan Roth Contributions & Conversion Feature

Making Roth Contributions: Unlike the Solo 401(k) plans offered by most financial institutions, self-directed Solo 401(k) plan document sponsor companies typically contain a built-in Roth subaccount, which can be contributed to without any income restrictions. Again, the main reason that the traditional financial institutions do not offer a designated Roth 401(k) feature is because of the perceived administrative complexity in keeping track of any pretax and Roth contributions.

Unlike an IRA, which has an income threshold limiting high-income earners from making after-tax Roth IRA contributions, no such limit exists for a Solo 401(k) plan. This means that unlike a Roth IRA, which limits individual Roth IRA contributions to $5,500 annually ($6,500 if the individual is fifty years or older), an individual using a Roth Solo 401(k) account in 2017 can make Roth contributions of up to $18,000 ($24,000 for those fifty or older) by the end of the year. This allows individuals to put away thousands of dollars more in tax-free retirement income than they would through a Roth IRA.

In addition, new tax rules allow plan participants to immediately convert employer profit-sharing contributions from pretax to Roth so long as the plan allows for the option. This means that a plan participant can make Roth contributions in 2017 up to $54,000 ($60,000 if over the age of fifty), almost *ten times* more than a Roth IRA.

With a designated Roth contribution, the employee irrevocably designates the deferral as an after-tax contribution that the employer must deposit into a designated Roth account. The employer includes the amount of the designated Roth contribution in the employee's gross income at the time the employee would have otherwise received the amount in cash if she had not made the election. It is subject to all applicable wage-withholding requirements. If you are a plan participant, you can make contributions to a designated Roth account and a traditional pretax account in the same year in any proportion you choose.

The Roth Solo 401(k) plan is a feature of a Solo 401(k) plan and not a separate plan. As long as the Solo 401(k) plan adoption agreements offers the option, Roth employee deferral contributions can be made by the plan participant to the designated Roth account. The plan simply needs to open a new bank account for the Roth contributions. It is common to include the word "Roth" or "R" on the new bank account name so that it is clear that the account is for Roth contributions.

As mentioned earlier, there is no wrong or right answer for whether one should make a pretax or after-tax (Roth) contribution. The main reason people contribute to a Roth Solo 401(k) plan is to generate tax-free income and gains from the investment. Remember, so long as the Roth Solo 401(k) plan account has been opened at least five years and you are over the age of fifty-nine and a half, all income and gains from your Roth Solo 401(k) are tax-free. This is known as a "qualified Roth distribution."

The advantage of contributing to a Roth Solo 401(k) account is that income and gains generated by the Roth investment can be tax-free and penalty-free so long as certain requirements are satisfied. On the other hand, the primary disadvantage of making Roth contributions versus pretax 401(k) plan contributions is that contributions to a Roth Solo 401(k) account are not tax deductible but would be if made to a pretax Solo 401(k) account. For that reason, most plan participants face an important decision when considering whether to make a Roth 401(k) contributions versus a pretax contribution. Essentially, you need to weigh the current benefit of a pretax 401(k) contribution tax deduction versus tax-free income and gains in the future. This is a conversation best had with your tax advisor, who will be able to provide you with a more complete picture as to the potential impact the decision will have on your income tax position.

The In-Plan Roth Solo 401(k) Conversion Option: Before 2010, converting pretax 401(k) plan funds to a Roth 401(k) plan was not commonly done. The Small Business Jobs Act of 2010, signed by President Obama, contained a little-known provision that went into effect on September 27, 2010, allowing for the conversion of a traditional 401(k) or 403(b) account to a Roth in the same plan if their employer offers one. However, the 401(k) plan participant (employee) must pay income tax on the amount converted.

For Solo 401(k) plans that include the Roth in-plan conversion option, the advantages of making a Roth 401(k) conversion are that distributions in retirement from accounts at least five years old are tax-free. The downside for making the conversion is that the tax must be paid on the fair market value of the 401(k) account at the time of conversion. In contrast, traditional 401(k) plans give you a tax break in the year you save for retirement but income tax is due upon withdrawal.

Before deciding whether you want to do a Roth 401(k) plan conversion, you will need to make sure that the plan indeed allows for that in-plan Roth conversions. Most traditional financial institutions do not allow for in-plan Roth conversions because of the accounting complexities, whereas most self-directed Solo 401(k) plan document providers do allow for in-plan Roth conversions. Once you have determined that your Solo 401(k) plan offers an in-plan Roth conversion, the next step is considering whether an in-plan Roth conversion ultimately makes financial sense. Some of the items to consider are:

- Do you have the ability to pay income taxes on the money you convert from your pretax Solo 401(k) plan?
- Based on your income tax bracket, does it make sense to pay the entire tax due in 2016? If you expect your income tax rate to go up, converting may be for you. If you think it will go down, then the opposite holds true.
- Do you anticipate withdrawing Roth Solo 401(k) plan funds for personal use within five years of conversion? If so, you may face taxes and penalties if you withdraw within five years.
- How confident are that your Roth 401(k) plan investments will be successful?

What Do You Need to Do If You Decide to Do an In-Plan Roth Conversion?: First, if you do not already have a bank account set up for your Roth contributions, a new bank account should be established. Roth contributions must be placed in a separate bank account where the Solo 401(k) plan participant can keep track of any contributions or distributions taken. Once the Roth account has been established, the plan participant must disclose to the plan administrator the value of the funds being converted or, in the case of an in-kind conversion, the plan asset being converted. Cash is easy to value for Roth conversion purposes, but an in-kind asset, such as real estate or a privately held stock interest, will likely need an independent valuation.

An independent valuation is important in the case of an in-kind conversion because the amount of tax due is based on the value of the asset being converted, not the price paid for the asset. So providing the IRS with an accurate and independent appraisal of the fair market value of the asset is crucial. The Roth conversion must be done before December 31 to be treated as converted in that year.

Since tax will be due on the in-plan Roth conversion, you will need to report the conversion transaction of the IRS. This is done via IRS Form 1099-R. The 1099-R will disclose to the IRS that a Roth conversion was made as well as its amount. A copy of the IRS Form 1099-R will also be provided to the plan participant who made the Roth conversion. An example of a completed 1099-R Form reporting a 401(k) plan Roth conversion can be found in Appendix C. When submitting the IRS Form 1099-R, you will also need to need to complete the Form 1096 (Annual Summary and Transmittal of US Information Returns). Additionally, the plan participant who made the Roth conversion must report the amount converted on IRS Form 1040, line 16A.

Will 2017 Be The Year of the Roth Conversion

President Donald Trump's tax plan has received significant amount of attention since his election victory. Even though most of the details are not yet known, a reduction in income taxes across the board, for individuals, businesses, investments are expected. President-elect Trump's tax rate reductions are not expected to be enacted until at least 2017, but if and when enacted, could potentially offer taxpayers contemplating a Roth conversion with an opportunity to defer taxes on the conversion amount by holding off to at least 2017. In general, the amount of taxable income on a Roth conversion is based on the fair market value of the IRA assets subject to the conversion. The converted Roth amount is then added to the taxpayer's gross income on the IRS Form 1040 and is then subject to tax, subject to the applicable tax rates. For example, under 2016 current tax rates, if John had gross income of $45,000 and wishes to convert $50,000 of pre-tax retirement funds to Roth, John would be subject to tax on $95,000 and his tax bracket would have gone from 25% to 28%. Whereas, if John waited until at least 2017 when the Trump tax plan was enacted, and assuming the tax plan rates promoted by President Trump during his campaign were passed, the $95,000 of income would be subject to a tax of 25%. However, with a low tax rate of just 12% for income under $75,000 under the Trump tax plan, John would have the option to do partial Roth conversions over multiple years keeping his annual gross income under $75,000 and taking advantage of the lower tax rate.

The ability to generate tax-free income and gains using a Roth 401(k) plan presents many valuable tax-planning opportunities. The election victory of Donald J. Trump and his plan to lower individual income tax rates could make the Roth conversion more tax friendly for taxpayers after 2016.

"Checkbook Control" Option

When it comes to determining what type of Solo 401(k) qualified retirement plan is best suited for your investments goals, it is important to look at all the investment options the plan provides. The traditional financial institutions are in business to make money by selling financial investment products—not real estate or other alternative assets. Therefore, they don't offer alternative asset investment options. This has created a small industry for a group of self-directed Solo 401(k) plan document sponsor companies who essentially make money by selling the self-directed plan documents, which allow for alternative asset investments, such as real estate. The self-directed plan documents sponsored by these companies typically also include the loan feature and Roth component.

Unlike a Solo 401(k) plan offered by most financial institutions and passive custodians, with a self-directed Solo 401(k) plan the plan account can be opened at most local banks in your community or town and is not required to be open at the financial institution that provided the plan documents or at a trust company or custodian in another state. The Solo 401(k) plan bank account will typically come with a checkbook that will allow the trustee of the Solo 401(k) plan, which is typically the business owner, the ability to make nontraditional investments such as real estate by signing a check or even executing a wire transfer.

This is quite different than a financial institution plan that will not allow you to make nontraditional investments or a custodian controlled self-directed Solo 401(k) plan, which will not offer a checkbook with the account. The appealing aspect of having "checkbook control" by serving as trustee of the Solo 401(k) plan held at a local bank is that you have the ability to make investments quickly, which can help get an offer accepted for a real estate investment property

A World of Investment Opportunities

Remember, the ability to make certain investments such as in real estate depends on the 401(k) plan documents that are adopted. Even though the IRS allows 401(k) plan funds to be invested in real estate, there is no requirement that a Solo 401(k) plan document offers you that right. As we will examine in detail shortly, almost all the major financial institutions do not allow for nontraditional or alternative asset investments with a Solo 401(k) plan (such as real estate, precious metals, and private business investments) for the simple reason that they don't make any money or earn any fees when you make these investments. A traditional financial institution, such as Vanguard or Bank of America, makes money when you buy the financial products they offer, which are typically stocks, mutual funds, ETFs, and other equity types of investments. For someone who wants to have the ability to make traditional as well as alternative asset investments with their Solo 401(k) plan, using a self-directed Solo 401(k) plan document sponsor company or trust company that offers plan documents that allow for alternative asset investments is generally your only option.

For those reasons, one of the main factors determining whether your business should adopt a financial institution supported plan, a custodian controlled plan, or a self-directed plan, is the type of investments you would like to make with your plan. If you feel comfortable that all your 401(k) plan assets are in the financial markets, then a financial institution supported plan could work well. If you want to diversify your 401(k) plan assets and are interested in having the option to buy real estate and precious metals, or doing hard money lending or private business investments, then custodian controlled or self-directed IRA LLC Solo 401(k) plan could be a viable option. It is good practice to work with a tax expert and investment advisor when determining which type of Solo 401(k) plan would suit your retirement and investment goals.

We spent a significant amount of time in prior chapters reviewing the main reasons why you would want to consider making alternative asset investments with your Solo 401(k) plan funds, such as investment diversification, hedging against inflation or a falling US dollar, as well as gaining the ability to invest in what you know well or understand. While everyone's interests will vary, the great news is that you have many options through the Solo 401(k).

A Solo 401(k) plan offers you the ability to use your retirement funds to make almost any type of investment on your own without requiring the consent of any custodian or person. The IRS and Department of Labor only describe the types of investments that are prohibited, which are very few.

So what kind of investment opportunities are available to you? The list includes:

- Residential or commercial real estate
- Domestic of foreign real estate
- Raw land
- Foreclosure property
- Mortgages
- Mortgage pools
- Deeds
- Private loans
- Tax liens
- Private businesses
- Limited liability companies
- Limited liability partnerships
- Private placements
- Precious metals and certain coins
- Stocks, bonds, and mutual funds
- Foreign currencies

Reasons to Purchase Nontraditional Assets with Your Solo 401(k) Plan

Diversification

In general, most Americans have an enormous amount of financial exposure to the financial markets. Whether it is through retirement investments such as IRAs or 401(k) plans, or personal savings, many of us have most of our savings connected in some way to the stock market. In fact, over 90 percent of retirement assets are invested in the financial markets. With what is believed to be approximately $25 trillion in retirement assets as of 2014, you can see the scope of that exposure. Investing in nontraditional assets such as real estate offers a form of investment diversification from the equity markets.

In general, the more diversified your portfolio, the greater the chance that your assets will offer lower correlation, meaning they are less likely to move in the same direction. However, diversification does not assure profit or protect against loss. The use of nontraditional asset classes can help protect your portfolio when the market is down and help protect you from losing more than the market.

Invest in Something You Understand

Many Americans became frustrated with the equity markets after the 2008 financial crisis. Thankfully, we have seen the financial markets rebound since then and have even seem some years of over 20 percent growth in the equity markets. Nevertheless, many Americans are still somewhat shell-shocked from the market swings and not 100 percent sure what exactly goes on in Wall Street and how it all works.

Real estate, in comparison, is often a more comfortable investment for the lower and middle classes because they grew up exposed to it, whereas the upper classes often learned about Wall Street and other securities during their younger years and college days. Everyone has heard someone talk about the importance of owning a home or the amount of money that can be made by owning real estate. From Donald Trump to reality TV, real estate is fast becoming mainstream and one of the most trusted asset classes for Americans. It is, of course, not without risk, but many retirement investors feel more comfortable understanding the real estate market and buying and selling real estate than they do stocks.

Inflation Protection

Rising food and energy prices, coupled with high federal debt levels and low interest rates, have recently fueled new inflationary fears. As a result, some investors may be looking for ways to protect their portfolios from the ravages of inflation. It is a matter of guesswork to estimate whether these inflation risks are real, but for some retirement investors, protecting retirement assets from inflation is a big concern. Inflation can have a nasty impact on a retirement portfolio because it means a dollar today may not be worth a dollar tomorrow. Inflation also increases the cost of things that are necessary for humans to live and enjoy life, such as bread, gas, shelter, clothing, and medical services. This decreases the value of money so that goods and services cost more.

For example, if someone had a 401(k) plan worth $250,000 at a time of high inflation, that $250,000 will be worth significantly less or have significantly less buying power. This can mean the difference between retiring and working the rest of your life. Buying hard assets is seen as one way of protecting your assets against inflation. Many investors have long recognized that investing in commercial real estate can provide a natural protection against inflation, as rents tend to increase when prices do, acting as a hedge against inflation.

Hard Assets

Many nontraditional assets, such as real estate and precious metals, are tangible hard assets that you can see and touch. With real estate, for example, you can drive by with your family, point out the window, and say, "I own that." For some, that's important psychologically, especially when there are concerns about financial instability, inflation, and/or political or global upheaval.

Let's go into a few of those opportunities in more detail so that you understand the finer points.

Real Estate

Real estate has become one of the most popular nontraditional investment options for Solo 401(k) plan investors. (We'll discuss the details further in Chapter 7.) Real estate offers diversification from overexposure to Wall Street for both personal and retirement funds. After the 2008 financial crisis, many retirement investors began to appreciate the importance of having a well-balanced and diversified retirement portfolio that can help protect against another financial crisis. People generally like to invest in something they know and understand. Real estate is reemerging as an asset class that more Americans have confidence and comfort in compared to the vagaries of stock market fluctuations. Buying tangible assets such as real estate is seen as a solid way of protecting retirement savings from the threat of inflation.

In addition, all income and gains from real estate owned in a Solo 401(k) plan are exempt from tax, making real estate an even more powerful investment. For example, if you purchased a piece of property with your Solo 401(k) plan for $100,000 and you later sold the property for $300,000, the $200,000 of gain appreciation would generally be tax-free. Whereas if you purchased the property using personal funds (nonretirement funds), the gain would be subject to federal income tax and, in most cases, state income tax.

The IRS allows you to use a Solo 401(k) to purchase real estate or raw land as long as your plan allows for it. Remember, it is up to the plan documents whether nontraditional investment options are permitted to be made with plan funds. In general, most financial-institution adopted plans do not allow for real estate investments, while a custodian-directed and open-architecture self-directed Solo 401(k) plan will allow for the real estate investment option. Then since you are the trustee of the 401(k) plan, making a real estate investment is as simple as writing a check from your 401(k) plan bank account.

Do I Need an LLC to Buy Real Estate?

There is no need to establish an LLC to make your real estate investment using Solo 401(k) plan assets. The plan itself can make real estate and other investments without the need for an LLC because the plan is a trust, and the trustee, on behalf of the trust, can take title to a real estate asset.

Tax Liens

Tax lien and tax deed investments have become popular investment choices for many Solo 401(k) plan participants. Beginning in 2009, as foreclosures continued to pile up, many properties were saddled with unpaid property taxes. For some investors, this created a great investment opportunity.

Tax collectors in twenty-nine states; Washington, DC; Puerto Rico; and the Virgin Islands use tax lien sales to force owners to pay unpaid property taxes. The process varies by state, but here's how it generally works: When property owners don't pony up for their property taxes, tax collectors wait the time period required by state law and then put those unpaid property taxes up for auction. The time period varies from just a few months to several years, depending on the state.

In most states, the person willing to pay the most cash for the tax lien wins the auction. Some states, however, have a bid-down process, where investors' bids indicate how much interest they're willing to accept on their investment, and the lowest bidder wins. Whatever method is used, the tax collector takes the payment for the overdue taxes from the winning bid. In exchange, the purchaser gets a lien on the property. As the winning bidder, you'd get a return on your investment in one of two ways: interest on your bid amount or ownership of the property.

With a tax deed, on the other hand, you will actually own the property in which the owner has been delinquent in paying the property taxes. A tax deed sale generally involves property being sold by a taxing authority or the court to recover delinquent taxes.

The IRS permits the purchase of tax liens and tax deeds with a Solo 401(k) plan. The advantage of purchasing tax liens or tax deeds with a Solo 401(k) plan is that your profits are tax deferred back into your retirement account until a distribution is taken. In the case of a Roth Solo 401(k) plan, all gains are tax-free. Once again, you have "checkbook control" and can make purchases on the spot without custodian consent.

Loans and Notes

The IRS permits using 401(k) funds to make loans or purchase notes from third parties. By using a Solo 401(k) plan to make loans or purchase notes from third parties, all interest payments received are tax deferred until a distribution is taken. In the case of a Roth Solo 401(k) plan, all gains are tax-free. When engaging in private lending transaction or purchasing notes, it is important to make note of the IRS prohibited transaction and disqualified person rules, which are found in IRC 4975. See Chapter 6 for a detailed description of the prohibited transaction and disqualified person rules.

For example, if you used a Solo 401(k) to loan money to a friend, all interest received would flow back into your 401(k) plan tax-free. Whereas if you lent your friend money from personal funds (nonretirement funds), the interest received would be subject to federal and in most cases state income tax.

Private Businesses

With a Solo 401(k), you are permitted to purchase an interest in a privately held business that is engaged in any type of business activity. The business can be established as any entity other than an S corporation (i.e., LLC, C corporation, or partnership) When investing in a private business using 401(k) funds, it is important to keep in mind the "Disqualified Person" and "Prohibited Transaction" rules under IRC 4975 and the "Unrelated Business Taxable Income" rules under IRC 512. It is a good idea to consult a retirement tax professional to develop the most tax-efficient structure for using your Solo 401(k). Plan to invest in a private business. These rules will be explained in greater detail in Chapter 6.

Precious Metals and Coins

You can also use your Solo 401(k) plan assets to make investments in precious metals and certain coins. The advantage of using a Solo 401(k) plan to purchase precious metals and/or coins is that their values generally keep up with or exceed inflation rates better than other investments. In addition, an argument can be made that IRS approved metals and/or coins (bullion) can be held in the name of the 401(k) plan at your local bank's safe deposit box, eliminating depository fees. A more detailed explanation of the rules involved in purchasing precious metals or IRS-approved coins can be found in Chapter 7.

Foreign Currencies

Your Solo 401(k) plan documents permit the purchase of foreign currencies, even including Iraqi dinars. Many investors believe that foreign currency investments offer liquidity advantages compared to the stock market as well as significant investment opportunities. Again, all foreign currency gains generated are generally tax deferred until a distribution is taken, and in the case of a Roth Solo 401(k) plan, all gains are tax-free.

Stocks, Bonds, Mutual Funds, and CDs

In addition to nontraditional investments such as real estate, a Solo 401(k) may also be used to purchase stock, bonds, mutual funds, and CDs. The advantage of using a Solo 401(k) plan with "checkbook control" is that you are not limited to just making these types of investments and you can open a stock trading account with any financial institution.

According to the Investment Company Institute, as of December 31, 2014, 401(k) plans and other defined contribution plans held an estimated $6.8 trillion in assets and represented approximately 28 percent of the $24.7 trillion US retirement market. The majority of 401(k) plans limit investments to stocks and mutual funds. It's likely that a significant amount of the 47 million or so IRAs are invested in the equities market, too. Accordingly, it's easy to conclude that stocks, mutual funds, ETFS, and other equities are by far the most popular investment for retirement accounts, including Solo 401(k) plans.

No one is arguing against stocks as the best retirement investment. Indeed, history has shown that owning stocks is one of the easiest and most profitable ways to grow your wealth over the long term. From January 1, 1900, through December 31, 2013, for example, the average return of the S&P 500, which tracks the 500 largest stocks based on market capitalization, was 11.60 percent. In comparison, the average S&P 500 return from January 1, 2000, through December 31, 2000, was just 5.52 percent.

Stocks have proven to be a good investment over time. Could you do better with a different investment? Possibly. The bigger concern, however, is that such heavy exposure to the US equity markets carries some risk. Diversification is a must when it comes to retirement planning.

Can You Take a Loan from Your Solo 401(k) Plan?

Another really great feature of a Solo 401(k) plan is the ability to use it as a source of funds when it would be to your advantage to tap in to your retirement savings. The loan feature is unique to a 401(k) plan, but the plan adoption agreement must include the option in the plan in order for the loan to be available to an eligible plan participant. In the case of a Solo 401(k) plan, most financial-institution-provided plans, which are typically offered for no fee, do not offer the loan feature because these institutions only make money when the 401(k) plans are being invested and not when they are being pulled out for personal purposes. In contrast, most of the custodian-directed and open architecture Solo 401(k) plan document providers will offer the loan feature. Again, the plan documents will determine whether the loan feature will be available for your particular Solo 401(k) plan.

With a Solo 401(k) plan loan, you can access your retirement funds without tax or penalty by taking out a loan using the accumulated balance of your Solo 401(k) plan as collateral. Such a loan is permitted at any time, and you can borrow up to either $50,000 or 50 percent of your account value, whichever is less.

This feature makes the Solo 401(k) plan unique among retirement savings plans and particularly attractive to many sole proprietorships and small business owners. There is no loan feature available with any type of IRA, including a SEP-IRA or SIMPLE IRA. The Solo 401(k) loan feature is really the only way you can use retirement funds for personal use without triggering a tax or penalty. The loan feature is truly helpful because it allows you to use the retirement funds and do a prohibited transaction and not pay a tax or penalty.

Plan loans from the Solo 401(k) are legal because of a limited statutory exception to the prohibited-transaction rules as stated in IRC 4975(d)(1). Specifically, IRC 72(p) and the 2001 EGGTRA rules allow you to borrow money from your Solo 401(k) plan tax-free and without penalty. As long as the plan documents allow for it and the proper loan documents are prepared and executed, you can take such a loan for any reason. If the loan payments are made on time, there are no penalties or taxes due.

There are thousands of ways to use your Solo 401(k) plan loan. In fact, you can use your Solo 401(k) loan for practically anything as long as that activity is not illegal. There is no need to worry about IRS-prohibited transactions because the Solo 401(k) loan is exempt from the reach of the prohibited-transaction rules.

What could you possibly do with such a loan? Here are some ideas and popular ways to use Solo 401(k) loan proceeds:

- Obtain immediate funds for your business.
- Help pay personal expenses.
- Lend to a third party at a higher interest rate.
- Invest in a real estate project that offers a higher rate of return than Prime plus 1 percent.
- Consolidate your debt and help pay it off.
- Pay for college expenses.
- Pay for unexpected emergencies.
- Avoid distribution penalties while using up to $50,000 immediately without restrictions.
- Invest in a new franchise or business.
- Make an investment (such as a tax lien, private placement, or mortgage pool) that will generate a higher rate of return than Prime plus 1 percent.
- Invest in some transaction that would otherwise be prohibited under IRC 4975.

In short, you can have quick, easy, and inexpensive access to $50,000 for any reason.

In addition, you are not limited to taking or making only one loan, but those loans together must not exceed $50,000 or 50 percent of your account value, whichever is less, with some stipulations. Specifically, the total amount you can borrow can't, when added to the balance of all other outstanding loans, exceed the lesser of:

- $50,000 that is reduced by the highest loan outstanding balance (HLOB) of any other loans during the plan
- More than half of your vested current plan outstanding balance (POB) or $10,000

Here are some examples to explain how those restrictions apply:

Joe

Joe is a software consultant who runs his business as a sole proprietor. Joe adopted a Solo 401(k) plan and rolled in $40,000 from a former employer retirement plan. Joe has some credit card debt with high interest rates and is looking to use the Solo 401(k) loan feature to pay off that debt. This would allow him to replace his high credit card debt with a lower interest rate. Furthermore, in paying back to his plan, he would also be increasing the value of his plan. The maximum Joe could borrow from his Solo 401(k) plan would be $20,000: 50 percent of his account value since he had less than $100,000 in his plan.

Amy

Amy is a doctor and operates her business as an S corporation. She also provides consulting services to various clients who receive a 1099. Amy adopted a Solo 401(k) plan and rolled in $200,000 from a former employer retirement plan. Amy's parents have run into some medical problems recently and have accumulated excessive medical bills that are forcing them to consider bankruptcy. Amy spoke to her CPA because she was looking for a way to help her parents out and pay off some of those bills.

The CPA mentioned that the Solo 401(k) plan Amy adopted included a loan option that would allow her to borrow up to $50,000. Amy then asked about the interest rate and was told that the lowest interest rate allowed by law is Prime as per the *Wall Street Journal*, which as of December 31, 2016 was 3.75 percent. The CPA also mentioned that the loan would have to be paid back over a five-year period at least quarterly. Amy did the math and figured if she borrowed the full $50,000, she would be paying back about $915 to her plan each month or about $2,745 if she elected to make quarterly loan payments. Amy felt that this was doable, plus she liked the fact that she would be increasing the value of her plan at the same time.

Steve

Steve is in the real estate business and has a LLC through which he buy and sells real estate and offers management services. Steve has a Solo 401(k) plan for his LLC, which he adopted several years ago, and has $60,000 in his Solo 401(k) plan account. Steve is finally ready to pop the question and propose to his girlfriend of four years, Jackie, but is short about $12,000 for the engagement ring he was looking at. Steve was talking with this father about his financial problem, and his father mentioned that his friend at work used the 401(k) plan loan feature from his company plan to help pay for his engagement ring. Steve likes that idea very much, completes the Solo 401(k) plan loan kit, and borrows $13,000 from his Solo 401(k) plan.

Even though Steve was able to borrow up to $30,000, he really only needed $13,000 for the ring, so he just borrowed the $13,000, which he plans to pay back monthly over a five-year period. This is a great way for Steve to get money tax-free and penalty-free from his plan without having to incur credit card debt with excessive interest rate charges. Plus, his plan will actually be growing from the loan payments he makes. Steve, and later Jackie, see this as a win-win situation.

Ben

Ben, a documentary filmmaker, is the sole participant of the Ben Smith Documentary Films Solo 401(k) plan. He is also the plan trustee and administrator. Ben's plan account value is $135,000. One year ago, Ben decided to borrow $45,000 to invest in special camera equipment. He has repaid $5,000 of that loan through regular quarterly payments at an appropriate interest rate. Ben's loan balance is now $10,000, but he wants to take out another loan.

In fact, Ben is only able to borrow another $7,500. This is because he is allowed the lesser of A or B:

A. $50,000, reduced by the highest loan outstanding balance (HLOB) ($15,000) of any other loans from the plan during the one-year period ending on the day before the date upon which the loan is to be made, which would be $35,000

B. The greater of one-half of Ben's retirement value of the nonforfeited account balance minus the outstanding loan balance ($15,000) or $10,000.

So if we did the calculation and multiplied 0.5 (or one-half) by Ben's outstanding loan balance (35,000), which equals $17,500, minus his outstanding loan balance of $35,000, we would get $7,500. Since $7,500 in formula B is less than $35,000 in formula A, Ben would only allowed to borrow an additional $7,500 from his plan.

Repayment Terms

Your Solo 401(k) loan is a loan and not a gift, so like all loans it does need to be paid back. In fact, you must repay the loan over an amortization schedule of five years or less on at least a quarterly payment frequency basis.

You must pay interest on the loan, set at a reasonable rate, generally interpreted as the Prime interest rate as per the *Wall Street Journal*. Some plan administrators will set the minimum loan amount as the Prime interest rate plus 1 percent. For example, as I write this passage, the Prime interest rate is 3.75 percent, which has increased somewhat in 2016 from prior years due to higher interest rates.

Huh?

Why would you ever want to charge yourself a higher interest rate for your Solo 401(k) plan loan? Actually, when you think about it, there's an amazing logic to the idea.

Take the example of Jeff, a successful dentist with a practice that has no full-time employees other than himself and his wife. Jeff and his wife are able to max-out their employee deferral and employer profit-sharing contributions each year. However, Jeff and his wife would still like to add more money to his plan if possible. Jeff discussed this dilemma with his CPA, who mentioned that if he and his wife took out a Solo 401(k) loan and charged themselves a high interest rate, making sure it stayed under the usury or loan-shark interest rate rules in their state, they could actually put an amount of money into their plan that exceeds their annual limitation amount. Jeff mentioned that he doesn't need the money, but his CPA told him he could use those funds as he sees fit, but it would allow him to defer additional funds into his plan.

His CPA gave him an example. Assuming Jeff and his wife each borrowed $50,000 from the 401(k) plan, instead of using an interest rate of 3.75 percent, they could select a 10 percent interest rate. This would allow them each to defer an extra $14,000 or so in the plan over a five-year period.

Not bad!

Your loan payments must include both principle and interest. In general, it is not permitted to make balloon payments to repay your loan. However, most loan documents do allow for loan prepayment without penalty.

Can You Borrow from Your Roth Account?

A Solo 401(k) includes pretax and after-tax (Roth) funds. It is possible to take a loan from the Roth portion of a Solo 401(k) plan as long as the plan documents permit it.

Using Roth 401(k) funds for a loan does trigger some potential tax ramifications if you default. In such a case, the determination of what portion of the Roth funds are distributed tax-free and what portion is subject to tax, and potentially subject to a 10% early distribution penalty, is looked at on a pro rata basis. Determining the tax implication on a defaulted Roth Solo 401(k) plan loan is quite complex, and it is one of the reasons why some 401(k) plan administrators only allow for pretax funds to be used for a loan.

How Do You Apply for a Solo 401(k) Loan?

In order to take out a Solo 401(k) loan, the first step is to make sure your plan documents allow for it. As explained earlier, many of the Solo 401(k) plans that are provided by large financial institutions do not allow loans. The reason is simple: your financial institution does not want to get involved in the administration of your loan and would rather invest your funds in the financial products they sell. Think about it: the less money stays in their account, the less money available to them for investment or to generate fees.

Once you have determined that your Solo 401(k) plan loan documents allow for a loan to be taken, the next step is to determine how much you can borrow. To calculate the amount, you must determine the fair market value of your plan assets with the understanding that, in general, the maximum loan amount you can take is $50,000 or 50 percent or your account value, whichever is less.

In determining the fair market value of your plan assets, if your plan is all in cash, then that is clearly not an issue as the fair market value of the plan assets would equal the cash in the plan. However, if the plan's assets consist of nontraditional asset types (such as real estate, notes, or private business investments), then you need an independent third party to provide an opinion on the value of those assets so you can determine your maximum loan amount. This would not be an issue when it is crystal clear that the plan assets are over $100,000, since you would be entitled to borrow-up to the maximum $50,000 amount.

After that, you simply need to contact your plan administrator to apply for the loan and complete the necessary loan documents. Typically, with a Solo 401(k) plan, you serve as your own plan administrator, so getting loan approval is pretty easy. In fact, I have yet to hear of a Solo 401(k) loan that has been denied by the person looking to use the money.

The loan paperwork generally includes a loan agreement as well as a "Truth and Lending Disclosure Statement" that will provide an overview of all the terms of the loan. This will include the amount, the payment schedule, the applicable percentage of interest, and other details. In general, your spouse will also be required to sign the loan agreement, but most loan documents do not require the signature of a notary.

Having said all that, your loan application will be governed by your plan documents, so it is possible that your application process may have some unusual details or requirements. Please read them thoroughly.

Who Is Responsible for Administering Your Solo 401(k) Plan Loan?

Your Solo 401(k) plan loan is a private loan between you, the plan participant, and the plan. The loan documents are not filed with the IRS or any government agency. Accordingly, the administration of the loan is the responsibility of the plan administrator.

In most cases with a Solo 401(k) plan, you are both the plan participant and the administrator. It is in your capacity as administrator that you will administer the loan. The plan administrator (probably you) and the plan participant (you again) should both keep copies of the plan documents.

In general, there is not much work involved in administering a Solo 401(k) plan loan. The plan administer must make sure that all loan payments are being in full and in a timely manner. That's pretty much it. In the case where a plan participant wishes to take one or more additional loans, the plan administrator should be certain that the plan allows for multiple loans and that the plan participant has not exceeded the permitted loan threshold.

When Loans Go Bad

What happens if you miss a loan payment? Loan payments must be made in a timely manner or they will be considered delinquent. A delinquent loan is not the same as a defaulted loan. A "defaulted loan" is an IRS defined term, and a 401(k) plan loan is deemed to be in default when it no longer meets the requirements found in Treasury Regulation 1.72(p)-1.

A 401(k) plan would only be considered in default under the following circumstances:

- The 401(k) plan loan is not paid within the least permissible term of the loan (usually five years).
- The 401(k) plan loan is not paid according to the amortization schedule, with loan payments made at least quarterly and including interest and penalty.
- The 401(k) plan loan exceeds the maximum allowable amount.
- An event designated by the 401(k) plan occurs.

If there is a default, you can try to cure the default if the plan documents allow for a cure period. In such a case, the plan documents may allow for a certain period of time for you to make up the missed payments. This cure period cannot extend beyond the end of the calendar quarter in which the loan payment was missed.

If you do default on a plan loan, you will trigger a deemed taxable distribution. This is not a real distribution, but it is treated as such for tax purposes. This means that the entire loan balance or the loan amount above the allowable limit (if the maximum loan amount is exceeded) is considered a taxable distribution in the taxable year that the amount is deemed distributed.

The deemed distribution is considered a table event and is subject to a 10 percent early distribution penalty if you are under the age of fifty-nine and a half in the year of default. Even if your plan loan is in default and those funds are deemed distributed, you must still repay your loan. The loan repayment amount is actually treated as an after-tax contribution to your plan.

You cannot roll over the deemed distribution from your 401(k) plan loan default into another retirement account. Once the distribution occurs, those funds become personal assets and are no longer considered retirement assets. However, the amount of the defaulted loan, even if it goes unpaid, is still considered an outstanding loan when calculating the amount available to you for future loans.

It is possible, however, to roll over your outstanding Solo 401(k) loan to a new qualified plan so you are not in default. Most plan documents will not allow a plan participant with an outstanding loan to roll the outstanding loan to another 401(k) plan. In fact, some plans will not allow you to roll funds out of the plan until the loan has been paid off or the participant takes the loan as a distribution. That being said, there are plan docs that allow for an outstanding loan to be rolled into another 401(k) plan that offers a loan program. It all depends on the plan documents that govern your new plan.

For example, you can never roll over an outstanding loan into a new IRA because IRAs do not permit loans. The key is whether your new employer's plan allows for the rollover of outstanding loans and similar loan provisions. When a loan cannot be rolled over into a new retirement plan, you must either pay the remaining loan off (including principle and interest) or treat the outstanding loan balance as a taxable distribution.

Comparing the Solo 401(k) Plan with Other Retirement Savings Plans

To get a really clear picture of the advantages of the Solo 401(k) plan, let's compare it with other traditional retirement savings plans.

Solo 401(k) versus SEP-IRA

As explained earlier, before the EGTRRA became effective in 2002, there was no compelling reason for an owner-only business to establish a Solo 401(k) plan because the business owner could generally receive the same benefits by adopting a profit-sharing plan or a SEP-IRA. After 2002, EGTRRA paved the way for an owner-only business to put more money aside for retirement and to operate a more cost-effective retirement plan than a SEP-IRA or 401(k) plan.

The SEP is a pure profit-sharing employer-sponsored retirement plan that allows for a tax-deductible contribution equal to the smaller of $54,000 or 25 percent (20 percent if sole proprietorship) of compensation for 2017.

The Solo 401(k) has the following advantages:

- **Higher maximum contribution:** As I've already mentioned, a Solo 401(k) plan allows you to make an employee salary deferral contribution and an employee profit-sharing deferral contribution. In 2017, a SEP-IRA, on the other hand, only allows for a profit-sharing contribution equal to the lesser of $54,000 or 25 percent (20 percent in the case of a sole proprietorship or single-member LLC) of the earned income or compensation earned via the business; and it does not have an employee salary deferral contribution. So if you are sixty years old and have an S corporation from which you earn $100,000 in self-employment wages according to your W-2 form, then you can put $24,000 plus $25,000 (which is 25 percent of $100,000) or approximately $49,000 into your Solo 401(k). Whereas if you established a SEP-IRA, you can only defer 25 percent of $100,000 or $25,000.
- **Catch-up contributions:** With a Solo 401(k), you can contribute an extra $6,000 if you are over fifty years of age. The SEP-IRA does not allow a catch-up contribution.
- **Roth feature:** A Solo 401(k) plan can be made in either pre-tax or after-tax (Roth) formats. A SEP-IRA only permits pretax contributions.

- **Tax-free loan option:** A Solo 401(k) permits you to borrow up to $50,000 or 50 percent of your account value, whichever is less. This loan can be used for any purpose. A SEP-IRA does not allow you to borrow any money from your account without triggering a prohibited transaction.
- **Invest in real estate and use leverage with no additional tax:** With a Solo 401(k), you can make a real estate investment using nonrecourse funds without triggering the Unrelated Debt Financed Income rules and the Unrelated Business Taxable Income (UBTI) tax (IRC 514). These rules will be discussed in greater detail in Chapter 7. This is not possible with a SEP-IRA, as using SEP-IRA funds to purchase real estate using a nonrecourse loan would trigger the Unrelated Business Taxable Income tax.

Solo 401(k) versus SIMPLE IRA

A SIMPLE IRA plan can be established by an employer who has fewer than a hundred employees who will receive at least $5,000 in compensation from the employer in the preceding calendar year. A SIMPLE IRA plan is similar to a Solo 401(k) plan, as both are funded by employee deferrals and additional employer contributions. However, a SIMPLE IRA has a lower deferral limit and uses an IRA-type trust to hold contributions for each employee, rather than a single plan.

The SIMPLE IRA has all of the same disadvantages as the SEP-IRA relative to the Solo 401(k) with one big exception: the SIMPLE IRA has an even lower deferral limit of $12,500 (for 2017) and a catch-up contribution that is just $3,000. In addition, the employer must provide either:

1. A dollar-for-dollar match of up to 3 percent of compensation to all who defer
2. A 2 percent nonelective contribution to all employees who are eligible to participate in the plan

Solo 401(k) versus a Defined Benefit (DB) Plan

The one major advantage of establishing a DB plan is that you can sock away a whole lot of money for retirement—far more than any other retirement plan. For example, in 201 the annual benefit cannot exceed the lesser of:

- 100 percent of the participant's average compensation for his or her highest 3 consecutive calendar years; or
- $215,000 for 2017.

A DB plan identifies the specific benefit that will be payable to you at retirement. Your basic retirement benefit is usually based on a formula that takes into account such factors as the number of years a participant works for the employer (years of service) and the participant's salary. Your retirement benefit is generally provided in the form of regular payments over your lifetime beginning at what the plan calls "normal retirement age," which is typically age sixty-five.

While it is really nice to know how much money you will have at retirement or payout, some DB plans do not adjust your future payouts to keep pace with inflation. In addition, you generally don't have much say in how the money is invested. Moreover, you can't choose to invest more in the plan, and the yearly maintenance fees for the plan can become significant. That being said, one of the major advantages of a DB plan is that there is no effort required on your part. The company that provides the DB plan is responsible for making all contribution and investment decision, which, when you are self-employed, is *you*. However, the DB plan sponsor bears the investment risk associated with the plan. In a weak market, higher contributions will be required to compensate for lower-than-expected investment return to satisfy the defined contribution requirement.

In sum, most business owners who elect to adopt a DB plan are doing it because substantial benefits can be provided and accrued within a short time, even with early retirement, and the plan provides a predictable benefit.

I won't go into more detail about DB plans for a simple reason: they are increasingly uncommon. Today, there are about 38,000 insured DB plans in the United States, compared to 114,000 in 1985. DB plans offer substantial tax-deductible retirement contributions and a significant and predictable future retirement income. They generally appeal to business owners who would like to shelter the largest percentage of their income or make the largest retirement plan contribution possible under IRS rules. However, the DB is one of the most costly types of retirement plans to adopt and administer, and has rigid annual funding requirements. Generally speaking, it is falling by the wayside.

The Roth Solo 401(k) Secret

The Roth Solo 401(k) plan is the ultimate tax-free retirement solution for the self-employed. With federal and state income tax rates expected to increase in the future, gaining the ability to generate tax-free returns from your retirement investments when you retire is the last surviving legal tax shelter. With a Roth Solo 401(k), you can make almost any investment tax-free, including real estate, tax liens, precious metals, currencies, options, and private business investments, and once you hit the age of fifty-nine and a half, you will be able to live off your Roth 401(k) assets without ever paying tax. Imagine if someone told you that if you started making Roth 401(k) contributions in your forties and that by just generating a modest rate of return, you could have over a million dollars tax-free when you retire. With a Roth 401(k), you can live off the Roth 401(k) investment income tax-free or take a portion of your Roth 401(k) funds and use it for any purpose without ever paying tax.

The Roth Solo 401(k) Plan Advantages

The Power of Tax-Free Investing

One of the main attractions of the self-directed Roth Solo 401(k) plan is the fact that qualified distributions of Roth earnings are tax-free. As long as certain conditions are met and the distribution is a qualified distribution, the Roth Solo 401(k) plan participant will never pay tax on any Roth distributions received. The advantage of contributing to a Roth Solo 401(k) plan is that income and gains generated by the Roth 401(k) investment can be tax-free and penalty-free so long as certain requirements are satisfied. Unlike pretax Solo 401(k) plan contributions, contributions to a Roth Solo 401(k) are not tax deductible.

The power of tax-free investing can be best illustrated by way of the following examples:

- **Example 1:** Joe, a self-employed consultant, began funding a Roth Solo 401(k) plan with $3,000 per year at age twenty and wishes to continue through age sixty-five. At age sixty-five, Joe would wind up with $2.5 million at retirement (assuming a long-run annual compound growth rate in stocks, which was 9.88 percent from 1926 to 2011). Not a bad result for investing only $3,000 a year!
- **Example 2:** Ben, a self-employed real estate agent who is thirty years old, began funding a Roth Solo 401(k) plan with $8,000 and wants to know how much he will have at age seventy if he continues to make $8,000 annual contributions and is able to earn at an 8 percent rate of return. Ben did some research and was astonished that at age seventy he would have a whopping $2,238,248 tax-free, which he can then live off or pass to his wife or children tax-free.
- **Example 3:** Mary, a self-employed real estate investor who is thirty-five years old, began funding a Roth Solo 401(k) plan with $13,000 and wants to know how much she will have at age seventy if she continues to make $13,000 annual contributions and is able to earn at a 10 percent rate of return, which she felt was possible based on her past real estate investment returns. Mary did some research and was astonished that at age seventy she will have a whopping $3,875,649 tax-free to live off of or pass to her husband and children tax-free.

While it may be hard to believe that putting away just a few thousand dollars a year in a Roth Solo 401(k) plan can leave you with millions of dollars tax-free, it's simple. Just make annual contributions to your Roth Solo 401(k) plan and generate tax-free returns from making real estate or other investments with your Solo 401(k) plan.

High Contributions

A Roth Solo 401(k) combines features of the traditional 401(k) with those of the Roth IRA. Like a Solo 401(k) plan, the Roth Solo 401(k) plan is perfect for any self-employed individual or small business owner with no employees. The Roth Solo 401(k) plan contains the same advantages as a Solo 401(k) plan, but contributions are made with after-tax dollars as with a Roth IRA. While you don't get an upfront tax-deduction, the Roth 401(k) account grows tax-free, and withdrawals taken during retirement aren't subject to income tax, provided you're at least fifty-nine and a half, and have held the account for five years or more.

The Roth Solo 401(k) can offer advantages to self-employed individuals who wish to maximize their ability to generate tax-free retirement savings while receiving the ability to invest in real estate, precious metals, private businesses, or funds tax-free and without custodian consent.

Unlike a Roth IRA, which limits individual Roth IRA contributions to $5,500 annually ($6,500 if the individual is fifty years or older), in 2017 with a Roth Solo 401(k) account an individual can make after-tax (Roth) contributions of up to $18,000, or $24,000 for those fifty or older by the end of the year. This allows you to put away thousands of dollars more in tax-free retirement income than you would through a Roth IRA.

A Roth Solo 401(k) is perfect for sole proprietors, small businesses, and independent contractors such as consultants. The Roth Solo 401(k) plan is unique and so popular because it is considered the last remaining legal tax shelter available. There are so many features of the Roth Solo 401(k) plan that make it so appealing and popular among self-employed business owners.

Unlimited Investment Opportunities

With a Roth 401(k) plan or Roth 401(k) plan subaccount, you can invest your after-tax Roth 401(k) plan funds in real estate, precious metals, tax liens, private business investments, and much more tax-free. Unlike a pre-tax 401(k) plan, in a Roth 401(k) account all income and gains flow back tax-free to your account. As long as you have reached the age of fifty-nine and a half, and have had the Roth 401(k) account opened at least five years, you can take Roth 401(k) plan distributions tax-free. In other words, you can live off your Roth 401(k) plan assets or income tax-free. With federal income tax rates expected to increase, the ability to have a tax-free source of income upon retirement may be the difference between retiring early or not.

Loan Feature

While an IRA offers no participant loan feature, the Roth Solo 401(k) allows participants to borrow up to $50,000 or 50 percent of their account value (whichever is less) for any purpose at a low interest rate (the lowest interest rate is Prime, which is 3.75 percent as of December 31, 2016). This offers a Roth Solo 401(k) plan participant the ability to access up to $50,000 to use for any purpose, including paying personal debt or funding a business.

Offset the Cost of Your Plan with a Tax Deduction

By paying for your Solo 401(k) with business funds, you will be eligible to claim a deduction for the cost of the plan, including annual maintenance fees. The deduction for the cost associated with the Solo 401(k) plan and ongoing maintenance will help reduce your business's income tax liability, which will in turn offset the cost of adopting a self-directed Solo 401(k) plan. The retirement tax professionals at the IRA Financial Group will help you take advantage of the available business tax deduction for adopting a Solo 401(k) plan.

Cost-Effective Administration

In general, the Roth Solo 401(k) plan is easy to operate. There is no annual filing requirement unless your Solo 401(k) plan exceeds $250,000 in assets, in which case you will need to file a short information return with the IRS (Form 5500-EZ).

Exemption from UDFI Tax

When an IRA buys real estate that is leveraged with mortgage financing, it creates Unrelated Debt Financed Income ("UDFI"), a type of Unrelated Business Taxable Income (also known as "UBTI," or "UBIT") on which taxes must be paid. The UBTI tax is approximately 40 percent for 2016. However, with a Roth Solo 401(k) plan, you can use leverage without being subject to the UDFI rules and UBTI tax. This exemption provides significant tax advantages for using a Roth Solo 401(k) plan versus an IRA to purchase real estate.

The Solo 401(k) Wins Every Time

When Congress put EGTRRA in effect in 2002, it did a real favor for self-employed Americans. After decades of being disadvantaged when it came to taxation and retirement savings, the Solo 401(k) plan makes it possible for the self-employed to build their wealth faster than ever. With its high annual contributions, tax advantages, Roth feature, and loan component, the Solo 401(k) enables you to save far more money than any other retirement savings plan, except the DB plan, while retaining the simplicity, low cost, and flexibility that every self-employed person wants.

It's not often that the government delivers more than expected, but in the case of the Solo 401(k), we really lucked out. Now let's look first at what you can't do with a Solo 401(k) before we move on to what you can do.

CHAPTER 6

Rules for Prohibited Transactions

THE US GOVERNMENT CREATED THE Solo 401(k) to give you a mechanism for saving a lot of money for retirement. It's the IRS's job to make sure that you do so in a way that does not break any tax law. You are, after all, contributing to your Solo 401(k) by deferring tax payments. And your Solo 401(k) plan offers you tremendous latitude and flexibility in terms of options for how you can use and invest that money. But if you do something with those assets that the government thinks will not help you accumulate savings for retirement or otherwise enables you to take unfair potential advantage of the tax benefits you have been given, the IRS will ask you to pay tax on that money and (if you are under fifty-nine and half years old) a penalty as well.

The tricky part is that neither the IRS nor the Department of Labor tells you what you *can* invest in or how you *should* use your Solo 401(k) assets, they only tell you what you *can't* invest in or how you *can't* use those assets. Nevertheless, these limits and restrictions, which we call "prohibited transactions," are very important to understand and follow if you wish to gain maximum advantage from the work you are doing to create and grow your Solo 401(k) retirement assets.

In this chapter, we'll look at prohibited transactions that are restricted because they pertain to "disqualified persons," "conflicts of interest," and "self-dealing." Most Americans have never heard of the prohibited-transaction rules for good reason—most retirement investors use their retirement funds to buy traditional financial assets, such as stocks, mutual funds, and ETFs. In such cases, the change of engaging in a prohibited transaction is slim. If you are considering nontraditional investments such as real estate with your Solo 401(k) plan, the prohibited-transaction rules become very important. Prohibited transaction rules can be harsh, but they are easily avoidable. As long as you stay away from breaking the rules, you will have no reason to fear the IRS or Department of Labor when making 401(k) investments.

Before examining the prohibited-transaction rules in detail, you may be wondering why the IRS governs these rules for a 401(k) plan. Remember, a Solo 401(k) plan is not an ERISA 401(k) plan, so the IRS rules and not the ERISA rules would govern. Through an arrangement between the IRS and the Department of Labor, it is the Department of Labor's responsibility to determine whether a specific transaction is prohibited and to issue prohibited transaction exemptions. When the IRS discovers what appears to be a prohibited transaction in an individual's retirement account, it turns the matter over to the Department of Labor to make the determination. The Department of Labor reviews the situation and responds to the IRS, which in turn responds to the taxpayer.

We will also look at exceptions and exemptions to these restrictions, as well as certain categories of transactions that are not allowed with a 401(k) plan, such as the purchase of collectibles. Though there are many different scenarios stipulated in IRC Section 4975 and extensive case law clarifying those scenarios, the restrictions themselves are not complicated and I've simplified them as much as possible to make them easier to follow. Even so, it can be helpful to get advice from a tax professional or Solo 401(k) expert just to make sure you're on the straight and narrow path.

Disqualified Persons

If Solo 401(k) transactions are restricted, it is likely because they pertain to a "disqualified person." We'll go into more detail shortly about those transactions. But first, we need to clarify one thing: Who does the IRS consider to be a "disqualified person"?

Generally, this is referring to *you* (the Solo 401(k) plan participant) and most of *your immediate family*, including your direct lineal ancestors or descendants, as well as *any business entities* that hold a controlling equity or management interest in your Solo 401(k) plan.

Specifically, a disqualified person is:

A. **You** as the Solo 401(k) participant or any person with authority for making Solo 401(k) plan investments
B. **A trustee or custodian**, or a person providing services to the Solo 401(k) plan
C. **The owner** of the business that establishes the Solo 401(k) plan, which is usually you, a self-employed person
D. **An employee organization**, any of whose members are covered by the Solo 401(k) plan
E. **A 50-percent owner** of C or D
F. **A family member** of A, B, C, or D, which includes your spouse, your parents and grandparents, your children and grandchildren and their spouses, but not brothers, sisters, aunts, uncles, cousins, stepsiblings, or friends
G. **A partnership, corporation, trust, or estate** more than 50 percent owned or controlled by A, B, C, D, or E
H. **A 10-percent owner, officer, director, or highly compensated employee** of C, D, E, or G
I. **A 10-percent or more partner or joint venturer** of C, D, E, or G

In order to determine whether a proposed transaction is a prohibited transaction and violates IRC 4975, it is important to examine all the parties engaged in the proposed transaction rather than just the Solo 401(k) plan participant. Pursuant to Internal Revenue Code Section 4975, a Solo 401(k) plan is prohibited from engaging in certain types of transactions. The types of prohibited transactions can be best understood by dividing them into three categories: *direct prohibited transactions*, *self-dealing prohibited transactions*, and *conflict of interest prohibited transactions*.

Direct or Indirect Prohibited Transactions

What is a direct or indirect prohibited transaction? Essentially, it is a transaction between the Solo 401(k) plan and a disqualified person that either directly or indirectly *personally* benefits a disqualified person. It is important to remember that the main purpose behind the IRS prohibited-transaction rules is to make sure that the use of retirement funds is in no way directly or indirectly personally benefiting the plan participant or any of his or her lineal descendants. From the IRS's point of view, if you want to make personal use of your 401(k) plan funds to help yourself or a close family member and you are under age fifty-nine and a half, then take a distribution and pay the tax and penalty.

The IRS has provided the 401(k) plan participant with a tax deduction in the anticipation that the benefit provided to the taxpayer would be paid back in the form of taxation on the appreciated assets of the 401(k) plan at a later time. The IRS and Department of Labor need to protect their distribution rules to make sure that the IRS and Treasury receive the taxes they believe they deserve from retirement distributions.

The distinction between a direct and indirect prohibited transaction is as follows. A *direct prohibited transaction* is the simplest type of prohibited transaction to uncover because it deals with scenarios involving a disqualified person and the retirement account directly. An *indirect prohibited transaction* deals with transactions that do not appear to directly benefit a disqualified person but could indirectly do so based on certain facts and circumstances. For example, using your Solo 401(k) plan to pay your personal credit card bill would be a clear direct prohibited transaction, whereas using your Solo 401(k) plan to invest in a company in which you own 15 percent might be considered an indirect prohibited transaction based on certain facts and circumstances.

Specifically, you cannot use your Solo 401(k) plan to do the following with a disqualified person:

- Sell, exchange, or lease property
- Lend money or extend credit

- Furnish goods, services, or facilities
- Transfer income or assets

Here are some scenarios pertaining to IRC 4975(c)(1)(A) that illustrate prohibited transactions to do with directly or indirectly selling, exchanging, or leasing property to a disqualified person.

Direct and Indirect Prohibited Transaction Examples

- **4975(c)(1)(A): the direct or indirect sale, exchange, or leasing of property between an IRA and a "disqualified person"**
  - Joe **sells** an interest in a piece of **property** owned by his Solo 401(k) plan to his **son**: PROHIBITED.
  - Beth **leases real estate** owned by her Solo 401(k) plan to her **daughter**: PROHIBITED.
  - Mark uses his Solo 401(k) plan funds to purchase an LLC interest owned by his **mother**: PROHIBITED.
  - Victor **leases** an interest in a piece of **property** owned by his Solo 401(k) plan to his **son**: PROHIBITED.
  - Tracy **sells real estate** owned by her Solo 401(k) plan to her **father**: PROHIBITED.
  - Ben **sells real estate** he owns personally to his **Solo 401(k) plan**: PROHIBITED.
  - Jason **transfers property** he owns personally to his **Solo 401(k) plan**: PROHIBITED.
  - Katy **purchases real estate** with her Solo 401(k) plan funds and **leases** it to her **son**: PROHIBITED.
  - David uses his Solo 401(k) plan funds to **purchase an interest in an entity** owned by his **father**: PROHIBITED.
  - Ted **transfers property** he owns personally subject to a mortgage to his **Solo 401(k) plan**: PROHIBITED.

- Sally **uses personal funds to pay expenses** related to her **Solo 401(k) plan real estate investment**: PROHIBITED.
- Jane **uses personal funds to pay taxes and expenses** related to her **Solo 401(k) plan real estate investment**: PROHIBITED.

- **4975(c)(1)(B): the direct or indirect lending of money or other extension of credit between an IRA and a "disqualified person"**
  - Ted **lends** his **wife** $70,000 from his Solo 401(k) plan: PROHIBITED.
  - **Mary personally guarantees** a bank loan to her Solo 401(k) plan to purchase real estate: PROHIBITED.
  - Dan uses his Solo 401(k) plan funds to **lend an entity** owned and controlled by his **father** $18,000: PROHIBITED.
  - Ken **lends his son** $4,000 from his Solo 401(k) plan: PROHIBITED.
  - Rick **uses the assets** of his Solo 401(k) plan **as security** for a loan: PROHIBITED.
  - Brandon **uses his personal assets as security** for a Solo 401(k) plan **investment**: PROHIBITED.
  - Chuck uses Solo 401(k) plan funds to **lend an entity owned and controlled by his father** $45,000: PROHIBITED.
  - Eric **acquires a credit card for his Solo 401(k) plan bank account**: PROHIBITED.

A Real-Life Example

Peek v. Commissioner, 140 TC 12 (2013): In Peek, the Tax Court held that a personal guarantee by an IRA owner of a loan to the owner's IRA is a prohibited transaction as a loan of money or extension of credit between a plan and a disqualified person under Code Sec. 4975(c)(1)(B). But what if the loan was not made directly to the IRA but instead was made to an entity owned by the IRA? Is a personal guarantee by the IRA owner of such a loan a prohibited transaction? That was the subject of the Peek case.

Peek involved two IRA owners (Mssrs. Fleck and Peek) who jointly invested in a corporation (FP) formed by them to acquire the assets of another company (AFS). The IRAs were the only shareholders of FP. FP acquired the assets of AFS in exchange for a combination of cash and notes, including a promissory note from FP, to the sellers secured by personal guarantees from both IRA owners.

Mssrs. Fleck and Peek were fiduciaries of their respective IRAs due to retaining authority and control over such IRAs and thus were disqualified persons under Code Sec. 4975(c)(1)(A), and each IRA constitutes a "plan" under 4975(e)(1). Notwithstanding, they argued that because their personal guarantees did not involve the plan itself (since the guarantees were between the disqualified persons Fleck and Peek and an entity other than the IRAs themselves) the guarantees were not prohibited. This argument was flatly rejected by the Tax Court, which noted that 4975(c)(1)(B) also prohibits indirect loans and/or extensions of credit between a plan and a disqualified person and that the "obvious and intended meaning" of (c)(1)(B) "prohibited Mr. Fleck and Mr. Peek from making loans or loan guarantees either directly to their IRAs or indirectly to their IRAs by way of the entity owned by the IRAs."

It is also prohibited, according to IRC 4975(c)(1)(C), to use your Solo 401(k) plan to directly or indirectly furnish goods, services, or facilities to a disqualified person:

- **4975(c)(1)(C): the direct or indirect furnishing of goods, services, or facilities between an IRA and a "disqualified person"**
  - Andrew **buys a piece of property** with his Solo 401(k) plan funds and **hires his father to work on the property**: PROHIBITED.
  - Rachel **buys a condo** with her Solo 401(k) plan funds and **personally fixes it up**: PROHIBITED.

- Betty **owns an apartment building** with her Solo 401(k) plan and **hires her mother to manage the property**: PROHIBITED.
- Bill **purchases a condo** with his Solo 401(k) plan funds and **paints the walls without receiving a fee**: PROHIBITED.
- Henry **buys a piece of property** with his Solo 401(k) plan funds and **hires his son to work on the property**: PROHIBITED.
- Mary **buys a home** with her Solo 401(k) plan funds and **her son makes repairs for free**: PROHIBITED.
- Beth **owns an office building** with her Solo 401(k) plan and **hires her son to manage the property for a fee**: PROHIBITED.
- Jackie **owns an apartment building** with her Solo 401(k) plan funds and **has her father manage the property for free**: PROHIBITED.
- Doug **receives compensation from his Solo 401(k) plan for investment advice**: PROHIBITED.
- Matt **acts as the real estate agent for his Solo 401(k) plan**: PROHIBITED.

A REAL-LIFE EXAMPLE

IN RE: CHERWENKA, Cite as 113 AFTR 2d 2014-2333 (508 B.R. 228), (Bktcy Ct GA), 03/06/2014. When it comes to performing services by a "disqualified person" with respect to real estate owned by a retirement account, IRC Section 4975(c)(1)(C) is clear that a prohibited transaction occurs in the instance of the furnishing of goods, services, or facilities between a plan and a disqualified person What is not so clear is what actually constitutes "services" when it comes to a "disqualified person" and his or her real estate investment. The Cherwenka case involved a Georgia statutory bankruptcy estate exemption for IRAs, which covered a self-directed IRA held by Michael Cherwenka who was in business of "flipping houses. Michael Cherwenka established a self-directed IRA to buy real estate. In Cherwenka, the court considered whether a debtor could exempt a self-directed IRA utilized to invest in distressed real properties and have the IRA realize profit from the later sale of these properties. The court agreed that the Cherwenka was a "disqualified person" under IRC Section 4975. It was argued that Cherwenka performed work on the properties by researching and identifying the subject properties, appointing and approving work on the properties, and overseeing payment from the IRA custodian for such work and those acts constitute prohibited transactions under IRC Section 4975(c)(1)(C) as direct and indirect services by a "disqualified person". The Court disagreed and held that such a position requires the Court to read out of the statute the word "transaction." There is no evidence that Cherwenka engaged in any transaction. A transaction includes an exchange of goods or services and the evidentiary record does not include that Cherwenka received anything in exchange for his alleged services. In fact, Cherwenka testimony included that he received no money, discount, or other benefit for the identified activities he undertook with the IRA.

The Cherwenka case is really the first case that offers a detailed framework about the type of activities or tasks a retirement account real estate investor can perform without triggering the IRC 4975 prohibited transaction rules. In the case, Cherwenka was not compensated for any real property research he performed, nor was he compensated for any recommendations, management or consulting services he provided relating to how the retirement account owned properties were improved before resale. Cherwenka explained his role in buying and selling of these properties as being limited to identifying the asset for purchase and later selling the asset. Cherwenka engaged contractors to decide or oversee the scope of work with improved properties. Cherwenka testified that he "read and approved" the expense forms prior to the IRA custodian paying funds to reimburse the submitted expenses. Contractors were paid by the job, which accounted for labor costs, but no management fee or additional cost was included in the expenses submitted to the IRA custodian. Cherwenka stated he would inspect or confirm that work was completed through site visits or communication with his "team" before he would approve expenses to be paid by the IRA custodian.

Because most retirement account real estate investors tend to perform the same sort of tasks that Cherwenka performed, such as locating the property, reviewing transaction documents, engaging contractors to perform property improvements, inspection of improvements, approval of expenses, and coordinating with IRA custodian regarding the real estate, the case offers a clear blueprint for the type of activities or tasks that a self-directed IRA or Solo 401(k) plan real estate investor can do without violating the IRC Section 4975 prohibited transaction rules.

More Indirect Prohibited Transaction Examples

Unlike a direct prohibited transaction where there is a direct transfer of funds between the plan and a disqualified person or a direct benefit received by the plan participant from the plan, an indirect prohibited transaction, as the name suggests, involves some type of winding or circuitous relationship between the plan and a disqualified person that still could trigger the prohibited-transaction rules. Subject to any exemptions under Internal Revenue Code Section 4975(d), an indirect prohibited transaction generally involves one of the following:

- **4975(c)(1)(D): the direct or indirect transfer to a "disqualified person" of income or assets of an IRA**
  - Ken is in a financial jam and **takes** $32,000 from his Solo 401(k) plan to **pay a personal debt**: PROHIBITED.
  - John uses his Solo 401(k) plan to **purchase a rental property** and hires his friend to manage the property. The **friend then enters into a contract with John and transfers those funds back to John**: PROHIBITED.
  - Melissa **invests** her Solo 401(k) plan funds **in a real estate fund** and then **receives a salary for managing the fund**: PROHIBITED.
  - Jim **uses a house** owned by his Solo 401(k) plan **for personal use**: PROHIBITED.

- Seth **deposits** Solo 401(k) plan funds in **to his personal bank account**: PROHIBITED.
- Spencer **buys precious metals** using his Solo 401(k) plan funds and **uses them for personal gain**: PROHIBITED.
- Bryan **purchases a vacation home** with his Solo 401(k) plan funds and **stays in the home on occasion**: PROHIBITED.
- Elliot **buys a cottage on the lake** with her Solo 401(k) plan funds and **rents it out to her daughter** and son-in-law: PROHIBITED.
- Allison **purchases a condo** using her Solo 401(k) plan on the beach and **lets her son use it for free**: PROHIBITED.
- Kelly **invests** her Solo 401(k) plan funds in an investment fund and then **receives a salary for managing the fund**: PROHIBITED.
- Larry uses his Solo 401(k) plan funds to **purchase real estate and earns a commission** as the real estate agent on the sale: PROHIBITED.
- Steve uses his Solo 401(k) plan funds to **lend money to a company he owns and controls**: PROHIBITED.
- Gordon **invests** his Solo 401(k) plan funds into **a business he owns 75 percent of and manages**: PROHIBITED.

Self-Dealing Prohibited Transactions

"Self-dealing" is a term used for a situation that arises when someone benefits on both sides of a deal. According to 4975(c)(1)(E), self-dealing, which is a form of an indirect prohibited transaction, occurs when you directly or indirectly use the income or assets of your Solo 401(k) plan to further your own interests or benefit your own accounts. The following transactions would be prohibited because they involve self-dealing:

- **4975(c)(1)(E): the direct or indirect act by a "disqualified person" who is a fiduciary whereby he/she deals with income or**

assets of the IRA in his/her own interest or for his/her own account

- Debra, who is **a real estate agent,** uses her Solo 401(k) plan funds to **buy a piece of property *and* earns a commission from the sale**: PROHIBITED.
- Ben wants to buy a piece of property for $120,000 and would like to own the property personally but does not have sufficient funds. As a result, Ben **uses $110,000 from in his Solo 401(k) plan *and* $10,000 personally to make the investment**: PROHIBITED.
- Nancy uses her Solo 401(k) plan funds to **invest in a real estate fund managed by her son,** *and* **Heidi's father receives a bonus** for securing Nancy's investment: PROHIBITED.

- Karen **makes an investment** using her Solo 401(k) plan funds **into a company she controls, which will benefit her personally**: PROHIBITED.
- Brett uses his Solo 401(k) plan funds to **invest in a partnership with himself personally in which he and his family will own greater than 50 percent of the partnership**: PROHIBITED.
- Pam uses her Solo 401(k) plan funds to **invest in a business she and her husband own and operates, and she and her husband earns compensation from the business**: PROHIBITED.
- Rick uses his Solo 401(k) plan funds to **lend money to a business in which he controls and manages**: PROHIBITED.
- Lance **invests** his Solo 401(k) plan funds **in a trust** in which Lance and his wife would gain a **personal benefit**: PROHIBITED.
- Helen uses her Solo 401(k) plan funds to **invest in a real estate fund managed by her son who receives a bonus for securing her investment**: PROHIBITED.
- Stanley **invests** his Solo 401(k) plan funds into **a real estate project that his development company will be involved in order to secure the contract**: PROHIBITED.

- Warren uses his Solo 401(k) plan funds to **invest in his son's business that is in financial trouble**: PROHIBITED.
- Alex uses his Solo 401(k) plan funds to **buy a note on a piece of property for which he is the debtor personally**: PROHIBITED.

Real-Life Examples

Rollins v. Commissioner, T.C. Memo 2004–60:

This is an important case in the self-directed IRA LLC context because it illustrates that one can engage in a prohibited transaction with an entity even if the entity is not per se a disqualified entity. The Rollins case also is important when examining whether a potential transaction could be considered an indirect prohibited transaction under IRC 4975.

The facts in Rollins are as follows: Mr. Rollins owned his own CPA firm. He was sole trustee of its 401(k) plan. Mr. Rollins used his plan to lend funds to three companies in which he was the largest (9 percent to 33 percent) but not controlling, stockholder. The companies had twenty-eight, seventy, and eighty other stockholders respectively. Mr. Rollins made decision for companies to borrow from his 401(k) plan. The loans were demand loans, secured by each company's assets. The interest rate was market rate or higher. Mr. Rollins signed loan checks for the plan and signed notes for borrowers. All loans were repaid in full.

Mr. Rollins acknowledged that he is a disqualified person with regard to the plan because he owns Rollins (the CPA Firm), but he contends that (1) none of the corporations that were the borrowers was a disqualified person, (2) none of the loans was a transaction between him and the plan, and (3) he "did not benefit from these loans, either in income or in his own account." The Tax Court held that a Code Section 4975(c)(1)(D) indirect prohibition did not require an actual transfer of money or property between the plan and the disqualified person. One of the more interesting parts of the Rollins case was the Tax Court's emphasis that the burden of proof as to whether an indirect prohibited transaction had occurred is the responsibility of the taxpayer.

At its core, the Rollins case is a burden-of-proof case that illustrates the breadth of the application of 4975(c)(1)(D), as well as the difficulty of meeting that burden of proof. Mr. Rollins was not a majority owner of any of the borrowers, but he was the largest shareholder for each company, and he also signed the notes for each borrower. The burden of proof was on Mr. Rollins that the transaction did not enhance or were not intended to enhance the value of his investments in the borrowers. That seems to be a very tough burden to meet, and moreover, as the Court noted, the fact that a transaction is a good investment for the plan has nothing to do with it. As such, caution should be exercised whenever a disqualified person is sitting "on both sides of the table."

ERISA Advisory Opinion Letter 93–33A:

In this advisory opinion, an IRA owner proposed to use his IRA to buy land and a building of a high school founded by his daughter and son-in-law, and lease the property back to the school at either fair market rent or lower rent depending on the school's ability to pay. Presumably, this was a non-profit organization, without stockholders.

The IRA owner, having discretion to invest the IRA's assets, was a fiduciary and a disqualified person. The IRA owner's daughter and son-in-law were the sole directors and officers of the school. As such, by virtue of 4975(e)(2)(F), they also were disqualified persons. Consequently, the Department of Labor concluded that the proposed sale–leaseback transaction would constitute the use of IRA assets for the benefit of disqualified persons (the IRA owner's daughter and son-in-law) in violation of 4975(c)(1)(D).

It seemed that the major factor here was the arrangement to lease back the property at a rent dependent on the school's ability to pay. In fact, the Department of Labor broadly took the view that either 4975(c)(1)(D) or

(E) would be violated if a transaction were part of an agreement, arrangement, or understanding in which the fiduciary caused plan assets to be used in a manner designed to benefit any person in whom such fiduciary had an interest that would impact the exercise of his or her best judgment as a fiduciary.

Conflict-of-Interest Prohibited Transactions

In life, conflicts of interest are sometimes clear and sometimes vague. When it comes to Solo 401(k) prohibited transactions, a conflict of interest occurs, according to 4975(c)(i)(F), when a disqualified person is connected to a transaction involving the income or assets of your Solo 401(k) plan. So, for example:

- **4975(c)(i)(F): receipt of any consideration by a "disqualified person" who is a fiduciary for his/her own account from any party dealing with the IRA in connection with a transaction involving income or assets of the plan**
  - Jason uses his Solo 401(k) plan funds to **loan money to a company that he manages and controls, and also owns a small ownership interest in**: PROHIBITED.
  - Cathy uses her Solo 401(k) plan to **lend money to a business that she works for in order to secure a promotion**: PROHIBITED.
  - Eric uses his Solo 401(k) plan funds to **invest in a fund that he manages and where his management fee is based on the total value of the fund's assets**: PROHIBITED.

Real-Life Example

Technical Advice Memorandum 9118001: In this Technical Advice Memorandum, the IRS concluded that loans made by a law firm's pension and profit-sharing plans to its clients to provide those clients with financial support while they were awaiting settlement on their lawsuits were prohibited transactions under both Sections 4975(c)(1)(D) and 4975(c)(1)(E) of the Code. The law firm's partners, who were fiduciaries with authority over plan assets, directed a bank, as the plan trustee, to lend clients money pending the outcome of their suits. The district office contended that this is a transaction prohibited by Section 4975(c)(1)(D) since the partners of the law firm were acting as a lending institution and that the law firm was indirectly using and benefiting from plan assets. The taxpayer disagreed, arguing that the loans were made to clients from the plan assets solely to benefit plan participants and that it is a common business practice in personal injury law firms to advance funds to clients who are awaiting settlement.

The IRS determined that the loans were prohibited under Section 4975(c)(1)(D) because the employer, who is a disqualified person under section 4975(e)(2)(C), benefited from the use of plan assets. As the IRS stated, here the parties benefiting from the loans (i.e., the party whose business objective is being served) are the partners in the law firm. It did not matter that the clients could have received loans elsewhere or that the loans were good investments, nor did it matter that it was common practice for law firms to advance funds to clients pending the conclusion of their lawsuits. So long as a benefit is derived by a disqualified person through the use of a plan asset, the transaction is prohibited under Section 4975(c)(1)(D).

Statutory Exemptions

In order to allow some wiggle room when it comes to navigating the prohibited-transaction rules for certain specific circumstances, Congress created several ways to grant exemptions from the very broad prohibited-transaction rules. The most popular way for satisfying a prohibited-transaction exemption is the statutory exemption, since anyone who complies with the term of the statute will be able to benefit from the exemption. In such situations, Congress has decided to issue blanket prohibited-transaction exemptions permitting certain type of transactions, as long as certain requirements prescribed in the statute are met.

The most common prohibited-transaction exemption involves participant loans from a 401(k) plan. IRC 4975(d)(1) describes conditions under which loans are allowable. The majority of the statutory exemptions found under IRC 4975(d) are not commonly applied because of their specific application, such as the ability to invest plan assets in a bank deposit account where the bank is the employer, or investing plan assets in life insurance company products where the company is the employer.

Besides the 401(k) loan exemption, the other common prohibited transaction exemption often used is the ability for a disqualified person to contract with the plan in order to provide office space, legal, accounting, or other services necessary for the operation of the plan so long as reasonable compensation is paid. This exemption is often cited as a source of potential abuse because it allows for certain services and fees to be paid from the plan to a disqualified person. The exemption refers specifically to "necessary" services, which seems to imply only those required types of services that must be performed in order to maintain the legality of the plan, such as legal or accounting services. The exemption does not, on the other hand, allow one to provide services to a plan asset, such as serving as a real estate agent for a plan real estate purchase, painting the walls of an investment property owned by the plan, or taking a salary to manage the plan's investments.

In a perfect world, you would avoid this exemption and pay nondisqualified persons for any necessary services that must be performed in connection with the plan. Taking advantage of this statutory exemption could create some level of scrutiny, as the IRS could ask you to prove that the service and/or fee received in connection with the service performed was "necessary." The burden would be on the trustee to prove this to the IRS, and it is generally believed that hiring nondisqualified third parties to perform all services in connection with the plan, including any "necessary" expenses, is the best course of action.

The Department of Labor may also grant individual prohibited-transaction exemptions, which are generally released and made public as advisory opinions. The individual exemptions would only apply to the individual or entity that applied for the exemption and typically only as far as the specific fact pattern described in the application. Applying for an exemption does have some negatives, including cost, timing, and confirmation that a proposed transaction would violate the prohibited-transaction rules, which for some people is a negative since it could tip the Department of Labor to a potential transaction that was occurring under the radar of the IRS and Department of Labor. However, these individual exemption opinions tend to offer valuable insight into how the Department of Labor views a particular type of transaction, which can be quite helpful to tax practitioners in the area.

When it comes to the Solo 401(k), the statutory exemptions pertain to three areas:

- You can contract with a disqualified person for office space, legal, accounting, or other service that is necessary for the operation of your Solo 401(k) plan as long as reasonable compensation is paid. You can't, however, contract with yourself or the Solo 401(k) trustee for such services.
- A bank trustee can provide ancillary services to your Solo 401(k) plan.
- A disqualified person can receive benefits to which she may be entitled as a participant or beneficiary of the Solo 401(k) plan, so long as those benefits are consistent with the way the plan pays benefits to all other participants and beneficiaries.

Shareholder Restrictions

A Solo 401(k) plan cannot own stock in an S corporation because of the shareholder restrictions imposed on S corporations. S corporations are "C" corporations that elect to pass corporate income, losses, deductions, and credits through to their shareholders for federal tax purposes. To qualify for S corporation status, the corporation must meet the following requirements:

- Be a domestic corporation
- Have only allowable shareholders
  - Including individuals, certain trusts, and estates; and
  - Not including partnerships, corporations, or nonresident alien shareholders.
- Have no more than a hundred shareholders
- Have only one class of stock

Since a 401(k) plan is a trust that is not treated as a permitted shareholder for an S corporation, having a 401(k) plan invest and become a shareholder would violate the S corporation rules and cause the S election to be invalid. This would make the entity a C corporation again for tax purposes. A Solo 401(k) plan can, however, own stock in a C corporation.

The good thing when it comes to prohibited transaction penalties is that they are easily avoidable. In simple terms, just don't engage in a prohibited transaction and you'll have nothing to worry about. For most retirement investors who will be investing in stocks and other traditional financial products, there is really not much to worry about when it comes to a prohibited transaction. The risk of engaging in a prohibited transaction in such circumstances is almost impossible, especially if you are buying stocks, mutual funds, and ETFs from a major financial institution. However, those Solo 401(k) plan participants looking to make nontraditional investments (such as real estate, private loans, and precious metals) should make themselves aware of the prohibited-transaction rules because of the harsh penalties.

Under the Internal Revenue Code, if a disqualified person involved in a Solo 401(k) plan transaction violates the IRS prohibited-transaction rules, a penalty tax is assessed equal to 15 percent of the amount involved in the prohibited transaction for each year of the transaction.

The prohibited transaction penalty can be assessed annually and will be assessed against any disqualified person who participates in the prohibited transaction. Once the prohibited transaction has been identified, it must be corrected immediately—certainly within the taxable year. However, if the prohibited transaction is not corrected during the taxable year, then an additional penalty tax in the amount of 100 percent of the prohibited-transaction amount will apply.

To make the penalty for engaging in a prohibited transaction even harsher, the 15 percent and 100 percent penalty can be assessed against any disqualified person who participates in the prohibited transaction. Interestingly, a fiduciary to a plan who was only acting as a fiduciary and not involved directly in the prohibited transaction will not be subject to any penalty.

The prohibited-transaction rules are extremely broad. Thus, a Solo 401(k) plan participant looking to engage in certain nontraditional investments must be especially cautious about the prohibited-transaction rules and should consult a tax attorney or CPA with specific questions.

Collectibles

Imagine if you could buy a gold Rolex, antique Corvette, a Monet, or even your uncle's rare stamp collection with your Solo 401(k) plan. How great would that be? Unfortunately, the IRS would not share your excitement and in fact has taken the position that assets defined as "collectibles" are not suitable investments for retirement accounts, largely because the difficulty of ascertaining a fair market value as well as the lack of marketability. A Solo 401(k) plan cannot invest in collectibles as referenced in IRC 408(m) and defined below as:

- Any work of art
- Any metal or gem
- Any alcoholic beverage
- Any rug or antique
- Any stamp
- Most coins

Other types of popular collectibles that are not permitted to be purchased with retirement accounts are antique watches, diamonds, horses, and baseball cards. However, a Solo 401(k) plan, like an IRA, may purchase certain IRS-approved precious metals and coins.

The IRS does permit a retirement account to own certain gold coins (American Gold Eagle coins or coins at least 0.995 fine, meaning 99.5 percent pure), one-ounce silver coins minted by the Treasury Department, any coin issued under the laws of the federal government or any state, a platinum coin described in 31 USCS 5112(k), and gold, silver, platinum or palladium bullion of a certain fineness that is in the physical possession of a U.S. bank or depository.

A more detailed description of the rules surrounding the purchase of precious metals and IRS-approved coins can be found in the Chapter 7.

Life Insurance Contracts

Unknown to most people, life insurance can be purchased by a Solo 401(k) plan, whereas it is not permitted with an IRA, pursuant to IRC 408. In order to purchase life insurance via the plan, the Solo 401(k) plan documents would have to allow for the purchase of life insurance. In most plan documents, you would indicate this in the plan adoption agreement. This works if:

- The life insurance policy is owned by the plan and the death benefit is payable to the plan.
- Every year, the insured plan participant pays income tax on the dollar value of the actual insurance protection—approximately equal to the term insurance cost.
- Any death benefit in excess of the policy's cash value is tax-free to beneficiaries, and the cash-value portion of the death benefit can be rolled tax-free into an IRA.

The argument for buying life insurance with a 401(k) plan is that pretax funds can be used to pay the premiums instead of after-tax funds if you purchased the policy with personal funds.

Plan-Asset Rules

Now let's assume that you have looked at all the prohibited-transaction rules under IRC 4975 and 408, and feel pretty comfortable that your transaction would not be treated as a prohibited transaction. Then you are told that there is another set-of rules (called the "plan-asset rules") that you may need to look at before being certain that your transaction will not violate the prohibited-transaction rules.

Oh, great. Actually, it's not so bad.

In late 1986, the United States Department of Labor issued regulations (the "Plan-Assets Regulation") relating to the definition of "plan assets." The plan-asset rules were developed in order to examine situations when a 401(k) plan or IRA is invested in a pass-through entity, such as an LLC or partnership. They do this to determine how the use of the assets of the plan apply to the prohibited transaction and ERISA rules.

Under the plan-asset rules, if the aggregate Solo 401(k) plan ownership of an entity is 25 percent or more of all the assets of the entity, then the equity interests and assets of the "investment entity" are viewed as assets of the investing Solo 401(k) plan for purposes of the prohibited transactions rules, unless an exception applies. Also, if a Solo 401(k) plan or group of related qualified plans owns 100 percent of an "operating company," the operating company exception will not apply and the company's assets will still be treated as plan assets.

In summary, the plan-asset rules can be triggered if:

- 100 percent of an "operating company" is owned by one or more IRAs/401(k) plans and disqualified persons, in which case all the assets of the "operating company" are deemed plan assets, or assets of the IRA/401(k)
- 25 percent or more of an "investment company" is owned by IRAs/401(k) plans and disqualified persons, in which case all the assets of the "investment company" are deemed plan assets, or assets of the IRA/401(k). In determining whether the 25 percent threshold is met, all IRAs/401(k) owners are considered, even if they are owned by unrelated individuals.

So why do we care about the plan-asset rules? If the LLC or partnership that the retirement account invested in is owned 25 percent or more by retirement account investors, and the entity or fund does not meet one of the other exceptions under the Plan-Asset Regulations, then the assets of the fund will be deemed plan assets for purposes of ERISA and Section 4975 of the Code.

This means that:

- The pass-through entity or fund's manager would be treated as a fiduciary of each retirement account investor governed by ERISA, and the manager's activities would be subject to the general fiduciary requirements of Section 404 of ERISA.
- All of the fund's activities would be subject to the prohibited-transaction rules of Section 406 of ERISA and Section 4975 of the Code. Among other things, transactions with affiliates would be restricted and some types of performance fees charged by the fund manager would need to be structured to ensure compliance with applicable Department of Labor requirements.

In other words, violating the plan-asset rules could trigger some unexpected prohibited-transaction rule exposure and cause unexpected tax implications.

THE HEDGE-FUND PARTNER

John, a general partner at a hedge fund, wishes to invest his Solo 401(k) plan in the hedge fund he manages. If the percentage of John's Solo 401(k)/IRA ownership equals or exceeds 25 percent of the equity interests, then the fund's assets are considered "plan assets." That means that a transaction between John, as a disqualified person, and the fund, could be deemed a prohibited transaction.

Accordingly, John is not able to receive personal benefits from his Solo 401(k) plan investment into the fund. He is also not permitted to receive any management fees associated with the Solo 401(k) plan's ownership interest in the fund because he would be receiving a personal benefit from his Solo 401(k) plan. John's Solo 401(k) plan investment in the fund may also be deemed a direct or indirect prohibited transaction under Internal Revenue Code Section 4975.

ABC LLC

Jane's Solo 401(k) plan owns 100 percent of ABC LLC, which operates a retail store. ABC LLC makes a loan to Jane. The loan is subject to the plan-asset rules and will also be considered a prohibited transaction pursuant to Internal Revenue Code Section 4975. In addition, any income generated by ABC LLC that is allocated to the Solo 401(k) plan would also likely be subject to the Unrelated Business Income tax.

GROW LLC

Steve's Solo 401(k) plan owns 15 percent of GROW LLC, an investment company. Allen's IRA owns 20 percent of GROW LLC. Steve and Allan are unrelated. Since a 401(k) qualified plan and the IRA own more than 25 percent of GROW LLC, an "investment company," assets of GROW LLC, are plan assets and deemed owned by each IRA. Thus, if GROW LLC makes a loan to Steve's father, the loan would be a prohibited transaction under Internal Revenue Code Section 4975.

FAST LLC

Robert's Solo 401(k) plan invests in FAST LLC, which will purchase a gas station—it's considered an "operating company." Robert's Solo 401(k) plan will own more than 25 percent of Fast LLC. Robert will take an annual salary of $50,000 to run the gas station. The payment of the salary would be subject to the plan-asset rules and would also be a "prohibited transaction" under IRC Section 4975 because it is a case of self-dealing. In addition, any income generated by the gas station that is allocated to the Solo 401(k) plan would also likely be subject to the Unrelated Business Income tax.

Using the Solo 401(k) Plan Loan Feature

There is one way that a Solo 401(k) plan participant can use retirement funds and engage in any transaction, including a prohibited transaction, and that is the Solo 401(k) plan loan feature. Back in the previous chapter, we discussed how a 401(k) plan can offer a loan feature that would allow a plan participant to borrow $50,000 or 50 percent of their account value and use that loan for any purpose. Well, if one wanted to transact with a disqualified person—such as paying off personal debt, helping out a kid with school, financing a new personal business, or any other prohibited-transaction activity—the Solo 401(k) loan is the only way to do it without triggering a tax or penalty.

Note that it is a loan, so it does have to be paid back over a five-year period, at least quarterly, and at a set interest rate, but at least you will be paying your own plan back and not a bank or credit card company, and you will get tax-free and penalty free use of your Solo 401(k) plan funds to do anything you want, including engaging in a prohibited transaction.

Enough of No, On to Yes

In this chapter, we've said "no" an awful lot. Of course, it's critically important to understand what you can't do when it comes to the IRS. We need this information in advance before making important decisions about how we will invest or allocate our Solo 401(k) plan assets. Accordingly, I've run through all the scenarios in which prohibited transactions come into play and limit our choices, and when exemptions or exceptions might be allowed.

I highly recommend you consult with a Solo 401(k) or retirement savings tax expert. A little upfront investment in knowledge can save you much more in taxes, penalties, and wasted effort.

In the next chapter, we'll dive deeper into what you *can* do with your Solo 401(k) plan assets. Specifically, we'll look closer at what investments you can make and how those decisions will help grow your retirement assets and meet your individual needs and life goals.

CHAPTER 7

Making Investments with Your Solo 401(k) Plan

WHAT'S THE BEST WAY TO accumulate and grow your Solo 401(k) retirement savings? Most people believe that their Solo 401(k) must be invested in bank CDs, the stock market, or mutual funds. Why is that?

As I've mentioned a few times now, traditional financial institutions have no incentive to publicize or offer 401(k) plans or IRA account holders the ability to make nontraditional investments with their retirement funds. In contrast, the IRS does give retirement account holders the ability to make all sorts of traditional as well as nontraditional investments using 401(k) plan funds—you just need to make sure your plan documents allow for it.

The IRS can't force any of the major financial institutions to allow you to buy gold or real estate, or make private loans, but you do have options to go elsewhere. There are many plan document provider companies and very reputable banks and custodians that will allow you to take more control over your retirement future by building a well-balanced and diversified retirement portfolio using a Solo 401(k) plan. That's the beauty of the Solo 401(k): you have tremendous latitude and freedom to invest your plan assets and grow them in the way that suits your needs, interests, and personal expertise.

Despite all the detail in the previous chapter about prohibited transactions, there are actually very few restrictions on how you can invest your Solo 401(k) assets. The IRS is only worried about preventing you or a close family member from taking personal advantage of the funds in your Solo 401(k) plan for reasons other than accumulating retirement savings.

Below is a list of just a handful of the most popular types of investments available for retirement accounts. Remember, so long as your plan documents permit it and so long as the investment does not violate the IRS prohibited-transaction rules under IRC 4975 or is not a collectible pursuant to IRC 408(m), you can enjoy the benefits of tax-deferred or (in the case of a Roth 401(k) plan) tax-free income and gains.

- Domestic or foreign real estate
- Residential or commercial real estate
- Raw land
- Foreclosure property
- Mortgages
- Mortgage pools
- Deeds
- Private loans
- Tax liens
- Private businesses
- Limited liability companies
- Limited liability partnerships
- Private placements
- Precious metals and certain coins
- Stocks, bonds, and mutual funds
- Foreign currencies

That's quite a range of options. So let's look more closely at the main groups. I want to paint a clear picture of what you can do and provide you with some helpful tips for making investments that can enable you to achieve your investment goals.

Real Estate

Most people mistakenly believe that their 401(k) must be invested in bank CDs, the stock market, or mutual funds. Few investors realize that the IRS has always permitted real estate to be held inside 401(k) retirement accounts. Investments in real estate with a Solo 401(k) are fully permissible under ERISA. IRS rules permit you to engage in almost any type of real estate investment, aside from any investment involving a disqualified person.

What Are the Advantages of Using a Solo 401(k) to Purchase Real Estate?

Income or gains generated by a 401(k) plan generate tax-deferred/tax-free profits. Using a Solo 401(k) plan to purchase real estate allows the 401(k) to earn tax-free income/gains and pay taxes at a future date rather than in the year the investment produces income. For example, if you purchased a piece of property for $100,000 with your Solo 401(k) plan and later sold the property for $200,000, all $100,000 would go back to your Solo 401(k) plan without tax.

When I tell people this, some wonder about the advantages and disadvantages. They say, "Well, if I bought the property personally and held the property for at least twelve months, I would only have capital gains tax of 20 percent, which is not so bad."

That's true, but it is still 20 percent more than you would have to pay if you bought the real estate with your Solo 401(k) plan. And if you sold the real estate that you owned personally within twelve months, then the gain would count as a short-term capital gain and the ordinary income tax rate would apply, which can be as high as 39 percent without including state tax. Clearly, not paying tax on real estate provides far more advantages than even paying 20 percent tax let alone ordinary income tax rates.

Then they sometimes ask, "What about getting depreciation deductions? Aren't deductions tax beneficial? If I used my Solo 401(k) plan, I wouldn't receive a tax deduction because a Solo 401(k) plan is a tax-exempt plan."

Sure, getting depreciation for buying real estate has its advantages, since it does reduce the amount of tax you pay. But people forget that when you sell property, you will have to pick up the depreciation taken as ordinary income—this is referred to as "depreciation recapture." Tax deductions are swell, but they are certainly not as good as not paying tax. Ask any CPA or tax attorney which would be better: getting a tax deduction or not paying tax on gains. I would be shocked if anyone answered that a tax deduction would be preferred. That answer could change if the investment lost money—because when one makes a bad investment and loses money with a 401(k) plan, there is no net operating loss (NOL) benefit that can help reduce past or future income. However, the retirement account simply decreases in value and you have less money for retirement.

With a Solo 401(k), you can invest without paying tax and you will not have to pay taxes right away—or in most cases for many years to come. This allows your retirement funds to grow tax-free and all the income or gains from your real estate deals flow though to your 401(k) account without tax!

Types of Real Estate Investments

Below is a partial list of domestic or foreign real estate–related investments that you can make with a Solo 401(k):

- Raw land
- Residential homes
- Commercial property
- Apartments
- Duplexes
- Condos/townhomes
- Mobile homes

- Real estate notes
- Real estate purchase options
- Tax liens certificates
- Tax deeds

So How Does It Work?

For the purpose of discussing the steps involved in buying real estate, let's assume your Solo 401(k) plan account will be held at either a custodian-held self-directed account or via an open-architecture self-directed Solo 401(k) plan. The procedures for buying real estate discussed in detail below are typically the same for any IRS approved investment made via the Solo 401(k) plan.

1. Establish your IRS Compliant Solo 401(k) plan, whether via a trust company, custodian, or a document provider offering an open-architecture self-directed Solo 401(k) plan. The plan needs to be adopted and a custodian account or bank account should be established.
2. Make a tax-free transfer of retirement funds. Once the Solo 401(k) plan account has been opened, it is time to either transfer existing retirement funds to the plan account or make contributions to the plan account so funds are available for investment. In general, as long as the retirement funds are pretax and not a Roth IRA, the funds can be rolled into the Solo 401(k) plan without tax or penalty. This transfer is often referred to as a direct rollover. In most cases, the rollover of funds from another retirement account to a Solo 401(k) plan must be initiated by the plan participant typically via a rollover request or distribution form.

Unfortunately, Roth IRA funds cannot be rolled into a Solo 401(k) plan, but after-tax 401(k) plan funds can generally be rolled into a Solo 401(k) plan so long as the plan documents permit it. Hence, whether it is an IRA, SEP-IRA, SIMPLE IRA, 401(k) plan, 403B, 457B, or DB plan fund, the retirement assets, in cash or property (in-kind), can be rolled tax-free and penalty-free into a Solo 401(k) plan. For cash, the transfer can typically be done by cash or wire, whereas property is typically transferred by retitling the asset to show the change of ownership of the asset to the new retirement plan. It is advisable to work with a tax professional to assist in completing the rollover and ensuring that the paperwork is completed properly so that the transfer is done without tax. Also, there is typically no withholding that occurs on a transfer of retirement funds to the new plan.

Can Personal Funds Be Transferred into the Solo 401(k) Plan?

Unfortunately, no. Only pretax retirement funds and in some cases after-tax 401(k) plan funds can be transferred. Roth IRA funds may not be rolled into a Solo 401(k) plan, nor can Coverdale or 529 plan funds be rolled in or personal funds that you have saved for your retirement. Of course, one can make contributions of earned income to the plan, but only pretax retirement funds can generally be transferred or rolled into a Solo 401(k) plan.

Making the Real Estate Investment

As soon as the rollover retirement funds have been deposited into the new Solo 401(k) plan, either by check or wire, the trustee of the plan is now ready to make an investment. Hopefully, the trustee has performed the necessary due diligence required in order to have a high degree of confidence that the real estate investment will be a good one for the Solo 401(k) plan and also will not violate the IRS prohibited-transaction rules.

Buying Real Estate via a Custodian-Directed Solo 401(k) Plan

With a custodian-held Solo 401(k) plan, the Solo 401(k) plan account is generally held at the custodian or trust company. What this means in practice is that you don't have a checkbook or wire transfer abilities to make an investment even if you are the trustee of the plan. So how do you buy real estate? Essentially, you work with the custodian or trust company where the Solo 401(k) plan is held to make the purchase. The trustee of the plan would communicate, typically in writing via an investment authorization form or some similarly titled form, the details of the transaction, including the amount and the appropriate payment instructions whether by check or wire. The custodian or trust company would then cut the check or execute the wire transfer so that the Solo 401(k) plan could purchase the real estate.

Since the Solo 401(k) plan is a custodian-directed plan, the custodian is typically in control of the retirement funds and would need to be directed by the plan participant to make the investment. Now, this does not mean the custodian can just invest in anything she wants—absolutely not. The plan participant directs all plan investments and the custodian is not allowed by law to make any investment without that direction. Title to the property is typically in the name of the custodian as custodian of the plan. Therefore, if you established a Solo 401(k) plan called ABC Retirement Plan with XYZ trust company and purchased a piece of real estate, the title would generally be as follows: "XYZ Trust Company as Custodian of the ABC Retirement Plan."

Using a custodian-directed Solo 401(k) plan is a common way to buy real estate. The custodian will generally help you make sure your plan remains in IRS compliance while at the same time helping you facilitate traditional as well as nontraditional investments, such as real estate. To determine whether this is a viable option for you, closely examine the fees involved in maintaining the Solo 401(k) plan as well as any annual fees or transaction-specific fees for facilitation of Solo 401(k) plan investments.

How Do You Buy Real Estate with an Open Architecture Solo 401(k) Plan?

Unlike the custodian directed Solo 401(k) plan, which is generally held at a custodian or trust company and which you must go through to make investments, an open-architecture self-directed Solo 401(k) plan gives you, as trustee of the plan, greater control over the account and investments. A self-directed Solo 401(k) plan can generally be opened at most local banks, credit unions, and a majority of financial institutions, such as Fidelity. Accordingly, as trustee of the plan, you will have "checkbook control" over the plan assets. In practice, this means that when you open your Solo 401(k) plan bank account, you will receive a checkbook and wiring transfer authority so you can make an investment by simply writing a check or executing a wire transfer.

There are a number of Solo 401(k) document provider companies that will allow you to adopt an open-architecture self-directed Solo 401(k) plan. These companies have a different business model than a traditional financial institution such as Vanguard or E*Trade, for example. Essentially, document provider companies use a law-firm model to charge a flat fee for the plan documents and then a small annual fee for maintenance and compliance services. They do not offer any investment products for sale or investment advice. The plan documents they work with are generally prototype plan documents that have been preapproved by the IRS. The plan document adoption agreement typically contains a feature that allows the adopting employer to confirm that the plan will be trustee directed. By checking that the plan will be trustee directed, the adopting employer is basically stating that the plan will be a self-directed plan whereby the trustee will have full control over the plan's investments and assets, and not a bank or custodian.

Making investments with a self-directed Solo 401(k) plan is generally quick and easy. This is one of the primary advantages. As the trustee of the Solo 401(k) plan, you will have the freedom to make all investment decisions for your Solo 401(k) plan ("checkbook control"). A Solo 401(k) plan allows you to eliminate the expense and delays associated with a custodian so you can act quickly when the right investment opportunity presents itself. As trustee of the Solo 401(k) plan, you will be able to write a check or wire money from the 401(k) bank account to make an investment. In addition, you will not need to get your real estate investment documents signed by the custodian, as you can sign all real estate–related transaction documents for the benefit of the Solo 401(k) plan as the trustee for the plan.

When a real estate or other investment is made with your Solo 401(k) plan assets, the investment is made in the name of the Solo 401(k) plan. For real estate titling purposes, the common practice is for the trustee to hold title as trustee for the benefit of the plan. Hence, for example, if Joe Smith is the trustee of the ABC Inc. plan, when purchasing real estate the title of the property would be as follows: "Joe Smith as Trustee of the ABC Inc. Plan." Some title companies will allow title to be held simply in the name of the plan (i.e., ABC Inc. Plan) or in some case ABC Inc. Plan FBO (for the benefit of) Joe Smith. Essentially, as long as the plan name is in the title of the real estate and you will be using retirement funds, the titling is not a significant matter assuming the title insurance company or state rules approves the titling.

Do I Need to Use an LLC to Buy the Real Estate?

With a Solo 401(k) plan, the plan itself can make real estate and other investments without the need for an LLC—which, depending on the state of formation, could prove costly. Since a 401(k) plan is a trust, the trustee on behalf of the trust can take title to a real estate asset without the need for an LLC.

When making an investment with a Solo 401(k) plan, you have the option of making the investment directly with the Solo 401(k) plan or, alternatively, you can invest the funds in an entity, such as an LLC, which will be owned 100 percent by the Solo 401(k) plan and/or another retirement account or even personal funds from a nondisqualified person.

Using an LLC as an investment vehicle instead of the 401(k) plan itself offers the owner of the LLC—the Solo 401(k) plan—limited liability protection. What limited liability protection means is that the Solo 401(k) plan, as owner of the LLC, would generally be protected from any debt, liabilities, or obligations of the LLC. In other words, limited liability protection will protect all 401(k) plan funds held outside of the LLC from attack based upon a liability, debt, or obligation of the LLC.

Therefore, the LLC will not protect your Solo 401(k) plan funds held inside the LLC but will protect your Solo 401(k) plan assets held outside of the LLC. This could prove valuable to a number of retirement investors seeking to make nontraditional investments, such as real estate with 401(k) funds, as often your retirement account may be the most valuable asset. Protecting that from attack by creditors could be essential.

Along with limited liability protection, the LLC offers its owner(s) privacy, confidentiality, and discretion when making investments. Since most states do not require the name of the member(s) of the LLC to be made publicly available when forming an LLC, by using an LLC the 401(k) plan participant can generally shield his or her identity when making an investment. Whereas if the Solo 401(k) plan made the investment directly (without using an LLC), the trustee of the Solo 401(k) plan, which is typically the plan participant or the Solo 401(k) plan's name, would likely be included on all the real estate–related and title-related documents, and would be publicly available. In the case of an LLC, only the name of the LLC would be included, and identifying the owner of managers of the LLC could provide difficult, depending on the state.

Again, using an LLC wholly owned by a Solo 401(k) plan is not required and is not very popular, but it could serve your interests and prove useful to certain retirement investors looking to buy real estate with their Solo 401(k) plan funds and gain a level of added limited liability protection.

How Do You Structure the Purchase of Real Estate with a Solo 401(k) Plan

When using a Solo 401(k) to make a real estate investment, there are a number of ways you can structure the transaction in order to comply with IRS rules:

3. **Use your Solo 401(k) funds to make 100 percent of the investment:** If you have enough funds in your Solo 401(k) to cover the entire real estate purchase—including closing costs, taxes, fees, and insurance—you may make the purchase outright using the Solo 401(k) plan assets. In light of the IRS prohibited-transaction rules, all ongoing expenses relating to the real estate investment must be paid out of the Solo 401(k) bank account. In addition, all income or gains relating to your real estate investment must be returned to the Solo 401(k) bank account. Using only retirement funds to make an investment is the safest and cleanest way to make sure the investment does not run afoul of any of the IRS prohibited-transaction rules.
4. **Partner with family, friends, and colleagues:** If you don't have sufficient funds in your Solo 401(k) to make a real estate purchase outright, your Solo 401(k) can purchase an interest in the property along with a family member (nondisqualified person), nonlineal descendant, friend, or colleague. The Solo 401(k) plan would then coinvest with the third party or parties to make the investment. Typically this coinvestment is made through another entity, most commonly an LLC, that will be owned proportionally by the Solo 401(k) plan and the other nondisqualified investors. However, the investment can be made directly into the property whereby the property deed will include the name of the multiple owners. In order to protect the rights and interests of each of the investors, the coinvestors would then likely draft some sort of joint-venture agreement detailing the terms of the venture, including financial interests.

For example, your Solo 401(k) plan could partner with a nondisqualified family member, friend, or colleague to purchase a piece of property for $150,000. Your Solo 401(k) plan could purchase an interest in the property (i.e., 50 percent for $75,000), and your family member, friend, or colleague could purchase the remaining interest (i.e., 50 percent for $75,000). The title to the property would be in the name of each of the investors and then the investors would draft a joint-venture type of agreement outlining the terms of their venture.

All income or gain from the property would be allocated to the parties in relation to their percentage of ownership in the property. Likewise, all property expenses must be paid in relation to the parties' percentage of ownership in the property. Based on the above example, for a $2,000 property tax bill, the Solo 401(k) would be responsible for 50 percent of the bill ($1,000), and the family member, friend, or colleague would be responsible for the remaining $1,000 (50 percent).

How an LLC Can Make Your Life Easier

Investing with a nondisqualified family member, friend, or colleague does present several nice benefits, including securing the necessary funds to take advantage of an attractive real estate investment opportunity. But it also come with some risks, which exist anytime a joint-venture arrangement is entered into. The main type of risk presented by a joint-venture type of arrangement is making sure each partner lives up to the intended deal agreed upon by the partners, including profit split and sharing of expenses, as well as the determination of when to sell or not. In addition, there is also the risk of potentially being personally responsible for any claim or liability arising out of the property, assuming sufficient property insurance was acquired.

One popular way of removing a good chunk of the risks involved with making coinvestments involves the use of the LLC. An LLC is a legal entity that is treated as a pass-through entity for tax purposes but offers limited liability protection for corporate purposes. In other words, all profits and losses are "passed through" the business to each member of the LLC without any corporate tax, such as the case with a corporation. LLC members would then report profits and losses on their personal federal tax returns. You should note that in the case of a Solo 401(k) plan, no tax return is required to be filed because a Solo 401(k) plan is exempt from tax pursuant to IRC 401. When partnering up with a nondisqualified person to make real estate investments, using an LLC offers a number of advantages:

1. **Titling of real estate:** Since the Solo 401(k) plan and other non-disqualified investor(s) will invest in the LLC, and the LLC will be the party ultimately buying the real estate, the title of the real estate is in the LLC, which makes things a lot cleaner than having multiple parties on the deed.
2. **Papering the terms of the investment:** When establishing an LLC, the members (owners) of the LLC should prepare and execute an LLC Operating Agreement, which sets forth the specific terms in connection with the investment. The document should be prepared by an attorney who is familiar with the joint-venture arrangement in order to make sure that the agreed upon terms are properly reflected in the LLC Operating Agreement. Having the Operating Agreement should reduce any future misunderstandings and conflicts with the joint-venture partners. Also, it is much easier to share the profits and gains associated with the investment because they will be allocated to the LLC bank account and then can be sent to each partner's bank account as necessary.
3. **Limited liability protection:** Members of an LLC are protected from personal liability for business decisions or actions of the LLC. This means that if the LLC incurs debt or is sued in connection with any of its activities or investments, members' personal assets are usually exempt. This is particular important when it comes to retirement accounts, since many American's largest asset is their retirement account. That being said, limited liability protection would not prove very valuable if all the Solo 401(k) plan's assets were tied up in the Solo 401(k) LLC investment since limited liability protection only protects assets outside of the LLC not within the LLC.

For example, Joe has $100,000 in his Solo 401(k) plan and wanted to buy a piece of real estate for $200,000. Joe approached David, a friend who is quite well off, about partnering to buy the property. David agrees to invest the $100,000 along with Joe's $100,000 to buy the property. David recommends they form an LLC that would be owned proportionally by Joe's Solo 40(k) plan and David personally. The LLC Operating Agreement would show that Joe's Solo 401(k) plan and David personally each own 50 percent of the LLC, and also will set forth all the terms they agreed upon with respect to the management of the LLC and real estate project. Since Joe invested all his Solo 401(k) plan funds into the LLC to buy the real estate, if there were a claim or liability against the LLC, Joe's Solo 401(k) funds in the LLC could be subject to attack because the LLC only protects assets held outside of the LLC. Whereas if Joe had Solo 401(k) funds outside of the LLC that was invested elsewhere, those funds would be protected by using an LLC.

In general, using the LLC and an investment entity has some strong advantages when buying real estate with a Solo 401(k) plan, but it does come with some negatives. The first is cost. In most cases, it costs anywhere from $50 to $500 to form the LLC, and most states have annual fees anywhere from $25 to $800. So you must weigh the advantages of using an LLC as a Solo 401(k) plan investment vehicle against the cost of doing so. In addition, because the LLC will be owned by two or more persons and the real estate investment will be a joint venture between the Solo 401(k) plan and at least one other person or entity, the LLC will be required to file a partnership income tax return (IRS Form 1065) for federal and state income tax purposes. No federal income tax will be due, but a return must still be filed by April 15 of each year.

Isn't Partnering with a Family Member in a Real Estate Transaction a Prohibited Transaction?

Likely not, if the transaction is structured correctly. Whether a joint-venture transaction involving the Solo 401(k) plan and other joint-venture person(s) or entities(s) violate the IRS prohibited-transaction rules depends on the transaction. As a recap, in general a disqualified person is the Solo 401(k) plan participant and any of his or lineal descendants (i.e., parents, children, spouse, daughters-in-law, or sons-in-law), as well any entities controlled by such persons. In addition, because of self-dealing and conflict-of-interest prohibited-transaction rules under IRC 4975(c), even a minority interest in a company that the Solo 401(k) plan will be investing in could trigger a prohibited transaction.

For example, using a Solo 401(k) plan to invest in an entity that is owned by a family member who is a disqualified person will likely be treated as a prohibited transaction. Depending on the facts and circumstances, this may be the case even if the disqualified person would own less than 50 percent of the entity (remember the *Rollins* case from Chapter 6). However, partnering with a family member who is a nondisqualified person, such as a sibling, directly in an investment property would likely not be a prohibited transaction.

Can I Partner with Myself to Do a Solo 401(k) Plan Real Estate Investment?

One of the most popular questions I get from prospective real estate investors seeking to use retirement funds to make real estate investments is: Can I use some personal funds to coinvest with my Solo 401(k) plan funds? The majority of Americans have anywhere between $65,000 and $170,000 in a retirement account. A single-family home could easily exceed the amount of retirement funds held by that individual. With most banks are not overly eager to make real estate–related loans, especially nonrecourse loans, using personal funds along with your retirement funds to make an investment is very appealing. The problem with comingling retirement and personal funds to make an investment is that the IRS could argue that the transaction violates the IRS self-dealing and conflict-of-interest prohibited transactions pursuant to IRC 4975(c)(1(D),(E), and (F).

The IRS could easily make the case that using your retirement funds to make the real estate investment personally benefitted the individual, because without the retirement funds, the real estate investment could not have been made.

On the flip side, the IRS could also argue that using retirement and personal funds in the same real estate transaction could be considered the transfer, use by or for the benefit of a disqualified person of the income or assets of a plan. The analysis generally depends on the facts and circumstances involved in the transaction at issue, but any time personal and retirement funds are used together in one investment, the door is open for the IRS to argue that a prohibited transaction occurred. Since the burden lies on the taxpayer for proving a prohibited transaction did not occur, I always advise not to use any personal funds in connection with an investment involving retirement funds.

Recently, the legality of partnering with ones retirement funds to make real estate and other alternative asset investments has finally been reviewed by a Court of Law. In KELLERMAN, 115 AFTR 2d 2015-1944 (531 B.R. 219) (Bktcy Ct AR), 05/26/2015, a bankruptcy case, the court held that a partnership formed by a self-directed IRA and an entity owned by the IRA holder and his spouse personally was a prohibited transaction.

In the case, Barry Kellerman and his wife each own a 50 percent interest in Panther Mountain personally. To effect the acquisition and development of the four-acre property, the IRA and Panther Mountain formed a partnership whereby the IRA contributed property and Panther Mountain contributed property and cash. The case is a clear example that using retirement and personal funds in the same transaction can potentially trigger a self-dealing prohibited transaction under IRC 4975(c)(1)(D). By entering into a transaction with IRA funds that in some way directly or indirectly involves a disqualified person, in this case Panther Mountain, which was owned by the Kellermans' personally, the IRA owner then is saddled with the burden of proving the transaction does not violate any of the self-dealing or conflict of interest prohibited transaction rules under IRC Section 4975, a burden that as this case shows could be difficult to satisfy. As the court stated,

"Further, and cumulatively, Barry Kellerman transferred or used "the income or assets of [the IRA]" for the benefit of each of the aforementioned disqualified persons and as a fiduciary dealt with "the income or assets of [the IRA] in his own interest or for his own account. The real purpose for these transactions was to directly benefit Panther Mountain and the Kellermans in developing both the four acres and the contiguous properties owned by Panther Mountain. The Kellermans each own a 50 percent interest in Panther Mountain and stood to benefit substantially if the four-acre tract and the adjoining land were developed into a residential subdivision.

Anyone thinking of combining retirement and personal funds in the same retirement account investment should think twice. The Kellerman case is a great example why using retirement funds and personal assets in the same transaction is not advisable and highly risky as it can potentially trigger the IRC Section 4975 prohibited transaction rules.

What If I Have Enough in My Solo 401(k) Plan to Make the Investment, but I Still Think It Is a Good Investment for My Solo 401(k) Plan and Personal Funds?

This is another question I get often. The scenario is typically as follows. You are looking to buy a property and can make the investment personally or via your retirement account, since both include ample funds. But you want to own the property through some shared percentage of retirement account and personal funds. Is that permitted?

The problem is that any time retirement funds and personal funds are mixed in an investment, there is no guarantee that the IRS won't try to argue self-dealing or conflict-of-interest prohibited transaction pursuant to IRC 4975. With the burden of proof falling on the taxpayer to prove otherwise and with that proof being difficult to meet, it is best practice to stay away from using a combination of personal and retirement funds in a single real estate transaction (see the Kellerman case).

Can You Borrow Money for Your Solo 401(k) from a Nondisqualified Person?

When it comes to using a Solo 401(k) plan to buy real estate, the IRS allows you to seek outside financing from a nondisqualified person as long as the loan is not personally guaranteed by the Solo 401(k) plan participant or another disqualified person.

So What Is a Nonrecourse Loan?

A "nonrecourse loan" is a type of loan that is secured by collateral, which is usually property, such as real estate acquired by the Solo 401(k) plan. If the borrower defaults, the issuer can seize the collateral but cannot seek out the borrower for any further compensation, even if the collateral does not cover the full value of the defaulted amount. This is one instance where the borrower does not have personal liability for the loan.

Why Does the Loan Have to Be Nonrecourse?

Again, "prohibited transaction" is a transaction that, directly or indirectly, involves the loan of money or extension of credit between a plan and a disqualified person. Normally, when an individual purchases real estate with a mortgage, the traditional loan provides for recourse against the borrower (i.e., personal liability for the mortgage). However, if the 401(k) plan purchases real estate and secures a mortgage for the purchase, the loan must be nonrecourse; otherwise, there will be a prohibited transaction pursuant to IRC 4975(c)(1)(B), lending of money or the extension of credit between the plan and a disqualified person. A nonrecourse loan only uses the property for collateral. In the event of default, the lender can collect only the property and cannot go after the 401(k) plan itself.

How Hard Is It to Get a Nonrecourse Loan?

Nonrecourse loans are not especially common because of the added risk imposed on the lender in the case of a failure to pay. Unlike a traditional mortgage that you acquire when purchasing a home or commercial building, in the case of a default, the bank or lender could go after the individual borrower personally, which provides added security to the lender. Whereas in the case of a nonrecourse loan, the lender's only recourse against the nonpayment of the loan is to take the property that secured the loan back, which in a falling real estate market is not very attractive to banks or lenders. That being said, depending on your personal relationship with a bank or particular lender, it may be possible to get a nonrecourse loan.

In general, most banks and financial institutions will require at least 35 percent equity in the project before they will consider a nonrecourse loan. Of course, the more funds you are investing in cash, the easier it will be to secure a nonrecourse loan. Due to the limited number of banks that offer nonrecourse loans, there is a small industry of lenders that has emerged over the past ten years or so that specialize in nonrecourse lending. The terms of the nonrecourse loan are generally more expensive than a standard mortgage because of the risk the nonrecourse lender is taking with no personal guarantee. Also, most nonrecourse loans are for under five years and typically are for income-producing properties only and not raw land.

Is There Taxation on the Use of a Nonrecourse Loan by a Solo 401(k) to Buy Real Estate?

This topic will be discussed in greater detail later on in this chapter. But the ability to use a nonrecourse loan to buy real estate with a Solo 401(k) plan without tax is one of the primary benefits of using a Solo 401(k) plan as a real estate investment vehicle. The ability to use nonrecourse financing for real estate is a huge advantage because Solo 401(k) plans are exempt from any taxation in the Internal Revenue Code when nonrecourse leverage is used for real estate acquisition. This exemption does not apply to other retirement accounts, such as IRAs. Note that the exemption only applies to real estate and not to other types of nonrecourse financing, such as margin on stock.

Borrowing Money from Your Solo 401(k) Plan to Finance a Potential Real Estate Investment

As discussed earlier, one of the features of a Solo 401(k) plan is the ability to borrow up to $50,000 or 50 percent of the plan account value, whichever is less, and use those funds for any purpose. When it comes to real estate investing, the Solo 401(k) loan feature can be a valuable tool for using up to $50,000 to help make a personal real estate investment. The Solo 401(k) loan is a loan between the plan and the plan participant individually, so that the loan proceeds would then be able to be used by the plan participant personally to make a real estate investment. The Solo 401(k) plan loan funds cannot be used with other Solo 401(k) plan or other retirement funds to make the investment, as that would trigger a prohibited transaction since there would be a transaction involving personal and retirement funds. Accordingly, the Solo 401(k) loan feature could be a way for you to tap in to your Solo 401(k) plan to help make a personal real estate or other investment, but not for a Solo 401(k) plan investment.

For example, you can borrow up to $50,000 to use to purchase real estate for personal purposes, but the Solo 401(k) plan loan cannot be used in connection with any "disqualified person" retirement funds. Getting an extra $50,000 or so to help make a personal investment could come in quite handy, especially in light of the difficult lending market and the difficulty involved in getting a loan for a real estate project.

Beware of the Prohibited Transaction Rules

On the topic of prohibited transactions, you must also make sure that you're not engaged in any self-dealing when buying or selling real estate. In other words, if the purchase or sale directly or indirectly personally benefits you or a disqualified person, it would be a prohibited transaction. Similarly, no active services should be performed by you or a disqualified person in connection with the Solo 401(k) plan real estate investment. In other words, you cannot use a disqualified person as your real estate agent, tax accountant, advisor, property manager, and so on.

In addition to having "checkbook control" and freedom to make real estate investments through your Solo 401(k) plan, there are also significant tax advantages. Income or gains generated by Solo 401(k) investments create tax-deferred or tax-free profits the case of a Roth account. You are, in other words, free to defer taxes on gains or income to a future date when the distribution is taken, rather than pay them in the year the investment produces income. Pretax Solo 401(k) distributions are not required until you turn seventy and a half years old, and in the case of a Roth Solo 401(k) plan, all gains are tax-free.

For example, if you purchase a piece of property with your Solo 401(k) plan for $100,000 and you later sold the property for $300,000, the $200,000 gain appreciation would generally be tax deferred. If, on the other hand, you purchased the property using personal nonretirement funds, the gains would be subject to federal income tax and likely state income tax as well. On a percentage basis, the income from real estate and other alternative investments can be two to eight times higher than today's fixed income offerings, even after paying expenses such as property taxes and insurance. Meanwhile, the account holder can eventually reap the tax-free appreciation of the asset. For a foreign real estate investment, you also generally have the benefit of tax-free repatriation of income. This essentially means that when you make a real estate investment with your Solo 401(k) plan, the gains or income flow through your Solo 401(k) plan tax-free, helping you build your retirement assets.

In the case of an after-tax (Roth) account, you can also take personal ownership of the property when you turn fifty-nine and a half years old tax-free. So in other words, you can purchase that dream vacation property anywhere in the world, treat it as a real estate investment for a number of years while accruing the gains from rental income and appreciation, and then move on in when you celebrate your fifty-ninth-and-a-half birthday! Whereas if you used pretax 401(k) plan funds for the investment, you would be required to pay tax on the fair market value of the property when you reached the age of fifty-nine and a half.

HELPFUL TIPS

- The deposit and purchase price for the real estate property should be paid using Solo 401(k) plan funds or funds from a nondisqualified third party.
- No personal funds or funds from a "disqualified person" should be used.
- All expenses, repairs, and taxes incurred in connection with the Solo 401(k) plan real estate investment should be paid using retirement funds—no personal funds should be used.
- If additional funds are required for improvements or other matters involving the real estate investments, all funds should come from the Solo 401(k) plan or from a non "disqualified person."
- If financing is needed for a real estate transaction, only nonrecourse financing should be used. A "nonrecourse loan" is a loan that is not personally guaranteed and whereby the lender's only recourse is against the property and not against the borrower.
- With a Solo 401(k) plan, the use of a nonrecourse loan would not be subject to any tax pursuant to Internal Revenue Code Section 514, which is not the case with an IRA. This provides a very exciting investment opportunity.
- No services should be performed by the Solo 401(k) plan participant or "disqualified person" in connection with the real estate investment. In general, other than typical trustee type of services (necessary and required tasks in connection with the maintenance of the plan), no active services should be performed by the plan participant or a "disqualified person" with respect to the real estate transaction.
- Title of the real estate purchased should be in the name of the trustee for the benefit of the plan. For example, if Joe Smith is the trustee of ABC 401(k) Trust, title to any real estate purchased by Joe's plan would be as follows: "Joe Smith as Trustee of the ABC 401(k) Trust."
- Keep good records of income and expenses generated by the real estate investment.
- All income, gains, and losses from a Solo 401(k) plan real estate investment should be allocated to the Solo 401(k) plan.
- Make sure you perform adequate diligence on the property you will be purchasing, especially if it is in a state you do not live in.
- Make sure you will not be engaging in any self-dealing real estate transaction that would involve buying or selling real estate that will personally benefit you or a "disqualified person."

Foreign Currencies

You can also use your Solo 401(k) funds to purchase foreign currencies from any country in the world. Many people believe that such investments offer liquidity advantages compared to the stock market and represent significant investment opportunities in and of themselves.

As with real estate investments, all gains generated from your currency investments are tax deferred until a distribution is taken. Pretax distributions are not required until you turn seventy and a half years old, and in the case of Roth Solo 401(k) plan, all gains are tax-free.

If this approach to Solo 401(k) investing is appealing to you, we recommend that you have a solid background in trading currencies, as such investments can be highly volatile and may carry significant risk. If you're investing through a third party, please make sure that this group or individual has the knowledge to trade foreign currencies and that all securities licenses are in good standing.

You must make sure that all gains or losses from foreign currency transactions are allocated to your Solo 401(k) plan, and keep excellent records. You should also beware of leverage. It is allowable but would trigger the application of the UBTI under IRC 512 and subject you to a corresponding tax. No personal guarantee of any leverage or loan obligation is permitted.

Stocks, Bonds, Mutual Funds, and CDs

Naturally, in addition to nontraditional investments like real estate or foreign currencies, you may also use your Solo 401(k) to purchase stock, bonds, mutual funds, and CDs. Again, with "checkbook control," you can open a stock trading account with any financial institution.

Stocks and mutual funds continue to be the most popular investment for Solo 401(k) plans. This is especially true in the case of a financial institution–sponsored Solo 401(k) plan, which make up the most popular category of Solo 401(k) plans being adopted. These Solo 401(k) plans are typically quite restrictive and only permit the plan participant to make limited investments, such as stocks and mutual funds. The reason behind this is quite simple. Financial institutions make money when you hold funds at their institution and buy financial products such as stocks and mutual funds, which generate fees for them. With an estimated 24.7 trillion dollars in retirement funds available for investment as of December 31, 2014, you can imagine the enormous impact retirement funds have on the equity markets.

When purchasing stocks or securities with a Solo 401(k) plan, all income and gains, including dividends, flow back to the plan without tax.

With a Roth Solo 401(k) plan, all gains are tax-free. Whereas if you purchased stocks with personal funds, all income and gains would be subject to federal and, in most cases, state income tax.

As with foreign currency investments, if you will be investing with a third-party, perform adequate diligence on the individual and make sure he or she has the knowledge to trade stocks or securities and that all securities licenses are in good standing. And please beware of promoters promising high returns, especially those who do not work at reputable financial institutions.

Your brokerage account must be in the name of your Solo 401(k) plan, not a personal account. All income, gains, or losses from the stock investments should be allocated to the Solo 401(k) plan. Leverage is allowable but would compel you to pay a tax, since it would trigger the application of the UBTI rules under IRC 512.

Precious Metals and Coins

If you've watched enough late-night commercials, you may already know that precious metals such as gold, silver, platinum, and palladium can be purchased with retirement account funds. Precious metals and coins actually make excellent investment opportunities because their values generally keep up with or exceed inflation rates better than other investments. This should be no surprise, since precious metals are the original currencies of civilization and have been leveraged or exchanged throughout history. The purchase of bullion, in particular, is viewed as a surprisingly safe investment. Using a Solo 401(k) can be one of the most tax efficient ways to finance a precious metals purchase.

Only a handful of financial advisors are skilled in these specialized account structures, however, so you should seek the right level of guidance and expertise. There are a number of basic details to understand from the outset. For example, only IRS-approved metals and coins may be purchased. Moreover, these metals and coins must be purchased by your Solo 401(k) plan using plan funds or funds from a nondisqualified third party. As with other investments you make with your Solo 401(k) funds, all income, gains, or losses incurred should flow through your Solo 401(k) account.

When it comes to coins or metals, Internal Revenue Code Section 408 is generally the provision that applies. According to that provision, collectibles such as artworks, rugs, stamps, certain coins, beverages, and antiques are not allowed within a Solo 401(k).

What type of metals and coins are IRS approved? These are described in IRC 408(m). They include:

- One, one-half, one-quarter, and one-tenth ounce US gold coins are IRS approved (American Gold Eagle coins are the only gold coins specifically approved for IRAs). Other gold coins, to be eligible as IRA investments, must be at least 0.995 fine (99.5 percent pure) and be legal tender coins.
- One-ounce silver coins minted by the Treasury Department are approved.
- Any coin issued under the laws of any state are acceptable.
- A platinum coin described in 31 USCS 5112(k) is approved.
- Gold, silver, platinum, or palladium of a certain fineness that is in the physical possession of a trustee that meets the requirements of a trustees, as defined under Code Sec. 408(a), is IRS approved.

It's also important to comply with regulations for how you must hold or possess your metals and coins. The Technical and Miscellaneous Revenue Act of 1998 expanded the types of precious metals and coins that retirement account holders were allowed to invest their retirement assets in. In the case of IRS-approved precious metals (bullion), the Internal Revenue Code under Section 408(m) specifically states that they must be held in the "physical possession" of a US depository or at a US bank in the name of your Solo 401(k) plan. Other than the language in IRC 408(m), the IRS has not offered crystal-clear guidance on this issue, but their regulations do imply that precious metals (all bullion) should not be stored in the home or in the possession of the plan participant or any person who does not satisfy the definition of a trustee pursuant to the Internal Revenue Code.

How Do You Hold Physical Bullion in a Solo 401(k) Plan?

The IRS allows retirement funds to purchase gold, silver, platinum, or palladium bullion of a certain fineness that is in the physical possession of a trustee, as defined under Code Sec. 408(a). IRC Section 408(m) identifies what types of coins and precious metals (bullion) are permitted to be purchased using a retirement account, such as a Solo 401(k). IRC Section 408(m) also states that bullion (IRS-approved gold, silver, or palladium) must be held in the physical possession of a trustee described under subsection (a).

A "trustee" is defined in Internal Revenue Code Section 408(a) as a bank—as defined in subsection (n)—or a person who demonstrates to the satisfaction of the Secretary that the manner in which that person will administer the trust will be consistent with the requirements of this section. Internal Revenue Code Section 408(n) defines a "bank" as any bank (as defined in section 581) or an insured credit union, within the meaning of paragraph (6) or (7) of section 101 of the Federal Credit Union Act.

Section 581 defines a bank as a bank or trust company incorporated and doing business under the laws of the United States (including laws relating to the District of Columbia) or of any state, a substantial part of the business of which consists of receiving deposits and making loans and discounts; or of exercising fiduciary powers similar to those permitted to national banks under authority of the comptroller of the currency; and which is subject by law to supervision and examination by state, territorial, or federal authority having supervision over banking institutions. That also means a domestic building and loan association. The Code seems to suggest that precious metals cannot be held in a foreign bank account, since it would not satisfy the definition of a bank pursuant to IRC 541.

The question then becomes, what does "physical possession" mean? IRC Section 408(m) clearly states that gold, silver, or palladium bullion must be held in the physical possession of a US trustee, otherwise known as a US bank or financial institution.

Accordingly, if a Solo 401(k) plan account holder holds precious metals in a safe deposit box at a US bank in the name of the Solo 401(k) plan, would that be considered to be in the "physical possession" of a US trustee or bank and satisfy the definition under IRC 408(m)? An argument can then be made that precious metals are certainly not in the physical possession of the Solo 401(k) plan participant if held in a security deposit box at a US bank, since the metals will physically be held in a safe deposit box of a bank in the name of the Solo 401(k) plan. However, the safe deposit box could be considered to be is in the constructive control of the Solo 401(k) plan trustee, typically the same as the Solo 401(k) plan participant, since he or she has the keys for the box.

The Internal Revenue Code under Section 408 clearly states "physical possession" and not "constructive control." From a legal standpoint, possession is not defined to represent control, meaning you can be in possession of an item but not in control or ownership of it. Therefore, many tax practitioners take the position that holding precious metals in a safe deposit box in the name of the Solo 401(k) plan would satisfy the "physical possession" requirement under Internal Revenue Code Section 408(m).

Unfortunately, the IRS has not offered any clear guidance on this issue. What is clear is that, unlike IRS-approved coins, precious metals should not be stored in the home or possession of the Solo 401(k) plan participant or any person who does not satisfy the definition of a trustee according to the Internal Revenue Code. It is good practice to hold precious metals owned by a Solo 401(k) plan at an IRS-approved depository where it is clearly in the "physical possession" of a US trustee.

How Can You Hold IRS-Approved Coins with a Solo 401(k) Plan?

Here are the relevant sections in Internal Revenue Code Section 408(m) that relate to purchases of IRS-approved coins for retirement funds:

- Exception for certain coins and bullion: for purposes of this subsection, the term "collectible" shall not include—
  - Any coin which is—
    - A gold coin described in paragraph (7), (8), (9), or (10) of section 5112 (a) of title 31, United States Code
    - A silver coin described in section 5112 (e) of title 31, United States Code
    - A platinum coin described in section 5112 (k) of title 31, United States Code
    - A coin issued under the laws of any state
- 31 USC § 5112 refers to denominations, specifications and design of coins.
  - The Secretary of the Treasury may mint and issue only the following coins:
    - A dollar coin that is 1.043 inches in diameter
    - A half dollar coin that is 1.205 inches in diameter and weighs 11.34 grams
    - A quarter dollar coin that is 0.955 inch in diameter and weighs 5.67 grams
    - A dime coin that is 0.705 inch in diameter and weighs 2.268 grams
    - A five-cent coin that is 0.835 inch in diameter and weighs 5 grams
    - A one-cent coin that is 0.75 inch in diameter and weighs 3.11 grams (exceptions to this are described in the next section).
    - A fifty-dollar gold coin that is 32.7 millimeters in diameter, weighs 33.931 grams, and contains one troy ounce of fine gold
    - A twenty-five dollar gold coin that is 27.0 millimeters in diameter, weighs 16.966 grams, and contains one-half troy ounce of fine gold

    - A ten-dollar gold coin that is 22.0 millimeters in diameter, weighs 8.483 grams, and contains one-fourth troy ounce of fine gold and contains one-tenth troy ounce of fine gold
    - A five dollar gold coin that is 16.5 millimeters in diameter, weighs 3.393 grams, and contains one-tenth troy ounce of fine gold
    - A $50 gold coin that is of an appropriate size and thickness, as determined by the Secretary, weighs 1 ounce, and contains 99.99 percent pure gold
    - A $25 coin of an appropriate size and thickness, as determined by the Secretary, that weighs 1 troy ounce and contains .9995 fine palladium

- Notwithstanding any other provision of law, the Secretary shall mint and issue, in quantities sufficient to meet public demand, coins that—
  - Are 40.6 millimeters in diameter and weigh 31.103 grams
  - Contain 0.999 fine silver
  - Have a design—
    - Symbolic of Liberty on the obverse side; and
    - Of an eagle on the reverse side.
- The Secretary may mint and issue platinum bullion coins and proof platinum coins in accordance with such specifications, designs, varieties, quantities, denominations, and inscriptions as the Secretary, in the Secretary's discretion, may prescribe from time to time.

In addition, legislation in 1997 (Technical and Miscellaneous Revenue Act of 1988—TAMRA) further liberalized the rules for retirement accounts investing in IRS-approved metals and coins. This legislation made reference to specific definitions of acceptable coins in USCS, title 31; IRC sections 5112(a), (e) and (k): the Commodity Exchange coins that would not be treated as a collectible to "certain gold and silver coins issued by the US Government." This change resulted in a windfall for individual collectors as well as coin and precious metal dealers (all of the coins allowed must be minted by the US government or the states). In general, the American Eagle, American Buffalo, and state minted coins are the most popular type of IRS-approved coins that are purchased with retirement funds.

Now that you have a clear idea of the types of coins that the IRS allows you to purchase using retirement funds, the next question is, how can the coins be held without violating IRS rules?

Most people don't realize that a coin can be treated as bullion. As a result, based on the language in IRC 408(m)(3)(B), all coins, including American Eagle and State minted coins, can be held in the "physical possession" of a U.S. trustee. There is some debate online as to whether IRS approved coins must be held in the "physical possession" of a U.S. bank. Although bullion may be cast into bars or minted into coins, the defining attribute of bullion is that it is valued by its mass and purity rather than by a face value as money. Hence, it appears that the IRS intended that the "physical possession" requirement outlined for bullion in IRC 408(m)(3)(B) should pertain to precious metals as well as all coins, such as American Eagle coins, defined in IRC 408(m)(3)(A) since they can be defined as bullion. However, the Technical and Miscellaneous Revenue Act of 1988 does state that a retirement account may purchase state minted coins so long as a person holds them independent of the retirement account owner. The 1988 Act does not define "Person" and interestingly does not refer to the term "trustee." So can one hold IRS approved coins personally? IRS approved coins should not be held personally by the retirement account holder and should be held in the physical possession of a trustee, as defined in IRC Section 408. In addition, it may be wise to have some type of legal document or affidavit drafted stating that the IRS approved coins are being held solely for the benefit of the Solo 401(k) plan and not for any personal or other benefit. Most tax practitioners believe that it is best practice to hold all IRS approved precious metals or coins (both are treated as bullion) at a U.S. bank or depository, including American Eagle and State minted coins.

Most importantly, the freedom to buy precious metals and coins provides you with one more valuable tool in your retirement wealth-building portfolio. In today's volatile and complex marketplace, timing and pricing is everything. With "checkbook control," you can use your Solo 401(k) assets to execute, buy, and sell orders instantly, leaving no downtime for big swings in prices. The appreciation of your precious metals or IRS-approved coins also grows without tax. You can avoid all taxes until the money invested is withdrawn. You can also use a loan from your Solo 401(k) to finance your precious metals or coin purchase for personal purposes because you are able to borrow up to either $50,000 of 50 percent of your account value, whichever is less. And, unlike other investments into equities, bonds, or mutual funds, you have the ability to physically access your precious metals or coins by taking an in-kind distribution during a time of crisis or national emergency, mitigating the risk of an uncertain age.

The following are some helpful tips to keep in mind when purchasing IRS approved precious metals and/or coins with a Solo 401(k) Plan:

- Only IRS approved metals and coins may be purchased as per Internal Revenue Code 408(m)
- The IRS approved precious metals or coins being purchased by the plan should be paid using Solo 401(k) Plan funds or funds from a nondisqualified third-party
- With respect to IRS approved precious metals or coins (bullion), the metals should <u>not</u> be held in the personal possession of any individual and must be held in the "physical possession" of a U.S. depository or at a U.S. bank
- An affidavit signed by the trustee of the plan confirming that the IRS approved precious metals or coins are being purchased and

being held in the sole interest of the plan and not for any personal benefit is good practice
- A detailed inventory of the purchased metals and/or coins would be a good idea
- Copies of all contracts or invoices showing the purchase of the metals or coins would be helpful
- Pictures of the purchased precious metals and or coins would be helpful proof to show that the assets being held is what was purchased and that there has been no personal benefit derived from the transaction
- All income, gains or losses from the purchased precious metals or coins should be allocated to the Solo 401(k) Plan
- IRS approved precious metals should not be held at a bank outside the United States
- Perform adequate diligence on the dealer with whom you will be transacting for the purchase of metals or coins

Tax Liens

Real estate has long been considered one of the best areas of investment available to anyone. In a down market such as the one we have just experienced, many savvy investors make money in real estate by purchasing properties for a fraction of their value. How do they do this? By investing in tax lien and tax deed sales.

When a property owner falls behind on her taxes and fails to pay for one or more years, the local taxing authority has the legal right to plan a lien or repossess the property and sell it at auction to recoup the lost tax revenue. Lien laws vary in different areas, but in many cases properties may be acquired for a few thousand dollars, regardless of actual worth. At the same time, paying off the lien may cost more than the property is actually worth. It's important, therefore, to take the time to research each property carefully prior to sale day.

Tax lien sales usually happen at public auctions once or twice a year, although large urban areas may hold monthly auctions. There are two types of lien sales that happen at auctions: the tax lien certificate and the tax lien deed. Both can offer safe but profitable investment opportunities.

Tax lien certificate sales offer the delinquent homeowner one last chance to retain ownership of the property by using third-party investment money to pay off the taxes. This gives the homeowner more time to collect the money needed to pay his debt without losing his home. As an investor, if you bid on a tax lien certificate, you are essentially agreeing to loan the homeowner the money needed to pay all taxes due, and the homeowner, in turn, is agreeing to pay back the tax lien certificate holder with interest by a specified date. If the homeowner fails to pay the debt on time, the deed to the property is transferred to the investor for the amount paid on the taxes. In either case, you make a profit, either on the interest earned on the loan or by obtaining the property for a fraction of its value and reselling it.

Tax lien deeds sales are handled a bit differently, since the investor is actually bidding on or buying the property at the time of auction, with no responsibility to give the homeowner more time to pay the tax debt. Once the selling price is approved, the deed is automatically transferred to its new owner, giving the investor full reign as to what to do with the property next. You can renovate it, sell it as-is, or raze the existing house and build anew.

Investors usually pay more for properties in this type of sale, which may lower their profit margins compared to the acquisition of tax lien certificate properties. But many investors prefer outright purchases to eliminate problems with current homeowners. Either way, investing in tax liens or tax deeds can be a profitable and easy way to enter the real estate market in virtually any area.

As an investment, tax liens offer significant returns for a surprising amount of security. In fact, you can quickly double your money through such opportunities. For example, a tax lien certificate can earn up to 16 percent annually in your Solo 401(k). When you buy tax lien investments, you generally receive the amount invested plus interest within twelve months. If you continue to reinvest in tax liens year after year at 16 percent, you can potentially double your money in about 4.4 years.

Just as importantly, your money grows tax deferred or tax-free in the case of a Roth. You avoid all taxes until the money is withdrawn from your Solo 401(k). The money can be invested once, twice, or a thousand times and continue to grow without tax, so long as it is not withdrawn for personal use. You should not use personal checks, credit cards, or cash for such purchases; indeed, the deposit and purchase price for the tax lien or deed should be paid using your Solo 401(k) plan funds, or funds from a nondisqualified third party (but never personal funds or funds from a disqualified person). And of course, all gains or losses from your tax lien or tax deed investments should be allocated to your Solo 401(k) plan.

Tax liens are relatively safe because they are backed and leveraged by real estate and guaranteed by the governmental taxing authority. In most states, all junior liens, including mortgages, are wiped out when a property is foreclosed. This allows you to potentially receive a valuable piece of real estate for pennies on the dollar! There are risks, however, to any investment, so it is important to have a clear and detailed understanding of the process involved before engaging. But a well-educated investor can do very well, and you can use that knowledge to build your retirement wealth very quickly.

Loans and Notes

The IRS also allows you to use Solo 401(k) funds to make loans or purchase notes from third parties. By doing so, all interest payments received are tax deferred until a distribution is taken, and in the case of a Roth Solo 401(k) plan, all gains are tax-free. For example, if you used a Solo 401(k) to loan money to a friend, all interest received would flow back into your 401(k) plan tax-free. Whereas if you lent your friend money from personal (nonretirement) funds, the interest you received would be subject to federal and, in most cases, state income tax. When it comes to making hard-money loans to friends, colleagues, or any third parties, it is very important to be mindful of the IRS prohibited-transaction rules, which do not allow you to lend money to any disqualified person or disqualified entity.

Once again, the loan or note amount should be paid using Solo 401(k) plan funds or funds from a nondisqualified third party, and no personal funds or funds from a "disqualified person" should be used in the loan transaction, nor should a "disqualified person" be directly or indirectly involved. The loan or note should also have a stated interest rate of at least Prime so that an argument cannot be made that the loan is really a gift. All interest and principal associated with the loan or note should be allocated to your Solo 401(k) plan.

It is good practice to have the loan terms documented in a promissory note or loan agreement, even if you are dealing with a friend. And if you are acting as the lender, you should consider securing the loan with an interest or lien in an asset owned by the borrower. Additionally, read up on the prohibited-transaction rules to make sure you will not be engaging in any self-dealing loan transaction that would involve a loan or note that will personally benefit you or a disqualified person.

Private Businesses

With a Solo 401(k), you are also permitted to purchase an interest in a privately held business. The business can be established as any entity, such as a LLC, C corporation, or partnership, but not an S corporation since only individuals can generally be S corporation shareholders. When investing in a private business using Solo 401(k) funds, it is particularly important to keep in mind the "disqualified person" and prohibited-transaction rules, and it's a good idea to consult with a tax or retirement expert.

In order to avoid triggering the prohibited-transaction rules when making investments into a private business, you should be careful to not invest any retirement funds in any business in which you have a direct or indirect benefit in, including ownership, serving as officer or manager, and even being an employee in some cases. Remember, the *Rollins* case: Mr. Rollins owned a small percentage of a company and served as officer of the company without being an employee, and the Tax Court still ruled that the loan from his 401(k) plan to the company was a prohibited transaction. It's all about the facts and circumstances. How big is the company? Is it a public or private company? How many shareholders? Do you have any personal role in the company? Would the retirement investment personally benefit you in any way, directly or indirectly?

Certainly, using a Solo 401(k) plan to invest in a friend's private business—so long as you have no involvement in it and the investment is 100 percent passive—would not violate the IRS prohibited-transaction rules. Likewise, an employee of IBM or another large public company can use 401(k) funds to buy stock in the company they work for without triggering a prohibited transaction because of the size of the company and number of shareholders. In fact, Congress already thought of this and called the purchase of stock by a 401(k) plan of corporate stock "qualifying employer securities"—exempted from the prohibited-transaction rules under IRC 4975(d)(13)—an investment option, which most Solo 401(k) plans include.

Remember, "qualifying employer securities" are defined as corporate stock and not an interest in an LLC or partnership, and 401(k) plans cannot purchase the stock of an S corporation. Therefore, since almost all public corporations are C corporations, you can generally purchase qualifying employer securities of the company you work for. In fact, many entrepreneurs are using the strategy of buying "qualifying employer securities" in order to use 401(k) funds to help buy a new business or franchise without tax or penalty. This is often referred to as the rollover business start-up solution (ROBS).

But what about a private company in which you already own a small percentage or are an employee of? Would that violate the IRS prohibited-transaction rules? Unfortunately, there is no clear answer to this and you must examine the facts and circumstances in relation to the prohibited-transaction rules under IRC 4975 to see if a prohibited transaction would occur. Even if you own less than 50 percent of the private business and on its face the entity does not seem to be a disqualified person under IRC 4975, remember that the self-dealing and conflict-of-interest prohibited-transaction rules could still trigger a prohibited transaction. Just ask Mr. Rollins about that. Therefore, the safest approach is to not invest retirement funds in any private business in which you have a personal ownership in or are an employee of, or have any direct or indirect personal relationship with.

Once again, the deposit and purchase price for the business should be paid using Solo 401(k) plan funds or funds from a nondisqualified third party, and no personal funds or funds from a "disqualified person" should be used. The purchase of the stock or assets of the business should not directly or indirectly benefit you personally or any disqualified person in order to avoid self-dealing or issues with prohibited transactions.

As we'll soon discuss, the use of 401(k) funds to purchase a business operated via an LLC or partnership will potentially trigger the Unrelated Business Taxable Income (UBTI) rules under IRC 512 and a corresponding tax of up to 40 percent would be applied. But the purchase of stock in a C corporation would not trigger UBTI rules.

Most importantly, make sure you perform adequate diligence on the business you will be purchasing or investing in, especially if you will be buying stock or an interest and not the actual assets of the business.

Beware of Fraud

This is probably a good time to mention the importance of performing due diligence on any retirement account investment, especially if you will be investing with a third party. While using retirement funds can be a tax-efficient and safe way to invest, it is important to be mindful of potential fraudulent schemes when using a self-directed retirement structure.

Recently, the SEC issued an Investor Alert to warn investors of the potential risks of fraud associated with investing through self-directed IRAs and Solo 401(k) plans. The SEC noted that there has been an increase in reports or complaints of fraudulent investment schemes that utilize a self-directed retirement plan as a key feature. To view a copy of the SEC Investor Alert titled, "Investor Alert: Self-Directed IRAs and the Risk of Fraud," please see Appendix D.

No party can guarantee the success of any investment. It is important that each retirement account investor undertake his or her own evaluation of the merits of a proposal. You should check with regulators about the background and history of an investment and its promoters before making a decision and beware of potential fraudulent schemes when considering a self-directed retirement structure. You should also understand that the custodians of self-directed retirement account may have limited duties to investors and that the custodians and trustees for these accounts will generally not evaluate the quality or legitimacy of an investment and its promoters. As with every investment, retirement account holders need to undertake their own evaluation of the merits of a proposal and should check with regulators about the background and history of an investment and its promoters before making a decision.

What is Fraud?

Fraud occurs when a person or business intentionally deceives another with promises of goods, services, or financial benefits that do not exist, were never intended to be provided, or were misrepresented. Typically, victims give money but never receive what they paid for.

Who are the Victims of Fraud?

Virtually anyone can fall prey to fraudulent crimes. Con artists do not pass over anyone because of age, finances, education level, gender, race, culture, ability, or geographic location. In fact, fraud perpetrators often target certain groups based on these factors. There is almost $24.7 trillion dollars in retirement assets as of December 31, 2014, according to the Investment Company Institute. Most individuals have not been happy with their retirement account returns, don't expect to have enough retirement funds when they retire, and are looking for supercharged investment opportunities. This makes retirement account holders an enormous target for fraud.

Who Commits Fraud Crimes?

According to the US government, fraud criminals vary like their victims: educationally, socially, geographically, and financially. Most con artists make a career of their criminal activities. Some even join professional organizations to legitimize their schemes and project a respectable front.

What Are Some Common Types of Fraud?

The weapon of choice for fraud criminals is not a gun or a knife. Rather, it is most often a telephone, letter, glossy publication, or brochure offering free vacations, merchandise, investment opportunities, or services. Not all frauds involve the direct selling of goods to consumers. Some frauds target institutions or businesses. Examples include:

- Telemarketing fraud (telephone solicitation for phony goods or services)
- Mail fraud
- Health-care and insurance fraud
- Pension and trust-fund fraud
- Credit card and check fraud (including fraud by impersonation resulting from theft of mail or credit cards)
- Identity theft
- Fraud related to securities, commodities, and other investments

- Bank fraud
- Embezzlement
- Pyramid or Ponzi schemes
- Advanced-fee schemes
- Internet fraud

Tips to Avoid and Prevent Being Financially CHEATED:

- Shred financial documents and paperwork with personal information before you discard them.
- Protect your social security number. Give it out only if absolutely necessary or ask to use another identifier.
- Don't give out personal information over the phone, mail, or the Internet unless you know who you are dealing with.
- Don't give out passwords for any of your accounts to anyone.
- Don't give out your credit card numbers to any strangers.
- If you believe the contact is legitimate, go to the company's website by typing in the site address directly or using a page you have previously bookmarked, instead of a link provided in the e-mail.
- Review all offers in writing.
- Be wary of promises of quick profits, offers to share "inside" information, and pressure to invest before you have an opportunity to investigate.
- Be careful of promoters who use "aliases." Aliases are common online, and some promoters will try to hide their true identity.
- Words like "guarantee," "high return," "limited offer," and "as safe as a CD" are red flags.
- Watch out for offshore scams and investment opportunities in other countries.
- Watch out if a company is not registered with the SEC or the Secretary of State where it is located.
- Be wary if a financial advisor cannot be found through FINRA.
- Don't assume that people online are who they claim they are.
- Ask the online promoter whether and how much they are being paid to sell the product.
- Do business with people you know.
- Make sure you understand the investment before you invest your money.
- Take your time to make decisions.
- Be sure to talk over all financial decisions with a trusted family member, friend, or financial advisor.
- Report any frauds and any potential investment frauds affecting Americans to local, state, or federal regulators.
- Never make a check out to a financial advisor.
- Never allow statements or confirmations to be sent directly to your financial advisor without receiving copies.
- Recommendations from a sales representative based on "confidential information," an "upcoming favorable research report" a "prospective merger or acquisition," or the announcement of a "dynamic new product" are suspect.
- Never act on a recommendation from your sales representative that you make a dramatic change in your investment.
- Be wary if you experience pressure to trade the account in a manner that is inconsistent with your investment goals and the risk you want or can afford to take.
- Do not heed any assurances from your sales representative that an error in your account is due solely to a computer or clerical error. Insist that the branch manager or compliance officer promptly send a written explanation, and follow up to make sure the error is fixed.

In general, the best prevention technique is to identify and research the persons, products, and companies offering you their services. The more education and understanding of the product features you have, especially any investment products, the higher the level of scrutiny you can apply. In the event of any suspicious calls, e-mails, or personal solicitations, you should report them to the proper authorities.

Always take the time you need to understand and evaluate a potential investment. Make sure you understand the investment you will be making and thoroughly understand how the promoter will be able to generate the returns being promised. Also make sure the promoter of the investment has the necessary qualifications or licenses, if applicable, to offer the investment. Be cautious if a sponsor or advisor uses the affiliation as the reason to make the investment rather than relying on the underlying merits of the investment or trust in the sales person.

Using retirement funds to make traditional and alternative asset investments could prove to be a very financially rewarding decision. However, you must always diligently review the details of the investment and be on the lookout for investments that just seem too good to be true. Working with a tax professional in this regard is generally a good way to reduce the chances of having your retirement account investment become subject to a fraud.

Can Certain Solo 401(k) Investments Be Subject to Tax?

One of the advantages of using retirement funds through your Solo 401(k) to make investments is that, in most cases, all income and gains from the investments flow back to your 401(k) plan without tax. This is because a Solo 401(k) is exempt from tax, pursuant to IRC 401. Pursuant to IRC 512, most of the popular forms of income generated by a retirement income will be exempt from tax. This is why most American investors look at you funny when you start telling them about the Unrelated Business Taxable Income (UBTI) rules.

The IRS enacted a set of rules in the 1950s to prevent businesses from creating charities and then engaging in active trade or business via the charity to gain an unfair advantage through their tax-exempt status. The IRS did not want a for-profit company like McDonalds setting up a charity and running its business through that charity to generate tax-free profits. These rules, found in IRC 511–514, have become known as the UBTI rules. When UBTI rules are triggered, the income generated from those activities are generally subject to a maximum tax rate of 40 percent.

The good thing about the UBTI rules is that they won't apply to over 90 percent of American retirement investors because most types of income and gains generated by a retirement account are exempt. The Internal Revenue Code exempts dividends, interest, capital gains, royalties, and rental income from being subject to the UBTI tax rules. Even so, the UBTI rules are new and somewhat intimidating to most people when learning about them for the first time. For example, buying public stocks and mutual funds with a Solo 401(k) plan will not trigger the UBTI; neither would receiving a dividend from a public stock, or interest from a bond, or even rental income from an investment property. In the case of a Solo 401(k) plan, the UBTI tax is essentially triggered in two main types of investments:

1. Investing in an active trade or business via a pass-through entity, such as an LLC
2. Using margin when buying stock

Interestingly, using a nonrecourse loan to buy real estate with a Solo 401(k) plan will not trigger the UBTI tax, while it would with an IRA.

So How Is the UBTI Tax Triggered?

One of the advantages of using retirement funds, such as a Solo 401(k) plan to make investments is that in most cases all income and gains from the investment will flow back to the Solo 401(k) tax-free. This is because a 401(k) is exempt from tax pursuant to Internal Revenue Code 401, and Section 512 of the Internal Revenue Codes exempts most forms of investment income generated by a 401(k) and a Solo 401(k) from taxation. Some examples of exempt types of income include: interest from loans, dividends, annuities, royalties, most rentals from real estate, and gains/losses from the sale of real estate. In essence, since most Americans tend to purchase stock, mutual funds, precious metals, and real estate with their retirement funds, there is generally no immediate tax on the income or gains generated.

However, there are instances when a Solo 401(k) plan could make an investment and generate a category of income not covered by IRC 512, such as business income via a pass-through entity or the use of margin for stock purchases where a tax could be triggered. This tax is refereed to the unrelated business taxable income or UBTI.

What's the Story?

Back in the 1950s, Congress was concerned that for-profit companies would set up a charity and run their business through that charity and thus escape taxation forever, providing then with an unfair advantage because of their tax-exempt status. With that in mind, they created the UBTI rules under IRC 512. If the UBTI rules are triggered, the income generated from those activities will generally be subject to a maximum tax rate of 40 percent. Of note, a 401(k) or Solo 401(k) investing in an active trade or business using a C corporation will not trigger the UBTI tax. This is why most Americans using retirement funds to purchase public company stocks, which are in most cases C corporations, have never have heard of the UBTI tax.

What Is Unrelated Business Taxable Income?

UBTI is defined as "gross income derived by any organization from any unrelated trade or business regularly carried on by it," reduced by deductions directly connected with the business. The UBTI rules only apply to exempt organizations such as charities, IRAs, and 401(k) plans. With the enactment of ERISA in 1974, IRAs and 401(k) plans, which are considered tax-exempt parties pursuant to IRC 408 and 401 respectively, became subject to the UBTI rules. As a result, if an IRA or 401(k) plan invests in an active business through an LLC or partnership, the income generated by the IRA or 401(k) from the active business investment will be subject to the UBTI rules.

In the case of a Solo 401(k) plan, a transaction would not trigger the UBTI or UBIT rules if the transaction is not considered a trade or business that is regularly carried on. This typically involves passive types of activities that generate capital gains, interest, rental income, royalties, and dividends: the categories of income exempt according to IRC 512. However, if the tax-exempt organization—your Solo 401(k)—engages in an active trade or business that is regularly carried on (such as a restaurant, store, or manufacturing business), the IRS will tax the income pursuant to the UBTI rules.

The UBTI Tax Rate

IRC 511 taxes "unrelated business taxable income" (UBTI) at the rates applicable to trusts. Generally, UBTI is defined as gross income from an organization's unrelated trades or businesses, less deductions for business expenses, losses, depreciation, and similar items directly connected therewith. A Solo 401(k) plan subject to UBTI is taxed at the trust tax rate because an IRA is considered a trust. For 2016, a Solo 401(k) plan subject to UBTI is taxed at the following rates:

If Taxable Income is between:	The Tax Due Is:
0–$2,500	15 percent of taxable income
$2,501–$5,900	$375 + 25 percent of the amount over $2,500
$5,901–$9,050	$1,225 + 28 percent of the amount over $5,900
$9,051–$12,300	$2,107 + 33 percent of the amount over $9,050
$12,301+	$3,179.50 + 39.6 percent of the amount over $12,300

As you can see, the UBTI tax rates are pretty steep. In fact, they are higher than most individual's income tax rates as well as the corporate income tax rate. This is one of the main reasons why the UBTI tax rules are so important to understand and avoid if possible. In essence, the UBTI tax is imposed on the Solo 401(k) plan investment and actually creates a double tax regime since the UBTI tax will apply in the year the income or gain is realized and then also when the plan participant takes a distribution or is required to take a distribution after the age of seventy and a half. This is just another reason why it is important to be aware of the UBTI tax rules and their potential application to Solo 401(k) plan investments.

So How Do You Know If UBTI Will Apply to Your Solo 401(k) Plan Investment?

The UBTI generally applies to the taxable income of "any unrelated trade or business...regularly carried on" by an organization subject to the tax. The regulations separately treat three aspects of the quoted words "trade or business," "regularly carried on," and "unrelated."

1. **Trade or Business**: In defining "unrelated trade or business," the regulations start with the concept of "trade or business" as used by IRC 162, which allows deductions for expenses paid or incurred "in carrying on any trade or business." The idea of "trade or business" is generally defined by the IRS to include any activity carried on for the production of income from selling goods or performing services. The IRS took the position that income generated as dividends, interest, royalties, rental income, or capital gains should not be treated as "trade or business" income and thus, should not be subject to the UBTI tax rules.
2. **Regularly Carried On**: The UBTI only applies to income of an unrelated trade or business that is "regularly carried on" by an organization. Whether a trade or business is regularly carried on is determined in light of the underlying objective to reach activities competitive with taxable businesses. Short-term activities are exempt if comparable commercial activities of private enterprises are usually conducted on a year-round basis. In the case of a Solo 401(k) plan, the IRS generally takes the position that any income generated by an investment in a "trade or business" via a pass-through entity would likely be treated as UBTI, even if it is not regularly carried on, because any business activity for a Solo 401(k) plan will be treated as "regularly carried on."
3. **Unrelated:** In the case of an IRA or Solo 401(k) plan, any business activity will be treated as "unrelated" to its exempt purpose.

Is Real Estate a Trade or Business That Is Regularly Carried On?

Real estate is the one type of activity that generally causes confusion when it comes to determining whether the activity rises to the level of a trade or business carried on. When it comes to determining whether real estate activity rises to the level of an active trade or business, the IRS generally takes the position that a passive real estate activity is a real estate activity without material participation by the retirement account holder.

For example, making a real estate investment solely as a limited partner or LLC member is generally passive due to more restrictive tests for material participation. Clearly, purchasing a home to sell or a rental property would not be considered an active trade or business. But what about if you purchase five homes or a tract of land that you intend to develop? These are activities the IRS could argue rise to the level of an active trade or business regularly carried on. Unfortunately, it all comes down to the facts and circumstances involved, but there is some IRS guidance and case law that can help make a more comprehensive determination of whether the UBTI rules would apply.

What Are Some of the Factors the IRS or the Courts May Consider When Determining Whether a Real Estate Transaction May Be Subject to UBTI?

One of the foundation cases for examining the application of the UBTI rules in connection with making real estate transactions with tax-exempt funds is *Mauldin v. Comr. 195 F.2d 714 (10th Cir. 1952)*. In Mauldin, the court explained that there is no fixed formula or rule of thumb for determining whether property sold by a taxpayer was held by him primarily for sale to customers in the ordinary course of his trade or business. Each case must rest upon its own facts. The court identified a number of helpful factors to point the way, among which are the purposes for which the property was acquired (whether it was for sale or investment) and the continuity and frequency of sales as opposed to isolated transactions.

However, the Tax Court case of *Adam v. Comr. 60 T.C. 996 (1973), acq., 1974–1 C.B. 1* is probably the most helpful case in trying to determine whether the UBTI rules would apply to a real estate transaction involving a tax-exempt organization, such as a charity, IRA, or 401(k) plan. The Tax Court analyzed the following factors in determining whether the taxpayer was engaged in the operation of a trade or business:

1. **The purpose for which the asset was acquired:** For example, if you can show that the real estate asset was purchased solely for investment purposes and not for any ongoing business purpose, then this would help your argument that the real estate transaction should be excluded from the reach of the UBTI rules.
2. **The frequency, continuity, and size of the sales:** This factor is particularly significant in determining whether the sale constitutes a trade or business that is regularly carried on, within the meaning of Internal Revenue Code Section 512. It may range from a one-time sale of a parcel of land to many sales over a long period. If sales are infrequent (not continuous) and small, the retirement account will not likely be viewed as similar to a taxpayer engaged in a real estate trade or business. Conversely, as sales become more frequent, more continuous, and larger, they are more likely to be considered a trade or business that is regularly carried on, comparable to the commercial activity of a taxpayer in the trade or business of selling real estate.

In *Private Letter Ruling (PLR) 9247038*, the IRS issued a favorable ruling to an organization that planned to sell land in up to a fifteen sales spread over a five- to 10-year period. The reason for the number of sales over the time period was that the value of the land was such that it was unlikely that a single purchaser would be able to acquire the entire parcel. Also, market conditions dictated this sales process for the organization to receive maximum value and keep control of the pace and type of development that would occur after the sales. Similarly, in *PLR 9017058*, where the exempt organization was engaged in selling forty-five of sixty-eight lots, such sales were deemed to meet the exception from unrelated business income under IRC 512(b)(5). Although this quantity of sales is admittedly significant, external forces essentially dictated the high number of sales.

The organization first tried to sell the property in one block but was unsuccessful due to the high cost of developing the property in order to comply with local ordinances. According to the IRS, had the organization attempted to sell the entire property as a whole and had local ordinances required certain development prior to sale as residential property, it is possible that the high number of sales in this case would have resulted in UBTI.

So a limited number of sales is usually a "good fact" for purposes of the facts and circumstances test. However, you shouldn't assume that any set limit applies. Instead, you should remember that factors such as that frequency of sales and cost of the property to be sold and other market conditions play a part in the number of sales allowed and the time frame of the sales allowed. If the real estate investment has significant amounts of acreage or the cost of the property precludes finding one purchaser, then it is more likely that the organization will be permitted to sell the property in more than one transaction and still comply with the requirements of IRC 512(b)(5).

The most popular question I get in this area involves flipping real estate. Clearly one or two flipping transactions would not be considered an active trade or business and would not trigger the UBTI tax. The question then becomes, what happens if you do three, four, or even ten flipping transactions in a year? Would that be considered an active trade or business that triggers the UBTI tax? I can't tell you how many people I have talked to who have been frustrated by the lack of clarity over the number of real estate flipping transactions that would trigger a prohibited transaction. Again, you need to examine all the facts and circumstances surrounding the multiple-house flipping transactions in order to determine whether the transactions as a whole would constitute an active trade or business. It is important to work with a tax professional who can help you evaluate the transaction in that light.

3. **The activities of the seller in the improvement and disposition of the property:** The less extensive the improvements by the organization to the property, the more likely the sale will fall under the exclusion for unrelated business income under IRC 512(b)(5). In

PLR 8043052, an organization proposed selling a parcel of undeveloped raw land. The fact that the land had remained undeveloped was significant in determining that gains from the proposed transaction would not constitute unrelated business taxable income. Whereas in *PLR 8522042* the property in question consisted of both developed and undeveloped lands, these developed lands included residential land improved with single-family dwellings or condominium apartments. However, all the improvements were constructed by unrelated third parties. The absence of development activity by the organization demonstrated that it was not holding property for sale to customers in the ordinary course of trade or business.

4. **The extent of improvements made to the property:** The more minimal the activities of the owner in improving and disposing of property, the more likely its sale will meet the exclusion from unrelated business taxable income under IRC 512(b)(5). Of course, the greater the number of improvements allowed, the greater the likelihood of maximizing gain from the sale. So there is a balancing act that a retirement account holder must exercise when preparing land for disposition in order to maximize its return, while not acting too much like a dealer and triggering UBTI. The rational here is that the more improvements you are doing to the property, the more the activity looks like a real estate development business versus a passive real estate investment.

The IRS has ruled favorably on improvements made to property in accordance with city or local ordinances requiring the organization to construct a street as well as curb, gutter, sidewalk, drainage, and water supply improvements in order to subdivide the property for sale. In *PLR 8950072*, a tax-exempt foundation's largest asset was a parcel of unimproved real estate. The foundation was examining four ways of using the property: (1) continue leasing the property, (2) sell the property as is, (3) complete some preliminary development work (obtaining permits and approvals) and sell the property, or (4) completely develop the property before sale. The last alternative would provide the highest return. The IRS ruled that the first three alternatives would not subject the foundation to UBTI or adversely affect its exempt status. However, the last alternative, to assume all the responsibilities of development, would result in UBTI.

Aside from development activities, the lack of marketing of the property by the retirement plan helps differentiate it from a taxpayer in the trade or business of selling real estate. For example, in *PLR 8522042*, an organization's lack of promotional or development activity in connection with the proposed sale demonstrated that it was not holding property for sale to customers in the ordinary course of a trade or business. Moreover, the use of real estate brokers or other independent contractors is not determinative. Rather, the pertinent facts involve the extent of the activities of the organizations themselves in promoting and marketing the property.

5. **The proximity of sale to purchase:** In evaluating this factor, generally the longer the period between purchase and sale, the more likely the sale will be excluded from UBTI. For example, buying a home and then selling it thirty days after and then repeating this process several times in a year can give the impression that you are in the real estate flipping business rather than a passive investor. In contrast, buying a home and then selling it thirty days later but not buying another home for ten to fifteen months would make it much harder for the IRS to argue the retirement account is engaged in a trade or business and thus subject to the UBTI tax rules.
6. **The purpose for which the property was held during the taxable year:** In evaluating this factor, generally the longer the period between purchase and sale, the more likely the sale will be excluded from UBTI. For example, in *PLR 9505020*, the fact that a school received land by bequest and held it for a significant period of time was considered a favorable factor, and the IRS did not impose UBTI on the sale of the land when the school was facing condemnation proceedings and it did not actively advertise the sale.

Below are several real-life examples that shed some light on how the IRS treats certain real estate investments for purposes of determining whether they rise to the level of an active trade or business and, hence, be subject to the UBTI tax rules.

- In *Brown v. Comr, 143 F.2d 468 (5th Cir. 1944)*, the exempt taxpayer owned five hundred acres of unimproved land used for grazing purposes within its tax-exempt mission. The taxpayer decided to sell the land and listed it with a real estate broker. The exempt organization instructed the broker to subdivide the land into lots and develop it for sale. The broker had the land plotted and laid into subdivisions with several lots. Streets were cleared, graded, and shelled; storm sewers were put in at street intersections; gas and electric lines were constructed; and a water well was dug. Each year, twenty to thirty properties were sold. The court held that the taxpayer was holding lots for sale to customers in the regular course of business. The court identified the sole question for its determination as whether the taxpayer was in the business of subdividing real estate. The fact that the taxpayer did not buy additional land did not prevent the court from finding that the sales activities resulted in an active trade or business.
- In *Farley v. Comr., 7 T.C. 198 (1946)*, the taxpayer sold twenty-five lots out of a tract of land previously used in his nursery business but now more desirable as residential property. Since the taxpayer made no active efforts to sell and did not develop the property, the court described the sale as "in the nature of the gradual and passive liquidation of an asset." Therefore, the income derived from the sales represented capital gains income rather than ordinary income from the regular course of business as in the *Brown* case. In other words, the Tax Court treated the land investment as passive and not an active trade or business and as a result the transaction was not subject to the UBTI taxing regime.

- Dispositions of several thousand acres of land by a school over a period of twenty-five years does not constitute sale of land held primarily for sale to customers in the ordinary course of business, and thus gains are excludable under Internal Revenue Code Section 512(b)(5) (*PLR 9619069 [Feb. 13, 1996]*).
- Developing or subdividing land and selling a large number of homes or tracts of land from that development in a given period would likely be considered an active trade or business for UBTI purposes.

In general, if you make passive investments with your Solo 401(k) plan (such as stocks, mutual funds, precious metals, foreign currency, rental real estate, and so on), the income generated by the investment will not be subject to the UBTI tax. Only if your Solo 401(k) plan makes investments into an active business (such as a retail store, restaurant, real estate development, or software company) using a pass-through entity such as an LLC or partnership will your Solo 401(k) plan likely be subject to the UBTI tax.

For example, if a Solo 401(k) plan invests in an LLC that operates an active business such as a restaurant or gas station, the income or gains generated from the investment will generally be subject to the UBTI tax. However, if the Solo 401(k) plan invested in an active business through a C corporation, there would be no UBTI since the C corporation acts as a blocker, blocking the income from flowing through to the Solo 401(k) plan. This is why most Americans have never heard of the UBTI rules and why you can invest IRA and 401(k) funds into a public company, such as IBM, without triggering the UBTI tax. Remember that if an IRA or 401(k) plan makes a passive investment (such as rental income, dividends, and royalties), such income would not be subject to the UBTI rules.

How Do You Calculate and Pay the UBTI Tax If It Applies to a Solo 401(k) Plan Investment?

Once you have determined that the UBTI tax rules will apply to a Solo 401(k) plan investment, the next part is figuring out how much tax will be due. If an IRA or 401(k) plan generates gross income subject to UBTI of more than $1,000 during the taxable year, the retirement account must file IRS Form 990. Form 990-T is the tax form where a charitable organization or retirement account, such as an IRA or Solo 401(k), reports income that would be subject to the UBTI tax. In general, only income generated from an active trade or business via a pass-through entity, margin, or real estate acquisition indebtedness would be subject to the UBTI tax.

For retirement accounts Form 990-T is due on April 15. It is important to note that the IRS Form 990 is not part of your personal income tax return and is only being filed because a retirement account has generated UBTI. The UBTI tax is typically paid by the retirement account. It is a good idea to work with a CPA or tax professional to complete the IRS Form 990-T. In general, the IRS Form 990-T is completed like a corporate return and includes reporting all income and expenses related to the Solo 401(k) plan investment. To view a copy of IRS Form 990-T, please see Appendix E.

Generally, a Solo 401(k) plan filing Form 990-T must make installment payments of estimated tax if its estimated tax (tax minus allowable credits) is expected to be $500 or more. The organization must pay any tax due in full by the due date of the return without extensions.

Exceptions to the UBTI Rules

As discussed earlier in the chapter, there are some important exceptions from the UBTI rules. The exemptions from the UBTI rules generally include the most popular categories of investment activities for retirement accounts, dividends, interest, annuities, royalties, most rentals from real estate, and gains/losses from the sale of real estate. Since the majority of those income categories reflect the most popular investments made using retirement funds, almost all retirement account investors will never have to worry about the UBTI rules. Investments such as stocks, mutual funds, ETFs, precious metals, real estate, and interest from a loan or bond, dividends from a stock would be exempt from the UBTI tax and flow back to the retirement account without tax.

Using Leverage to Buy Real Estate with a Solo 401(k) Plan

Sometime it helps to have a good lobbyist. To some people, that's the only explanation why 401(k) plans have been allowed to use nonrecourse financing for real estate acquisitions and not be subject to the UBTI and unrelated debt finance income tax ("UDFI").

What Is a Nonrecourse Loan?

A nonrecourse loan is a type of loan that is secured by collateral, which is usually property. If the borrower defaults, the issuer can seize the collateral but cannot seek out the borrower for any further compensation, even if the collateral does not cover the full value of the defaulted amount. This is one instance where the borrower does not have personal liability for the loan. The reason only nonrecourse loans can be used when investing in real estate with retirement funds is that IRC 4975(c)(1)(B) prohibits a disqualified person from lending money or providing any other extension of credit between with a retirement account. Since a nonrecourse loan does not require the disqualified person to extend any credit because there is no personal guarantee, only a nonrecourse loan can be used when using leverage to purchase real estate with a retirement account.

Unlike an IRA, using nonrecourse financing to purchase real estate will not trigger the UBTI tax since it will not be treated as UDFI. An exception exists for 401(k) qualified retirement plans but not IRAs under Internal Revenue Code Section 514(c)(9) when using "debt financed property" to acquire real estate. "Debt-financed property" refers to borrowing money to purchase the real estate (i.e., a leveraged asset that is held to produce income).

In the case of a Solo 401(k) plan, UBTI does not apply to UDFI. The UDFI rules apply when a 401(k) plan uses leverage to acquire property such as real estate. According to IRC 514(c)(9), a 401(k) qualified plan is not subject to the UDFI rules and thus the UBTI tax if nonrecourse leverage is used to acquire property such as real estate. With the UBTI tax rates at close to 40 percent, the Solo 401(k) plan offers real estate investors looking to use nonrecourse leverage in a transaction with a potentially valuable tax efficient investment solution.

UBTI and Real Estate Investments

Although there is little formal guidance on UBTI implications for Solo 401(k) plans investing in real estate, there is a great deal of guidance on UBTI implications for real estate transactions by tax-exempt entities. In most cases, purchasing real estate with a Solo 401(k) plan will not trigger any UBTI tax. That is because most real estate investments typically done in a retirement account will not rise to the level of a trade or business. Most retirement investors will purchase a home, apartment, building, or piece of land and primarily hold it for rental or sale purposes. Furthermore, because most people have limited retirement resources, it is generally very difficult to be able to purchase and sell multiple real estate properties in a year or develop land for business purposes, including multiple-home development. That being said, there are certainly instances where a real estate transaction or series of real estate transactions must be examined to determine whether the level of activity would rise to a trade or business and thus trigger the UBTI tax. The six factors outlined in the *Adams* case and discussed in detail earlier in this chapter is a good place to start. The main factors most tax professionals look at are:

1. **The intent of the investor:** Was the investment meant to be a one-off investment, or is this part of a series of ongoing related investments that could be considered part of a business?
2. **The frequency, continuity, and size of the investments:** Of course, the more real estate transactions in a given year, the easier it would be for the IRS to determine that all the real estate transactions make up part of a single real estate business. The same argument goes for the size of the real estate investments and how frequently they are being done. If a Solo 401(k) plan investor is buying and selling properties on an ongoing and continual basis, the

real estate will look a lot like inventory, which would make the real estate activities subject to the UBTI rules. In examining these factors, the IRS would likely look at all the activities of the retirement account in a given year and even possibly over a number of years to examine whether the activity could be deemed a business activity. Of course, the closer the proximity of sale to purchase, the greater argument the IRS could make that the real estate is inventory and not an investment to be held for investment or rental purposes.

3. **The extent of improvements made to the property:** The more improvements and work done to the property, the easier it would be to argue that the property is part of a business. This is especially the case for raw land. Whereas in the case of improvements made to a home, in general there would typically not be any UBTI tax on the income or gain from the sale of the home, with raw land, building multiple homes on acquired land or subdividing the land and then developing each separate parcel for sale looks a lot more like a business in the eyes of the IRS than if the property was held for rental or sale and only minimal improvements t it were made. In general, gains and losses on dispositions of property are excluded from UBTI unless the property is inventory or property held primarily for sale to customers in the ordinary course of an unrelated trade or business. This exclusion covers gains and losses on dispositions of property used in an unrelated trade or business, as long as the property was not held for sale to customers. In addition, subject to a number of conditions, if a retirement account acquires real property or mortgages held by a financial institution in conservatorship or receivership, gains on dispositions of the property are excluded from UBTI, even if the property is held for sale to customers in the ordinary course of business.

The question that needs to be addresses is whether the real estate investment would be considered an active trade or business for UBTI purposes. In other words, what level of real estate transaction must you cross before triggering the UBTI tax? Unfortunately, there is no clear test.

In general, as we have just reviewed, the IRS has a number of factors it will examine to make a determination. First, they'll look at the frequency of the transactions: How many flipping transactions are done in a year? Second, they'll examine the intent: Were you intending to engage in an active trade or business? Third, they'll also look at the scope of other activities of the retirement account to determine whether the activity is part of a business activity or a passive investment. In other words, whether your real estate transactions triggers the UBTI tax, which is taxed at a maximum tax rate of close to 40 percent in 2016, depends on the facts and circumstances.

Types of Real Estate Purchases That Typically Trigger UBTI

The reason there has been added focus on real estate as an investment class in connection with the application of the UBTI rules is that real estate can be generally passive or active. The only way to decide is through a facts and circumstances test. A business investment, on the other hand, is usually fairly clear. If you invest in a restaurant, store, consulting business, factory, or online venture, it is easy to say whether you are investing in a business that, if operated though a pass-through entity (i.e., an LLC), would trigger the UBTI tax rules.

Buying Real Property versus Personal Property

If you are sticking to the basics—buying land for resale or buying a home or apartment unit for rental or resale—such income and gains would generally be exempt from tax. Earlier we looked at scenarios where engaging in multiple real estate transactions in a year on an ongoing and continual basis could trigger the UBTI tax, as well as development activity with respect to the rental property. However, there are other real estate–related activities that could trigger the UBTI tax, such as investing in a hotel, motel, mobile home park, or storage facility. All these activities are real estate–related and generate rental income, but they are also more businesslike than buying a home or land.

When looking at a real estate venture that generates rental income, the determination of whether the activity that would trigger UBTI tax rules depends on the nature of rent payments. The IRS will look at whether the rental income is based off personal property versus real property or if the rents depend on the income or profits derived by a person from the property.

Generally, in the situation where payments for the use or occupancy of rooms and other space where services are also rendered to the occupant (such as in hotels, boarding houses, or apartment houses furnishing hotel services, as well as in tourist camps or tourist homes, motor courts or motels, or for the use or occupancy of space in parking lots, warehouses, or storage garages), such rental income does not constitute rent from real property and such rental activities are generally subject to the UBTI tax. This actually makes sense, because when you consider the activities that generate the rental income, those tend to look more like a business than a real estate investment.

This is especially true in the case of a real estate activity that involves a hotel or motel, where services are considered rendered to the occupant if they are primarily for his convenience and are other than those usually or customarily rendered in connection with the rental of rooms or other space for occupancy only. The supplying of maid service, for example, constitutes such service, whereas the furnishing of heat and light, the collection of trash, and the cleaning of public entrances, exits, stairways, and lobbies are not considered as services rendered to the occupant. This is why, for example, receiving rental income from an office building would likely not trigger the UBTI tax, while it would in the case of a hotel. Accordingly, payments for the use or occupancy of entire private residences or living quarters in duplex or multiple housing units, of offices in any office building, and so on, are generally treated as rent from real property and not subject to the UBTI tax rules.

How Do You Avoid UBTI?

In general, if you make passive investments with your Solo 401(k) plan, the passive income generated by the investment will generally not be subject to the UBTI tax. Only if your Solo 401(k) plan will be making investments into an active business—such as a retail store, restaurant, or software company using a pass-through entity such as an LLC or partnership or that will involve margin or leverage not for real estate acquisition purposes—your Solo 401(k) plan likely be subject to the UBTI tax.

It is important to remember that most investments that your Solo 401(k) plan might make are exempt from UBTI. In other words, in most cases making investments with a Solo 401(k) plan will not trigger any tax until a distribution is taken, or none at all in the case of a Roth Solo 401(k) plan. Some examples of exempt types of income include: interest from loans, dividends, annuities, royalties, most rentals from real estate, and gains/losses from the sale of real estate. However, if you will be investing in an active trade or business via a pass-through entity such as an LLC or using margin to buy stock, then you must be mindful of the UBTI rules. A 40 percent tax or so on what you believed to be tax-free income or gains can quickly change how attractive those investments look.

The key, of course, is determining whether the activity you will be engaging in will rise to the level of a trade or business. In most cases, this determination is quite easy, since it would be clear whether the underlying investment activity is a business, such as restaurant, store, or factory. The case for real estate is somewhat more complex, and a number of factors must be examined in order to properly determine whether the UBTI tax rates would apply. As explained, factors such as the type of real estate investment, the frequency and continuity of the real estate activity, whether the real estate will be held for rental or quickly sold after purchase, the extent of the development involved in the property, whether minor improvements to the home will be made or whether the land will be developed for multiple homes, and how quickly the property will be bought and sold, are some of the issues that need to be examined before engaging in certain types of real estate transactions to make sure the UBTI tax will not apply. If you fail to perform this analysis, you can turn a seemingly attractive tax-deferred or tax-free investment into a possibly tax inefficient retirement investment that may be better done with personal funds.

Using a Roth Solo 401(k) Plan to Buy Real Estate

Now that we have spent a considerable amount of time going through some of the types of investments you can make with a Solo 401(k) plan, as well as some of the hidden tax traps such as the UBTI, let's discuss an exciting retirement, tax, and investment feature of the Solo 401(k) plan: the Roth Solo 401(k) plan. Using a Solo 401(k) plan with a Roth component to purchase real estate or make other alternative asset investments is a very tax beneficial way to make such investments. With federal and state income tax rates expected to increase in the future, gaining the ability to generate tax-free returns from your retirement investments when you retire is the last surviving legal tax shelter.

By leveraging a Roth Solo 401(k) plan, you can make almost any investment tax-free, including real estate, tax liens, precious metals, currencies, options, and private business investments, What's more, once you hit the age of fifty-nine and a half you will be able to live off your Roth 401(k) assets without ever paying tax. Imagine if someone told you that if you started making Roth 401(k) contributions in your forties and generated a modest rate of return on your real estate investments, you could have over a million dollars tax-free when you retire. After reaching the age of fifty-nine and a half, if you have had the Roth Solo 401(k) plan open for at least five years, all income and gains from your Roth Solo 401(k) plan can be used tax-free and penalty-free. You can also pass the Roth Solo 401(k) plan funds to your spouse or children upon your death, allowing them to use the Roth funds for any purpose without paying tax.

Advantages of Buying Real Estate with a Roth Solo 401(k) Plan

Here are some of the advantages of buying real estate with a Roth Solo 401(k) plan:

POWER OF TAX-FREE INVESTING

One of the main attractions of the self-directed Roth Solo 401(k) plan is the fact that qualified distributions of Roth earnings are tax-free. As long as certain conditions are met and the distribution is a qualified distribution, the Roth Solo 401(k) plan participant will never pay tax on any Roth distributions received. The advantage of contributing to a Roth Solo 401(k) plan is that income and gains generated by the Roth 401(k) investments can be tax-free and penalty-free so long as certain requirements are satisfied. Unlike with a pretax Solo 401(k) plan contributions, contributions to a Roth Solo 401(k) are not tax deductible.

The power of tax-free investing can be best illustrated by way of the following examples:

- **Example 1:** Joe, a self-employed consultant, began funding a Roth Solo 401(k) plan with $3,000 per year at age twenty and plans to continue through age sixty-five. At age sixty-five, Joe will wind up with $2,500,000 at retirement (assuming a long-run annual compound growth rate in stocks, which was 9.88 percent from 1926 to 2011). Not a bad result for investing only $3,000 a year.
- **Example 2:** Ben, a self-employed real estate agent who is thirty years old, began funding a Roth Solo 401(k) plan with $8,000 and wanted to know how much he would have at age seventy if he continued to make $8,000 in annual contributions and was able to earn an 8 percent rate of return. Ben did some research and was astonished to learn that at age seventy he would have a whopping $2,238,248 tax-free, which he could then live off or pass to his wife or children tax-free.
- **Example 3:** Mary, a self-employed real estate investor who is thirty-five years old, began funding a Roth Solo 401(k) plan with $13,000 and wanted to know how much she would have at age seventy if she continued to make $13,000 annual contributions and was able to earn a 10 percent rate of return. She felt this was

possible based on her past real estate investment returns. Mary did some research and was amazed that at age seventy she would accrue $3,875,649 tax-free, which she could then live off or pass to her husband and children tax-free.

It's difficult for many people to comprehend that putting away just a few thousand dollars a year in a Roth Solo 401(k) plan can leave them with millions of dollars tax-free. But it's simple. Just make annual contributions to a Roth Solo 401(k) plan and then generate tax-free returns through real estate or other investments with a Solo 401(k) plan.

High Roth Contributions

A Roth Solo 401(k) combines features of the traditional 401(k) with those of the Roth IRA. Like a Solo 401(k) plan, the Roth Solo 401(k) plan is perfect for any self-employed individual or small business owner with no employees. The Roth Solo 401(k) plan contains the same advantages of a Solo 401(k) plan, but as with a Roth IRA, contributions are made with after-tax dollars. While you don't get an upfront tax deduction, the Roth 401(k) account grows tax-free, and withdrawals taken during retirement aren't subject to income tax provided you're at least fifty-nine and a half, and you've held the account for five years or more.

For the 2017 taxable year, an individual under the age of fifty can make a Roth Solo 401(k) plan contributions of up to $18,000. Whereas an individual over the age of fifty can make Roth Solo 401(k) plan contributions of up to $24,000 for the 2017 taxable year. As for the employer profit-sharing contributions, the employer may make contributions equal to 25 percent (20 percent in the case of a sole proprietorship of single-member LLC) of the plan participant's W-2 or self-employment income amount up to $54,000 ($60,000 for individuals over the age of fifty), including any employee deferrals made by the employee during the year.

The employer profit-sharing contributions must be made in pretax dollars, but as of 2013, those employer contributions can be converted immediately to Roth so long as the Solo 401(k) plan allows for in-plan Roth conversions. A tax would be required to be paid on the Roth conversion amount, but one would technically be able to make Roth contributions of up to $54,000 ($60,000 if over the age of fifty) for the 2017 taxable year, almost ten times the amount of an IRA.

Invest in What You Know and Understand

Most people mistakenly believe that their retirement funds must be invested in bank CDs, the stock market, or mutual funds. Few investors realize that the IRS has always permitted real estate to be purchased with retirement funds.

Investments in real estate with a Solo 401(k) are fully permissible by the IRS—it is even stated right on the IRS website. With a Roth 401(k) plan or Roth 401(k) plan subaccount, you can invest your Roth 401(k) plan funds in real estate, precious metals, tax liens, private business investments, and much more tax-free!

Unlike with a pretax 401(k) plan, with a Roth 401(k) account all income and gains flow back tax-free to your account. As long as you have reached the age of fifty-nine and a half, and have had the Roth 401(k) account opened at least five years, you can take your Roth 401(k) plan distributions tax-free. In other words, you can live off your Roth 401(k) plan assets or income tax-free. With federal income tax rates expected to increase, the ability to have a tax-free source of income upon retirement may be the difference between retiring early or not.

There are several key reasons why real estate has become one of the most popular nontraditional investment options for Solo 401(k) plan investors. The first is that real estate offers diversification from overexposure to Wall Street from both personal and retirement funds. After the 2008 financial crisis, many retirement investors began to appreciate the importance of having a well-balanced and diversified retirement portfolio that can help protect against another financial crisis. The second is that people tend to like to invest in something they know and understand. Real estate has fast become an asset class that more and more Americans have confidence in and have a greater comfort level with than trying to guess why stocks go up or down. The third is real estate is a hard asset you can touch and seem and therefore offers a level of confidence against any potential US inflation.

Buying hard assets such as real estate is seen as a solid way of protecting retirement assets from the threat of inflation. These advantages, coupled with the fact that all income and gains from real estate owned in a Roth Solo 401(k) plan are exempt from tax, makes real estate an attractive option for retirement investors.

Loan Feature

While an IRA offers no participant loan feature, the Roth Solo 401(k) allows participants to borrow up to $50,000 or 50 percent of their account value, (whichever is less) for any purpose at a low interest rate. (The lowest interest rate is Prime, which was 3.75 percent as of December 31, 2016). This offers a Roth Solo 401(k) plan participant the ability to access up to $50,000 for any purpose, including paying personal debt or funding a business. The Roth Solo 401(k) plan loan feature can also help a real estate investor fund personal real estate projects with up to $50,000 of retirement funds. This is especially attractive to real estate investors facing an unfavorable lending environment.

Use Leverage without Tax

When an IRA buys real estate that is leveraged with mortgage financing, it creates UDFI, a type of UBTI on which taxes must be paid. The maximum UBTI tax rate is close to 40 percent. Whereas with a Roth Solo 401(k) plan, you can use leverage without being subject to the UDFI rules and UBTI tax. This exemption provides significant tax advantages for using a Roth Solo 401(k) plan versus an IRA to purchase real estate. In other words, with a Roth Solo 401(k) plan, you can turbocharge your returns by using nonrecourse leverage to increase your real estate investment amount and generate tax-free returns without paying any UBTI tax.

Using the Roth feature of the Solo 401(k) plan is a really exciting way to generate tax-free wealth for you and your family. It also allows you to invest in what you know and understand. You must still be mindful of the prohibited-transaction rules and the potential application of the UBTI tax regime. Nevertheless, those advantages make a Solo 401(k) plan very attractive.

Bigger, Stronger, Faster

By reading this chapter, I hope that you see how much advantage you can gain by growing your retirement assets using a Solo 401(k). Rules exist, but in general, you have more independence and latitude in making your retirement investments. You can rely on your own experience and interests to make your decisions, and you have the freedom and flexibility to make those decisions when they suit you. And because of the tax advantages of the Solo 401(k), you can grow your assets much faster than you could in a traditional retirement account.

It's always important to consult a retirement or tax expert, but the pathway to becoming rich in retirement using a Solo 401(k) is wide open and smooth. In the next chapter, we'll look at some finer details that have to do with administering your Solo 401(k), including how and when you can get access to your plan funds.

CHAPTER 8

Administering Your Solo 401(k) Plan

One of the great features of the Solo 401(k) is that you can manage and administer it independently, without confusion. There are times when it helps to get the advice or assistance of a retirement account or tax expert, but even in those moments, you will know what is going on and be in control.

In this chapter, we're going to look closely at two moments that are important in managing your Solo 401(k) successfully. Specifically, these involve how to administer your Solo 401(k) and how to take distributions and access your retirement wealth.

It's EZ to Administer Your Solo 401(k)

In general, your Solo 401(k) plan is easy to operate. There are no annual filing requirements unless the fair market value of your Solo 401(k) assets exceeds $250,000 as of December 31 of the previous year. In other words, if your plan assets are less than $250,000 as of December 31 of the previous year, you have *no* filing requirements with the IRS with respect to your Solo 401(k). This sounds almost too good to be true, but it is.

The $250,000 Threshold

To determine whether your plan asset values equal $250,000, you will need to include the amount of cash and the fair market value of any assets owned by your plan as of December 31 of the previous year. In the case of real estate or other hard assets, it is good practice to have an independent party value the property in order to come up with an accurate value of the asset.

For most plan participants, attaining the value of your plan account as of December 31 is as simple as checking your online account or written account statement. But for plan participants who have made nontraditional investments, such as real estate, determining the value of the asset is somewhat more time consuming. If the value of your plan assets are close to the $250,000 threshold, it is good practice to file the Form 5500-EZ, as it is simply an information return and not a tax return, and there is really no downside to not filing.

Some people fear that filing Form 5500-EZ will put your plan on a direct path to an IRS audit. I've never seen evidence of that, and assuming you have an IRS letter of determination validating the legality of your plan and that you have not engaged in any IR prohibited transactions or violated the rules of the plan, you have nothing to worry about. If those total retirement assets exceed $250,000, you will need to file this short information return with the IRS.

This is one of the features that make the Solo 401(k) plan such an attractive retirement vehicle. In contrast, an ERISA 401(k) plan requires the adopting employer to comply with a set of complex testing and compliance rules. This includes a more detailed and comprehensive annual plan information return IRS Form 5500, which generally requires the services of a CPA or tax professional to complete and file.

With a Solo 401(k) plan, Form 5500-EZ is actually easy. The IRS really got it right and stayed in line with the spirit of a retirement plan for the self-employed that is easy to operate and administer. Most Solo 401(k) plan holders complete and file the IRS Form 5500-EZ on their own. It is, however, a good idea to have a tax professional review the form. To see an explanation of how to complete IRS Form 5500-EZ, please see Appendix F.

The IRS Form 5500-EZ is due on July 31 and is filed in paper form. For example, for a plan that was established in the previous year, 5500-EZ is due by July 31 of the following year. If you established your plan this year, then you would not need to file until next year. You should be aware that the IRS imposes a penalty of $25 a day (up to $150,000) for late or incorrect filings. You are permitted to seek an extension of three months when filing 5500-EZ, which would make your due date October 15. To file for an extension, you need to complete and file IRS Form 5558.

When Can I Get Access to My 401(k) Plan Funds?

There are only a few established ways to take money out of a Solo 401(k) plan. The most common method is via a distribution. "Distribution" is essentially a term for taking funds from a retirement account and turning tax-exempt funds into personal funds that are no longer exempt from tax. There are many different reasons for talking a distribution from your 401(k) plan before being required to do at age seventy and a half via the required minimum distribution rules, but most revolve around the ability to use the funds for personal purposes, such as for paying expenses. (Also, remember that you can use the loan feature as another way to take money out of your plan. Unlike with a distribution, there is no tax or penalty on your loan.)

While not ideal, taking a distribution from your 401(k) plan can be a big help if you need a bunch of cash right away. There are a two main negatives for taking a distribution: you will forfeit the benefits of tax-deferred compounding by cashing out the tax-deferred amount and you'll have to pay income taxes on your distribution for the tax year in which you take it out. In some cases, you'll also incur a 10 percent penalty, which can significantly cut into the amount you would be able to use.

For the most part, you may not take a distribution from your Solo 401(k) plan until a certain event occurs, often called a "triggering event." The actions that trigger a distribution under a Solo 401(k) plan will change depending on the type of plan documents you have adopted. Typically, distributions of elective deferrals cannot be made until one of the following occurs:

- You reach age fifty-nine and a half.
- The plan terminates and you do not establish or maintain a successor defined contribution plan.
- You have a severance of employment.
- You become disabled.
- You die.
- You incur a financial hardship.

Depending on the terms of the plan, distributions may be:

- Nonperiodic, such as lump-sum distributions
- Periodic, such as annuity or installment payments

Plan Termination

Plan retirement age ranges between fifty-nine and a half and sixty-five. Your Solo 401(k) plan documents (specifically, your plan adoption agreement and plan summary description document) will define the "normal retirement age" for your plan.

If your Solo 401(k) plan terminates, your plan documents will likely allow you to request distributions from your plan: in other words, the ability to roll over the retirement funds to an IRA or another 401(k) plan. In addition, most Solo 401(k) plans allow a plan participant who has left his or her job with the employer who adopted the plan the ability to receive distributions of the plan's vested account balance. Since in the case of a Solo 401(k) plan, the plan participant and plan owner are generally the same person, this means that if you close or sell your business or stop working, a triggering event occurs that allows you to access the plan funds through distribution.

Disability

You may also begin receiving distributions from your Solo 401(k) plan if you become disabled. It would be up to the plan participant to prove that he or she is disabled by providing supporting medical documentation to the plan administrator.

Death

Of course, all 401(k) plans allow the beneficiaries of a plan participant to begin receiving distributions upon that participant's death. It is common to name your spouse as your primary Solo 401(k) plan beneficiary unless he or she consents to the naming of another beneficiary.

Hardship Distributions

Your Solo 401(k) plan may also provide for hardship distributions if you have an immediate and heavy financial need. This need is determined based on all relevant facts and circumstances. Indeed, your financial need may be considered immediate and heavy by the IRS even if it was reasonably foreseeable or due to your own choices and decisions. Specifically, the IRS regulations consider the following to be financial hardships:

- Expenses for your medical care or the medical care of your spouse or dependents
- Costs directly related to the purchase of your principal residence (but not your mortgage payments)
- Tuition, related educational fees, and room and board expenses for the next twelve months of postsecondary education for you, your spouse, your children, or your dependents
- Payments necessary to prevent your eviction from your principal residence or foreclosure on your mortgage on that residence
- Funeral expenses
- Certain expenses relating to the repair of damage to your principal residence

Hardship distributions from a 401(k) plan are generally relegated to the amount of your elective deferrals and generally do not include any income earned on the deferred amounts. However, a plan can permit employer matching contributions and employer discretionary contributions to be included in hardship distributions. Hardship distributions cannot be rolled over to another plan or IRA. According to the IRS, a distribution is treated as a hardship distribution only if it is made on account of the hardship to satisfy the immediate and heavy financial need of the employee.

Hardship distributions are a permanent reduction of an account balance and cannot be repaid. They can have a significant impact on a plan participant's retirement account balance.

Immediate and Heavy Financial Need

You are not permitted to obtain a distribution, however, that exceeds the amount needed to relieve your immediate and heavy financial need. In addition, you are not allowed a distribution if your financial hardship need can be filled by other resources that are reasonably available to you, including:

- Your spouse's assets and any available assets of your children if they are minors
- Resources that could be obtained through reimbursement or compensation by insurance
- By liquidating your assets
- By ceasing to make elective contributions to your plan
- By other distributions or nontaxable loans from your plan
- By borrowing from commercial sources on reasonable terms in an amount sufficient to satisfy the need

After you have elected to take a hardship distribution from your Solo 401(k) plan, you are prohibited from making contributions to your plan and other retirement plans for at least six months after receiving your hardship distribution.

Hardship distributions are includible in gross income unless they consist of designated Roth contributions. They may also be subject to an additional tax on early distributions of elective contributions. Unlike loans, hardship distributions are not repaid to the plan. Thus, a hardship distribution permanently reduces your Solo 401(k) account balance.

To determine whether a hardship distribution is appropriate, the IRS looks at all relevant facts and circumstances. The place to start, of course, is your personal resources. However, your retirement assets are relevant in making an overall determination. Your resources are deemed to include the assets of your spouse and minor children when they are reasonably available to you. Thus, for example, a second home—whether owned by you or your spouse as community property, joint tenants, tenants by the entirety, or tenants in common—generally will be deemed a resource. Interestingly, the amount of an immediate and heavy financial need may include any amounts necessary to pay any federal, state, or local income taxes or penalties reasonably anticipated to result from the distribution.

An immediate and heavy financial need is a hardship that is generally not able to be relieved from other resources reasonably available to the plan participant:

- Through reimbursement or compensation by insurance or otherwise
- By liquidation of the employee's assets
- By cessation of elective contributions or employee contributions under the plan
- By other distributions or nontaxable (at the time of the loan) loans from plans maintained by the employer or by any other employer, or by borrowing from commercial sources on reasonable commercial terms in an amount sufficient to satisfy the need

According to the IRS, a distribution is deemed necessary to satisfy an immediate and heavy financial need if all of the following requirements are satisfied:

- The distribution is not in excess of the amount of your immediate and heavy financial need.
- You have obtained all distributions, other than hardship distributions, and all nontaxable (at the time of the loan) loans currently available under all your plans.
- You are prohibited, under the terms of the plan or an otherwise legally enforceable agreement, from making elective contributions and employee contributions to your plan and all other plans for at least six months after receipt of the hardship distribution.

Other Ways to Take a Distribution

Even if no triggering event has occurred, there may be other ways you can take money out of your Solo 401(k) plan as a distribution. These are often referred to as in-service distributions.

In general, there has to be a triggering event in order for you to get access to your retirement funds prior to the age of fifty-nine and a half. There is one major exception to this rule, and that is the in-service distribution option. An in-service distribution is when a participant, who is still employed by the plan sponsor, is allowed to take a distribution from the plan.

In-service withdrawals from 401(k) plans carry very specific restrictions. Only employer contributions are eligible for in-service distributions and not employee deferrals. What that means is that any employee deferral contributions made by the plan participant to the plan are not eligible for in-service distributions and are subject to the triggering rules described above. Only employer profit-sharing contributions can be used for an in-service distribution. The in-service distribution gets you access to your funds prior to turning fifty-nine and a half but will still require you to pay tax and penalty on the amount of the distribution.

In order to be eligible to take an in-service distribution of profit-sharing funds, your plan documents must allow for them. Even if the plan documents allow for in-service distributions, they will generally put restrictions on when the in-service distribution can be made. This could be the plan's normal retirement age, an early retirement age, or any age. It could also be after a fixed period of time. However, the contribution must be at least two years old or the account must be at least five years old.

Remember, if you are over fifty-nine and a half or can satisfy one of the triggering events, you will not need to worry about the in-plan service distribution rules, as you will have the ability to take a distribution of vested funds from the plan.

How Do I Take a Distribution?

Depending on the terms of your plan, the distributions you take may be "nonperiodic" lump-sum distributions or "periodic" distributions such as annuity or installment payments.

Specifically, if a distribution in excess of $1,000 is made and you (or your designated beneficiary) have waived the "Qualified Joint and Survivor Annuity" option, you may receive the funds as:

- A lump-sum payment
- A partial payment
- Installments payments not to exceed your life expectancy or the joint and last survivor life expectancy of you and your designated beneficiary
- By applying the distribution to a purchase of an annuity contract. Note that most Solo 401(k) plans do not require that plan distributions take the form of a life annuity or joint and survivor annuity as required under the Retirement Equity Act (REA) of 1984.

So what are the main differences between the different distribution options?

Lump-Sum Payment

First, let's talk about lump-sum distributions. These are the most popular distribution for most participants and they generally make the most sense. When most people retire or leave their employer, they want to receive all of their retirement funds in one large lump sum so that they can roll those funds into another retirement account, such an IRA, or take the money and live off it.

In a Solo 401(k) plan, a lump-sum payment is easily determined. It's the value of your vested account balance. A lump-sum distribution payment is taxable as ordinary income in the year it's received unless some of the contributions and earnings are because of Roth contributions. A lump sum is subject to the 20 percent federal income tax withholding.

Periodic Payments

If you're pleased with your 401(k) plan investment returns and don't want to switch investments or use a new financial institution for the rollover IRA investment, you may be able to receive a regular stream of income from your 401(k). Typically, most plans let you select an amount to receive monthly or quarterly, and you're allowed to change that amount once a year, although some plans allow you to do so far more frequently.

Installment Payments

An installment-payment distribution method is a periodic payment made for a specified period of time: for example, seven or ten years. Installment payments are not guaranteed for your lifetime, but instead your account balance is distributed in a number of periodic payments. When these payments are complete, you will have received your entire account balance and no more installment payments will be made.

Reporting a Distribution from Your Solo 401(k) Plan

In addition to reporting the amount of the distribution your personal federal income tax return (IRS Form 1040), the Solo 401(k) plan administrator will be required to complete and file with the IRS Form 1099-R. A copy form 1099-R will also be sent to the plan participant who took the distribution, which in the case of a Solo 401(k) plan is likely the same person as the plan administrator. The purpose of the 1099-R is to disclose to the IRS the amount of the distribution taken from the Solo 401(k) plan so that the IRS can verify that the amount is properly reported on the individual's personal tax return. An example of a completed 1099-R Form reporting a taxable distribution from a 401(k) plan can be found in Appendix J.

Required Minimum Distributions (RMDs)

Unfortunately, you can't keep your retirement funds in your account indefinitely. The required minimum distribution (RMD) rules are in place to stop you from accumulating wealth without tax. Just like the estate tax, the RMD rules are seen as a way of preventing wealth inequality, which could impact the overall economy. From the IRS's position, it would cause a major burden on the operation of the government if individuals were able to receive a tax deduction when making an IRA or 401(k) plan contribution, providing him or her with an immediate tax benefit as well as gaining the ability to generate tax-deferred growth for an unlimited period time.

Therefore, it is only fair that the period of tax-deferred growth be capped at some point and require you to pay tax on a percentage of the income that has grown tax deferred each year. Without the RMD rules, too much wealth would be concentrated in tax-exempt accounts, making it very difficult for the government to operate and offer the necessary services that our society needs and expects.

Generally, you have to start taking withdrawals from your retirement plan account when you reach age seventy and a half. For a Solo 401(k) plan, the RMD amount for a plan participant is equal to the plan account balance as of the last valuation date in the calendar year immediately preceding a year for which an RMD is due. However, if you are a participant in a 401(k) qualified retirement plan and are not a 5% or greater owner of the company sponsoring the plan, then you might be able to delay taking your distribution until you retire (even if you retire after age 701/2). Unfortunately, in the case of a Solo 401(k) Plan, the plan participant is generally more than a 5% owner of the company adopting the plan so this exception to the RMD rules is generally not applicable.

The required distribution rules apply only to your Solo 401(k) plan. In other words, you cannot satisfy your required minimum distribution by making a distribution from another plan. These rules are different than the rules that apply to satisfying RMD payments for an IRA. In the case of an IRA, the total RMD amount is calculated and can be satisfied from any IRA account.

For example, if you have three IRAs, each with a value of $30,000, and the annual RMD amount is $4,000, you can satisfy the RMD payment from any of the three IRA accounts and in any percentage. Your plan document ensures that these rules override any inconsistent distribution options available to you previously. As the plan administrator, you must determine the minimum amount required to be distributed each calendar year. You can obtain information to help you calculate the minimum distribution amount in IRS Publication 575, *Pension and Annuity Income.*

The "beginning date" for your required minimum distribution is April 1 of the first year after whichever of the following events is latest:

- The calendar year in which you reach age seventy and a half
- The calendar year in which you retire
- If you reach age seventy and a half on the date that is six calendar months after your seventieth birthday

For example, say you are retired and your seventieth birthday was June 30, 2013. You reached age seventy and a half on December 30, 2013. Turning seventy and a half was the later event, so you must take your first required minimum distribution (for 2013) by April 1, 2014.

In contrast, say you are retired and your seventieth birthday was July 1, 2013. Since you did not reach age seventy and a half until January 1, 2014, you do not have a required minimum distribution for 2013. You must therefore take your first required minimum distribution (for 2014) by April 1, 2015.

Even so, your plan may require that you begin receiving distributions by April 1 of the year after you reach age seventy and a half, even if you are not retired. Additional information to help determine your required beginning date is included in IR Publication 575.

Distributions after the Starting Year

The distribution required to be made by April 1 is treated as a distribution for the starting year. (The starting year is the year in which you reach age seventy and a half or retire, whichever applies.) After the starting year, you must receive your required distribution for each year by December 31 of that year. If no distribution is made in the starting year, two-year's worth of required distributions must be made in the next year (one by April 1 and one by December 31). (Publication 575 also includes information regarding the special rules covering distributions made after your death.)

Calculating Your Required Minimum Distribution

Your required minimum distribution is the minimum amount you must withdraw from your account each year. You can withdraw more than the minimum required amount. Your withdrawals will be included in your taxable income except for any part that was taxed before (your basis) or that can be received tax-free (such as qualified distributions from designated Roth accounts).

To determine your required minimum distribution for any year, take the account balance as of the end of the immediately preceding calendar year and divide it by a distribution period from the IRS's "Uniform Lifetime Table." The distribution period is based on IRS life expectancy tables—essentially the maximum number of years over which an individual is required to take distributions from his or her account. During an individual's lifetime, the RMD regulations provide that the distribution period for nearly all individuals is determined using the Uniform Lifetime Table, which can be found in the IRS Treasury Regulations. A copy of the Uniform Lifetime Table for 2016 can be found in Appendix G. A separate table is used if the sole beneficiary is your spouse who is ten or more years younger than you.

Examples of RMD Rules in Action

- Bill turned seventy on April 10, 2013, and had $140,000 in his plan as of December 31, 2013. Bill would be required to take an RMD of $5,109.49 by April 1, 2014. This is based on a withdrawal factor of 27.4 as per the IRS Uniform Lifetime Table.
- Jim turned seventy-two in 2013 and had $100,000 in his Solo 401(k) plan account. Jim would be required to take an RMD of $3,906.25 by December 31, 2014. This is based on a withdrawal factor of 25.6 as per the IRS Uniform Lifetime Table.
- Ben turned eighty-five in 2013 and had $40,000 in his Solo 401(k) plan account as of December 31 of that year. Ben would be required to take an RMD of $2,702.70 by December 31, 2014. This is based on a withdrawal factor of 14.8 as per the IRS Uniform Lifetime Table.

If you do not take any distributions, or if the distributions are not large enough, you may have to pay a 50 percent excise tax on the amount not distributed as required. To report the excise tax, you may have to file

Form 5329, *Additional Taxes on Qualified Plans (Including IRAs) and Other Tax-Favored Accounts.*

Required minimum distributions continue for your beneficiaries after you die. For the year of your death, your beneficiaries will take the same required minimum distribution that you would have received. For each year thereafter, the required minimum distribution will depend on the identity of your beneficiary and their individual circumstances.

Beneficiaries will calculate their required minimum distribution using the Single Life Table: Table I, Publication 590, *Individual Retirement Arrangements (IRAs).* To view a copy of the Single Life Table, please see Appendix H. The table shows a life expectancy based on your beneficiary's age. The account balance is divided by this life expectancy to determine your beneficiary's required minimum distribution.

Spouse Beneficiary and the RMD Rules

In order to determine how the RMD rules work in the case of the death of a plan participant, you must examine the makeup of the primary beneficiary. In other words, is the primary beneficiary of the Solo 401(k) plan account a spouse or nonspouse?

In the case of a spouse who is the sole designated beneficiary of the Solo 401(k) plan, he or she can:

- Treat an plan account as his or her own
- Base the RMDs on his or her own current age,
- Base RMDs on the decedent's age at death, reducing the distribution period by one each year
- Withdraw the entire account balance by the end of the fifth year following the account owner's death, if the account owner died before the required beginning date

When a Solo 401(k) plan participant dies before the required beginning date (prior to turning seventy and a half), the surviving spouse can wait until the owner would have turned seventy and a half to begin receiving RMDs or he or she could move the account into an IRA in his or her name if he or she was younger than the deceased spouse in order to prolong the requirement to take RMDs.

Since a Solo 401(k) plan is generally adopted by a sole proprietorship or small business with one owner, when the owner dies, the spouse beneficiary of the plan typically moves the funds to an IRA in his or her name. In a case where the deceased was over the age of seventy and a half, the designated beneficiary would need to continue to take RMDS from the Solo 401(k) plan account in the year of death but would then be able to move the funds to an IRA in his or her name where he or she would become subject to the IRA RMD rules.

Nonspouse Beneficiary and the RMD Rules

For a nonspouse who has been appointed beneficiary of a Solo 401(k) plan account from a deceased nonspouse, the IRS sets forth a number of options that the nonspouse can use to determine the amount of RMDs that must be taken.

- **Five-year rule:** Here, you would withdraw the entire account balance by the end of the fifth year following the account owner's death if the account owner died before the required beginning date.
- **Life-expectancy payments:** A nonspouse would be required to calculate the RMD amount using the single life expectancy of the oldest designated beneficiary in the year following the year of the plan participant's death:
    - If the Solo 401(k) plan participant died after RMDs began, it would revert to the longer of the:
        - Beneficiary's remaining life expectancy determined in the year following the year of the owner's death reduced by one for each subsequent year
        - Owner's remaining life expectancy at death, reduced by one for each subsequent year

- If the account owner died before RMDs began, the beneficiary's age at year's end following the year of the owner's death, reducing the distribution period by one for each subsequent year

Under the life expectancy payments option, RMD payments must begin by December 31 of the following year. Upon the death of a plan participant, a nonspouse beneficiary will directly roll over the plan account assets into an inherited IRA in almost all cases.

In the case of a Solo 401(k) plan, you would report an RMD distribution to the IRS using IRS Form 1099-R. An example of a completed 1099-R Form reporting a RMD can be found in Appendix I. As you will soon see, there is no withholding on RMD distributions. Of course, additionally you would report the RMD amount on your federal income tax return (IRS Form 1040).

Avoiding RMDs with a Roth Solo 401(k) Plan

Like a pre-tax Solo 401(k) Plan, a plan participant over the age of 701/2 must take RMDs from their Roth 401(k) account. This is quite different from the Roth IRA which does not require RMDs. So how could one circumvent the RMDs rules in the case of a Roth Solo 401(k) Plan? Firstly, a 401(k) plan participant with Roth funds that is nearing the age of 70 should start thinking about rolling the Roth 401(k) plan funds into a Roth IRA.

In general, one is able to roll retirement funds out of a 401(k) plan after reaching the age of 59½. The key is making sure that Roth 401(k) plan rollover to a Roth IRA is done prior to the plan participant reaching the age of 70. For example, if you have a Roth 401(k) Plan and are going to reach the age of 70 in 2017, you want to make sure that you have rolled the Roth 401(k) plan funds into a Roth IRA prior to December 31, 2016. The reason for this is that the RMD amount is based off the value of the retirement account as of 12/31 of the prior year. So if you left the Roth 401(k) plan funds in the 401(k) plan and rolled the funds into a Roth IRA in 2016, because there was a balance in the Roth 401(k) plan as of 12/31/2016, an RMD would be due from the Roth 401(k) plan in 2016. Going forward, after the Roth 401(k) plan participant reaches the age of 701/2; he or she can simply roll the Roth 401(k) funds into a Roth IRA and make sure that the Roth 401(k) plan balance is zero as of 12/31.

The fact that a Roth IRA holder is not required to take RMDs when reaching the age of 701/2 offers Roth 401(k) plan participants a convenient way to circumvent the Roth 401(k) plan RMD rules and allow their Roth funds to keep growing tax-free. The key is making sure that the initial rollover to a Roth IRA is done prior to 12/31 of the year before the Roth 401(k) plan participant reaches the age of 701/2 as well as making sure that in all subsequent years, the balance of the Roth 401(k) plan is zero as of December 31.

It is important to keep in mind that a Roth IRA has a separate five year clock from the 401(k) plan for purposes of satisfying the Roth qualified distribution rules. Therefore, if one has not established a Roth IRA prior to the rollover, that individual would be required to keep the rollover funds in the Roth IRA for five additional years before the Roth IRA funds can be distributed tax-free.

Alternatives to Taking a Distribution from a Solo 401(k) Plan

In general, the only way to take funds out of your Solo 401(k) plan is to take a distribution, which is generally subject to tax and potentially an early distribution penalty if you are under the age of fifty-nine and a half, and there is no hardship. However, there is one way you can take money out of the plan without tax or penalty, and that is the Solo 401(k) plan loan feature. This exception to the distribution rules applies only to 401(k) plans and not IRAs. Even better, there is no need for any triggering event or age requirement. As long as the plan documents include the loan option and it has been adopted as part of the plan, you can use the loan feature to pull money out of your Solo 401(k) plan without a triggering event and without any tax or penalty.

Loans

As discussed in Chapter 5, some Solo 401(k) plans permit you to borrow from your plan. The plan document must specify if loans are permitted. A loan from your Solo 401(k) plan is not taxable if it meets certain criteria.

Generally, if permitted by the plan, you may borrow up to 50 percent of your vested account balance up to a maximum of $50,000. The loan must be repaid within five years, unless the loan is used to buy your main home. The loan repayments must be made in substantially level payments, at least quarterly, over the life of the loan.

The Solo 401(k) plan loan feature is a great vehicle for getting access to retirement funds without paying tax or penalty. This is especially true if you are under the age of fifty-nine and a half, and don't qualify for any of the hardship distribution exceptions. In addition to getting access to your Solo 401(k) plan funds, using the loan feature will also allow you to grow your retirement account since the interest you pay back on the loan will go back to the plan.

Taxes on Early Distributions

The first thing to remember is that you need a plan triggering event before taking an early distribution from a 401(k) Plan so early distributions are not very common in a 401(k) Plan. In general, the only way a plan participant can get access to their 401(k) funds before the age of 59½ is to terminate employment or the company terminates the plan creating a triggering event. Taking an early distribution from a 401(k) plan does not make a lot of sense because of the 20% withholding tax. One would be better off rolling the funds to a Roth IRA and then taking a distribution from a Roth IRA which does not impose a withholding tax. Also, many 401(k) plans contain a loan provision that is generally more tax efficient than taking an early distribution.

Although taking a taxable distribution can give you access to the savings in your retirement plan, there are several things to consider when taking a lump-sum distribution. First, state and federal income taxes will take a "bite" out of your distribution. When you were making contributions to your Solo 401(k), you most likely did so with pretax dollars. In addition, employer contributions to a qualified plan on your behalf were also tax deferred. Upon distribution, you have to pay current income taxes on all pretax contributions and earnings.

There is a 20 percent mandatory federal income withholding tax that is applied to taxable distributions. If you elect to receive a check directly from your employer, you will only receive 80 percent of your distribution. In essence, if you expect to receive a check for $200,000, your employer will withhold 20 percent, or $40,000, and send you a check for $160,000.

If a distribution is made before you reach age fifty-nine and a half, you may be liable for a 10 percent additional tax on the distribution. This tax applies to the amount received that an employee must include in income.

There are exceptions. The 10 percent tax will *not* apply if distributions before age fifty-nine and a half are made in any of the following circumstances:

- Made to a beneficiary (or to your estate) on or after your death
- Made because you have a qualifying disability
- Made as part of a series of substantially equal periodic payments beginning after separation from service (termination of employment), and made at least annually for your life or life expectancy or the joint lives or life expectancies of you and your designated beneficiary (the payments under this exception, unless death or disability come into play, must continue for at least five years or until you reach age fifty-nine and a half, whichever is the longer period)
- Made to you after separation from service if the separation occurred during or after the calendar year in which you reached age fifty-five
- Made to an alternate payee under a "qualified domestic relations order" (QDRO)

- Made to you for medical care up to the amount allowable as a medical expense deduction (determined without regard to whether you itemize deductions)
- Timely made to reduce excess contributions
- Timely made to reduce excess employee or matching employer contributions
- Timely made to reduce excess elective deferrals
- Made because of an IRS levy on your Solo 401(k) plan
- Made on account of certain disaster for which IRS relief has been granted

Interestingly, unlike an IRA, there is no exception to the 10% early distribution penalty for a 401(k) plan for: (i) qualified first-time homebuyers, up to $10,000, (ii) qualified higher education expenses, and (iii) health insurance premiums paid while unemployed.

To discourage the use of retirement funds for purposes other than normal retirement, the law imposes a 10 percent additional tax on certain early distributions from some retirement plans. The additional tax is equal to 10 percent of the portion of the distribution that is includable in income. Generally, early distributions are those you receive from a qualified retirement plan or deferred annuity contract before reaching age fifty-nine and a half.

In the case of a Roth 401(k) account, distributions from a Roth 401(k) account that are not qualified may be subject to income tax and an additional 10% early-distribution penalty. A qualified distribution from a designated Roth account is not included in gross income. A qualified distribution is a distribution from a Roth 401(k) plan that meets both of the following two categories of requirements:

1. It occurs at least five years after the Roth 401(k) participant established and funded his or her first Roth 401(k) account.
2. It is distributed under one of the following circumstances:

- The Roth 401(k) plan participant is at least age 59½ when the distribution occurs.
- The Roth 401(k) holder becomes disabled before the distribution.
- The beneficiary of the Roth 401(k) plan participant receives the assets after the participant's death.

In the case of a Roth Solo 401(k) Plan distribution that is not qualified, the following chart summarizes the tax implications:

Roth 401(k) Distribution Scenario	**Taxation**
Under 59½ and Roth 401(k) account opened and funded less than 5 years	Income Tax and 10% penalty calculated on a pro rata basis between contributions and earnings
Under 59½ and Roth 401(k) account open and funded more than 5 years	Income Tax and 10% penalty calculated on a pro rata basis between contributions and earnings
Over 59½ and Roth 401(k) account open and funded less than 5 years	Income Tax calculated on a pro rata basis between contributions and earnings
Over 59½ and Roth 401(k) account open and funded more than 5 years	No Tax

In the case of a nonqualified Roth 401(k) distribution, in determining what portion of the distribution is considered to come from contributions as opposed to earnings, each distribution is simply treated on a pro-rata basis. If a Roth 401(k) distribution is a nonqualified distribution:

- The portion of the distribution that represents contributions to the account will be nontaxable (and not subject to the 10% penalty), and
- The portion of the distribution that represents earnings (i.e., growth) will be taxable and potentially subject to the 10% penalty.

This is in contrast to a Roth IRA which uses specific ordering rules to determine the tax treatment of Roth IRA nonqualified distributions,

For example, Jim currently has $20,000 in his Roth 401(k), of which $18,000 is from contributions and $2,000 is from earnings, any distribution will be considered to come 90% from contributions and 10% from earnings — meaning that 90% of the distribution will be nontaxable, and 10% will be taxable and possibly subject to a 10% penalty if Jim is under the age of 59½.

Taking Early Distributions From Funds Converted to a Roth 401(k)

The penalty rules regarding taking early distributions from Roth 401(k) plan conversion funds add a twist. The early withdrawal penalty applies to a distribution of conversion money from a Roth 401(k) assets if the plan participant is under the age of 59½ in a few situations.

1. The distribution is made within the five-tax-year period starting with the year that the conversion was distributed from a pre-tax 401(k) account; <u>and</u>
2. Only to the extent that the distribution is attributable to amounts that were includable in gross income as a result of the conversion.

In general, when thinking about taking early distribution from funds converted to a Roth 401(k) plan, one must consider that there could be a tax implication because of how the source of the Roth distributions are determined.

For example, Bill made a $20,000 conversion from his pre-tax 401(k) account to a Roth 401(k) in 2008. The entire amount converted was includable in Bill's income for 2008. Bill made no additional contributions or conversions to a Roth 401(k) in 2008 or in later years. In 2011, at the age of 65, Bill's 401(k) account was valued at $40,000. Bill withdraws $10,000 from the Roth 401(k). In order to determine what Bill would pay on the Roth 401(k) plan, the following distribution would be used: first, Bill would take the conversion amount (basis) and divide it by the total value of the 401(k) plan. Then Bill would multiply that percentage by the amount of the distribution. Based off our example, 50% of the $10,000 would be basis and 50% would be subject to income tax. Remember, no 10% early distribution penalty would apply because Bill is over the age of 59½.

It is important to remember that just because you made a Roth 401(k) contribution or did an in-plan Roth conversion, you are not able to make tax-free withdrawals from your designated Roth account at any time. Remember the same plan triggering rules that apply to pre-tax elective contributions also apply to designated Roth contributions. If your plan permits distributions from accounts because of hardship, you may choose to receive a hardship distribution from your designated Roth account. The hardship distribution will consist of a pro-rata share of earnings and basis and the earnings portion will be included in gross income unless you have had the designated Roth account for 5 years and are either disabled or over age 59 ½.

How Do You Report an Early Distribution on Your Income Tax Return?

Since taking a distribution of pretax retirement funds prior to the age of fifty-nine and a half is a taxable event and subject to the 10 percent early distribution penalty, the amount of the distribution and 10-percent penalty must be reported on your individual federal income tax return (IRS Form 1040) in the year after the distribution is taken. For example, if the early distribution was taken in 2013, the income must be reported by April 15, 2014. The early distribution penalty must also be reported on IRS Form 5329—Additional Taxes on Qualified Plans (Including IRAs) and Other Tax-Favored Accounts—if the distribution will be taxable.

Distributions from a qualified retirement plan are subject to federal income tax withholding. However, if your distribution is subject to the 10 percent additional tax, your withholding may not be enough.

Withholding Tax Rules

In 1993, Congress passed a mandatory withholding law. The law requires your plan administrator keep 20 percent of all qualified plan distributions to pay federal income tax before distributing the remainder to you. There are, however, some exceptions to the mandatory withholding rule. For example, amounts that are transferred directly from the trustee of your retirement plan to a trustee of another retirement plan or a custodian of an IRA are not subject to withholding (direct rollover).

When taking assets out of your Solo 401(k), the option of withholding comes up in the paperwork. Withholding results from an assumption by your 401(k) administrator and the IRS that you are spending the money. Indirect rollovers—where the 401(k) plan check comes to you—typically require a 20 percent withholding at the time of distribution. After the completed rollover, you have the option of making up the 20 percent withholding amount by adding to the account equal to the withholding amount and getting the withholding back in your tax return.

Also, Roth conversions are not subject to any withholding tax. However, in the case of direct rollovers (custodian-to-custodian), there is no withholding issue. Distributions generate a 1099-R or 1099-I form at the end of each year to account for the distributions to the IRS, including a Roth conversion. An example of a completed 1099-R Form reporting a taxable 401(k) plan distribution can be found in Appendix J.

Do All Distributions Need to Be in Cash?

For a traditional 401(k) plan, funds must be distributed upon the participant's request so long as the participant is eligible to receive a distribution. To initiate that action, a plan participant would complete a distribution request that designates which investments they would like to have liquidated and where the distribution funds should be sent. Distributions can be sent to the employee via a check or through a direct deposit into a bank account.

The Solo 401(k) is similar to most 401(k) plans in that the documents will allow for cash or in-kind distributions to be taken as long as a distribution is permissible. When taking a cash distribution, it is obviously quite simple to determine the value of the amount of the distribution: the value equals the cash amount. However, in-kind distributions—or distributions made in a form other than cash—are occasionally more difficult to calculate. For example, you could take an in-kind distribution in the form of real estate, stock, or IRS-approved metals. In such a case, how should you determine the value of those distributions?

Generally, the amount of the distribution is equal to the amount of the property being taken as a distribution, whether that property is real estate, stocks, gold, or something else. The value of such property needs to be based on a fair market, independent valuation. In the case of publicly traded stocks or securities, such information is readily available. However, it can be challenging to determine the fair market value of assets that aren't liquid or publicly traded such as real estate.

Any valuation you do obtain should be done by a licensed professional, such as a CPA or a real estate appraiser who is knowledgeable about the type of property or asset you are taking as an in-kind distribution. And the value they determine should be as close to the distribution date as possible so as to mitigate any swings in value or questions about accuracy. Such a formal appraisal is necessary because taking a distribution is a taxable event, which will require you to include the amount of the in-kind distribution on your income tax return as taxable income. The IRS will want to see that your valuation has been made by an independent person with proper credentials.

A cash distribution requires tax withholding. In the case of an in-kind distribution of your Solo 401(k) plan property, the IRC states that a plan administrator must satisfy the obligation to withhold on distributions of property other than employer securities, even if this requires selling all or part of the property and distributing the cash remaining after federal income tax is withheld. The IRS does, however, allow you to remit sufficient cash to satisfy the withholding obligation. In other words, you will not need to sell your property in order to pay the withholding taxes on it. You can pay the withholding tax in cash instead.

Making Your Solo 401(k) Work

As someone who develops the full range of retirement plans for many different clients, I can assure you that the Solo 401(k) is easy to administer. Basically, if your combined plan assets are less than $250,000, you do not need to file anything with the IRS. If they are over $250,000, you need to submit one form, which is very easy to complete and file.

Accessing your retirement wealth by taking a distribution is slightly more complicated but still very straightforward. There is nothing wrong with getting an expert to help you follow your plan documents and IRS regulations to the letter. Indeed, we highly recommend it. Getting it right the first time and every time will help you make the best plans for your retirement or the support of your beneficiaries while enabling you to preserve and maximize your retirement wealth. As cost-benefit equations go, this one is a no-brainer.

You've now received all the information you need to plan, create, manage, build, and access your Solo 401(k) retirement wealth. But to help bring everything back into focus, I want to tell you the stories of four people who made it all work—and retired rich in the process!

CHAPTER 9

Making Your Solo 401(k) Plan Happen

UNLESS WE MEET AND DISCUSS your work circumstances and retirement goals in some detail, I'll never know how your dreams for a wealthy and secure future can be realized. But because you are reading this book, I feel I can make a reasonable guess about some of the things that make you tick. Here's what I think:

- You are self-reliant and creative, and used to making things happen independently.
- You work at least part of the time for yourself, with your own small business or sideline, or have plans for doing so, and you appreciate the importance of discipline, organization, and planning, as well as the long-term payoff of steady progress.
- You are not as wealthy as you would like to be when you finish working.

I consult with thousands of people from every imaginable walk of life. And yet in spite of the differences in the careers they have chosen, the work they love to do, the needs they have, and their plans and dreams, they all have some strong characteristics and circumstances in common. Let me lay out five such examples now to give you a better sense of how a Solo 401(k) can support your goals and meet your needs.

Joe, the Hardware Store Owner

Joe is forty-five years old and lives in Wisconsin with his wife, an executive at a health-care company, and their three children. Joe worked for twenty years at a major hardware chain before he decided to become a business owner. Now he is the sole proprietor of Joe's Hardware Store. Joe has no full-time employees other than himself and his wife. While Joe has always been good with his own money, being a business owner has given him extra incentive to be hands-on and decisive.

Before Joe started his own business, he had accumulated $125,000 in his prior employer's 401(k) plan. But he had been frustrated with the performance of those funds, which were heavily invested in stocks and mutual funds. He knows that he'd like to direct his retirement funds in the future into nontraditional investments. In particular, Joe has a nose for real estate investments, and he's done well in that area before. Joe's friend Tim told him that he invested his IRA funds in real estate and he was sure that 401(k) plan funds could be used in the same way. Joe did some research online, and that's how he first learned about the Solo 401(k) plan. Joe was especially intrigued by the fact that this plan allowed him to make high deferral contributions as well as use the plan as a vehicle to make real estate investments.

Joe contacted his accountant and was told that according to the IRS, retirement funds, including 401(k) plan funds, can be invested in real estate. He was also surprised to learn that for 2017, the maximum deductible employee deferral contribution Joe would be eligible to make to his Solo 401(k) plan would be $54,000 since he is under fifty years old. In his first year as a business owner, Joe received a total of $55,000 of compensation from his shop. But he and his wife are actually able to live off her salary as an executive, so Joe would be able to save most of his solo business income tax-free in a Solo 401(k) retirement savings account and apply it to nontraditional real estate investments. This struck Joe as an unbelievable opportunity to take charge of growing his own retirement wealth, and he started looking at real estate opportunities in Wisconsin.

Joe's accountant told Joe that he could choose from a list of real estate options including residential homes, commercial property, apartments, duplexes, condos/townhomes, mobile homes, real estate notes, real estate purchase options, tax liens certificates, and tax deeds. The types of investments that could be made using Solo 401(k) plan funds are generally limited by the plan documents. As long as Joe is working with a self-directed plan document provider and not making a prohibited investment, Joe would be able to use his retirement funds to make a real estate investment on a tax-deferred basis without penalty.

Ready to roll, Joe established a self-directed Solo 401(k) plan using a plan sponsor company he found on the Internet and opened the plan account with a local bank. He titled his Solo 401(k) plan Joe Hardware 401(k) Trust. Joe will serve as trustee and plan administrator of the plan, and his local bank will serve as custodian of the account. He is pleased that, unlike an IRA where the custodian (bank) has annual reporting requirements (Form 5498), in a Solo 401(k) plan all reporting requirements are the responsibility of the plan administrator—not the bank. Moreover, because Joe would have less than $250,000 in his plan account, he would have no filing requirements with the IRS for his plan. Joe then completed a direct rollover form and rolled over his retirement funds tax-free from his previous 401(k) plan to his new Joe Hardware 401(k) plan account.

Joe scanned the market for the types of investments he wanted to make and found a nice foreclosed home in Wisconsin that he could rent out. But since he would be purchasing a home, Joe understood that no disqualified person (i.e., lineal descendants as in parents, grandparents, children, spouse, daughters-in-law, brothers-in-law, and so on) may live in the home or have any direct or indirect involvement with the property.

Joe also saw a duplex that intrigued him, but he could only afford half of the amount, so he knew he would be forced to partner up with a family member (nondisqualified person), friend, or colleague to complete the transaction or secure a nonrecourse loan. Joe decided against purchasing the duplex and decided to buy the foreclosed home instead. He was able to purchase the property for $87,000 and used his 401(k) plan funds to make the purchase in full. He acted as trustee of the plan and signed the purchase agreement. Title to the property was titled in the name of Joe's Solo 401(k) plan. Joe hired a property management company who was able to locate a tenant for the property. The property management company then began depositing rent checks directly into Joe's Solo 401(k) plan account.

Everything went great for a year, but then Joe's plans had an encounter with the bad economy. His business revenues declined significantly when a car plant in his town was suddenly closed and he was in need of a loan to pay off some personal debt. Joe remembered that his Solo 401(k) plan had a loan feature that would allow him to borrow $50,000 or 50 percent of his account value, whichever is less, and use that loan for any purpose, including paying off personal debt. At the time of the loan, the value of Joe's Solo 401(k) plan account was $140,000, so Joe was able to borrow up to $50,000 tax-free and penalty-free. Joe decided to borrow $20,000.

Since this was a loan and not a distribution, Joe understood that he was required to pay back the loan at least quarterly (he decided to pay it back monthly) at the lowest interest rate allowed by the plan documents, which was Prime as per the *Wall Street Journal*. As of the date of the loan, the Prime interest rate was 3.75 percent, so Joe's monthly loan payments on the $20,000 would be $361.60. Joe liked the loan idea because he was able to get access to these funds and use them for personal purposes without having to take a distribution and pay tax and penalty. Plus, he really liked the fact that he would be paying his plan back and not a bank or credit card company. This was especially true when he realized that at the end of the five-year loan, he would have paid $21,696 back to his plan, an increase of $1,696 to his plan overall.

Joe completed the plan loan kit, and as plan administrator of the plan, he approved the loan and wrote himself a check for $20,000. Joe then used the loan to pay off a number of personal and business debts without dipping into the savings account he shared with his wife.

The following year, business started to pick-up and Joe was able to take a salary of $60,000. Joe was eager to start making tax-deferred contributions to the plan. Since he was still under fifty years old, the maximum Joe would be able to defer from his plan would be $54,000 for 2017.

When it comes to making contributions to a Solo 401(k) plan, there are two parts to the process. First, there is the employee deferral portion that allows Joe to make pretax, after-tax, or Roth contributions up to $18,000 in 2017 (an amount that would be increased by $6,000 if Joe was over the age of fifty by way of a catch-up contribution). Second, Joe's business would be entitled to make a profit-sharing contribution based on Joe's self-employment income. In 2017, Joe would be able to make an employee deferral contribution close to 100 percent of his self-employment earnings up to the maximum of $18,000. That amount would be $24,000 if he was fifty or over.

Internal Revenue Code Section 404 states that the amount of employer contributions is limited to 25 percent of the entity's income subject to self-employment tax. Single-member LLCs or Schedule C sole proprietors must do an added calculation starting with earned income to determine their maximum contribution, which in effect brings the maximum 25 percent of compensation limit down to 20 percent of earned income. Thus, since Joe operated his business as a sole proprietorship, Joe's business would be entitled to make a profit-sharing contribution in 2017 equal to approximately 20 percent of $60,000 (the figure is actually based off $55,761.14, which is net of the FICA and self-employment tax Joe would have paid on his self-employment income).

Joe decided to maximize his employee deferral and make an $18,000 employee deferral to the plan. Joe made the pretax employee deferral contribution prior to December 31, even though he could have technically waited until filing his tax return since he operates his business as a sole proprietorship. After speaking with his accountant and analyzing the company's financials after year's end, Joe decided to make a maximum profit-sharing contribution of $11,152.23 to his plan (20 percent of his $55,761.14 net self-employment earnings). Joe made the profit-sharing contribution prior to filing his company's federal income tax return on March 15.

The following year, Joe's Solo 401(k) assets—specifically, the foreclosed home he purchased—lost some value due to fluctuations in the real estate market. After talking with his tax attorney about tax-planning opportunities, Joe began considering converting his pretax 401(k) funds into a Roth 401(k) plan. Joe knew that since 2016, Solo 401(k) plan participants were permitted to convert a portion or all of their 401(k) plan funds to a Roth Solo 401(k) account. Joe had read that many tax professionals expected tax rates to climb in the coming years and that if he could afford to pay the tax on a Roth conversion today, doing so would be a very wise and tax-efficient decision.

Joe, of course, had to run the numbers first to make sure he could afford to pay the tax on the amount of pretax 401(k) funds he wanted to convert into a Roth 401(k), which was $40,000. He was told by his accountant that he didn't have to convert his entire 401(k) balance at once and could do it over a period of years if he desired. Joe knew he would be able to pay the additional tax on the $40,000 Roth conversion amount, and he understood that the decision to do a Roth 401(k) conversion could be risky if the investments he made with the funds did not work out, since that would require Joe to pay tax on income he would never receive. Yet Joe felt very comfortable that the investments he would be making with the Roth funds would generate income that he would be able to live off tax-free once he turned fifty-nine and a half. In addition, Joe knew he would be satisfying the five-year holding rule since he was well under fifty-four years old.

Accordingly, Joe elected to convert $40,000 of his pretax 401(k) funds into a Roth 401(k) account. Joe simply opened a second account at the financial institution where his Solo 401(k) plan was established and included the word "Roth" in the name of the account so he would be able to differentiate between the two plan accounts. Joe's accountant notified him that the $40,000 of Roth conversion funds would be added to his income for the year and that he would be required to pay tax on that amount. The amount of Joe's Roth conversion would be included on Joe's federal income tax return (IRS Form 1040) under line 15a.

As plan administrator of his Solo 401(k) plan, Joe would issue an IRS Form 1099-R (Distributions from Pensions, Annuities, Retirement, or Profit-Sharing Plans, IRAs, Insurance Contracts, etc.) to himself and also send a copy to the IRS identifying the Roth conversion. Joe would need to include the amount rolled over in Box 1 (gross distribution) as well as include the taxable amount rolled over in Box 2a (taxable amount). Joe's accountant mentioned to Joe that Solo 401(k) plans are not required to withhold 20 percent for an in-plan Roth direct rollover. The 10 percent additional tax on early distributions under Internal Code Section 72(t) does not apply to any amount of an in-plan Roth rollover.

In addition to running his own business, being active with his retirement funds has been satisfying and productive for Joe. He no longer has to sit on his hands and see investment or tax-decision opportunities pass him by and go overlooked by a distant financial planner. He can work his own money, in the way that he understands best, to maximize the opportunities available to him.

Kathy, the Real Estate Agent

Kathy is sixty years old and lives and works in Texas as an independent real estate agent for a local brokerage company. Her husband passed away twenty years ago, and she has never remarried and doesn't have children, so she has been very independent in her work, life, and finances for a long time.

She works out of her house and is paid only on the commissions generated from the sale of homes she works on. Since she is an independent contractor and not an employee, Kathy's tax attorney suggested she form an LLC for limited liability protection. Kathy named her Texas LLC, Kathy Real Estate Investments LLC. She is the only owner of the LLC, and it has no employees other than her.

Seven years ago, based on the advice of her accountant, Kathy established a SEP-IRA at a local bank. Kathy was told that the SEP-IRA offered her the highest deferral opportunities, so she made annual deferral contributions each year. In 2016, Kathy earned $200,000 of self-employment income from Kathy Real Estate Investments LLC. Kathy was able to make a pretax SEP-IRA contribution of $38,000 to her SEP-IRA, or 20 percent of her net self-employment income of $190,272.45.

Shortly thereafter, Kathy spoke to her friend Fred, who is also a real estate agent and sixty-five years old. Fred mentioned that for the 2015 taxable year his accountant suggested he establish an individual 401(k) plan, which is often referred to as a Solo 401(k) plan. Fred also mentioned that he had a surprisingly successful 2014 and was able to defer almost $43,500 into his plan.

Kathy was very surprised that Fred was able to earn $200,000 in income, since he had only been a realtor for several years. She congratulated him on a successful year and cracking the $200K club. Fred answered that he had come nowhere near that level and had actually only earned $110,000 in income. This confused Kathy, who knew the deferral percentage of a SEP-IRA well, and she asked how he was able to put aside so much money when he earned almost 50 percent less than she did. Fred answered that for 2017, with a Solo 401(k) plan, he was able to defer a maximum amount of $60,000, $54,000, plus a $6,000 catch-up since he was over fifty—something the SEP does not offer.

Kathy was amazed by that number and asked Fred for more details. He explained that because a Solo 401(k) plan includes an employee deferral option in addition to a profit-sharing contribution, it actually allows you to make higher contributions than a SEP-IRA. Fred got out a cocktail napkin and began writing down numbers, showing Kathy how he was able to make an $18,000 employee deferral plus a $6,000 catch-up contribution, then also benefit from a profit-sharing contribution of 20 percent of his compensation, which came out to approximately $20,445.75 for 2017. Since he earned $110,000 in income, the profit-sharing contribution amount was based off $102,293.76:

- Net earnings: $110,000
- Calculate 1402(a)(12)deduction: $101,585
- Calculate Medicare and FICA: $15,542.51
- Half of self-employment tax: $7,771.24
- Self-employment income: $102,228.75

Thus, Fred was able to make the following contributions for 2017:

- Maximum 401(k) contribution: $18,000
- Maximum 401(k) catch-up: $6,000
- Maximum profit-sharing contribution: $20,445.75
- Maximum contribution: $44,445.75

Kathy was very impressed with what Fred had told her, so she decided to learn more about the Solo 401(k) plan. She spoke to a tax attorney and decided to establish a Solo 401(k) plan for her business. Since there is no exclusive plan rule for SEP-IRAs and Solo 401(k) plans, she decided to keep both plans open.

A month later, Kathy met Fred for coffee again and mentioned that she had established a Solo 401(k) plan for her business right away. She then asked Fred what type of investments he was doing with his retirement funds. Personally, she had been rocked by the recent turmoil in the stock market. Fred told Kathy that he had decided to purchase real estate with his retirement funds in addition to mutual funds. As a highly successful real estate agent, Kathy was surprised that she had never heard about this option before. Fred assured her that the IRS allows retirement funds to purchase real estate and even states so right on their website.

Kathy went home, did her own research, and set out to determine how she could roll over preexisting retirement funds from a SEP-IRA of $125,000. By rule, individuals may roll over pretax retirement assets in into an eligible employer-sponsored retirement plan if the plan document allows for it. After verifying that a retirement plan will accept IRA rollover contributions, an IRA holder may either directly or indirectly roll over eligible assets. Kathy's accountant gave her the option of doing a direct or indirect rollover. Kathy choose a direct rollover, which is when an IRA holder directly rolls over eligible IRA assets into an eligible retirement plan without tax or penalty and the check is issued in the name of the receiving plan for the benefit of the individual and forwarded as soon as administratively feasible. The sixty-day indirect rollover rule does not apply.

But Kathy wondered if a pretax Traditional IRA could be rolled into a qualified 401(k) plan? The answer, Kathy's accountant assured her, was yes. Only a Roth IRA could not be rolled into a 401(k) plan; all other pretax retirement funds could be rolled. This is because tax-free transfers of qualified plan distributions into other qualified plans, either directly or through intermediate IRAs, help make employee pension rights portable and thus fulfill an important objective of ERISA.

After Kathy rolled over her pretax retirement account of $125,000, she now had a mass amount of money that she wanted to use to invest. After weighing all of her investment opportunities, Kathy decided that she wanted to make an investment in real estate, just as Fred did. Kathy spoke with her tax attorney and confirmed that the plan she adopted allowed for the ability to make nontraditional investments such as real estate. She found a beach property and wanted to jump on it quickly. She knew that real estate was a great long-term investment, and the receipt of rental income and the appreciation of the property's value added to the appeal.

The biggest risks associated with real estate investments are changing economic and environmental conditions in a particular area. Also, because real estate is not cash or a marketable security, selling real estate can be more time consuming than selling a stock or mutual fund. Kathy considered the different ways to invest in real estate, including direct ownership, debt-financed ownership, mortgages, and real estate investment trusts. But Kathy knew that direct ownership was the most suitable vehicle for her given her expertise and experience, and because she had sufficient cash with which to make the investment. An IRA with sufficient liquid assets such as Kathy's could purchase real estate and hold it to generate tax-free income from rent and any gains on the property.

So Kathy rolled over the funds from her pretax retirement account (tax-free and penalty-free) to her Solo 401(k) plan. Kathy understood that no disqualified person (i.e., lineal descendants as in parents, grandparents, children, spouse, daughters-in-law, brothers-in-law, and so on) could use the home or have any direct or indirect involvement with the property, but that if she saw a property that intrigued her and could only afford half the amount, she could partner up with a family member (nondisqualified person), friend, or colleague.

Since Kathy was already sixty, she knew that she had been eligible since the age of fifty-nine and a half to take distributions for any reason from her retirement account without facing a 10-percent penalty. However, ordinary income tax would still be due on all contributions that were previously not taxable. If Kathy desired at that time, distributions in kind could be taken from her Solo 401(k), which means she could take property owned by the plan as a taxable distribution. By taking an in-kind distribution on her property asset, she ensured that even if the property loses money or goes down in value, she will only pay tax on the new house's fair market value compared to the purchase price.

For example, after Kathy purchased a home for $98,000, the housing market flopped two years later, causing her beach property to drop in value to $83,000. But due to this decrease in value, Kathy will only be responsible for paying taxes on the new value of the home instead of the purchased price of the home if she takes the home as an in-kind distribution.

Knowing the risks and having lots of retirement savings money to work with, Kathy set out to build her nest egg even faster than before. Her goal was and still is to keep working, because she enjoys work so much, but to retire in seven years much richer than she would have been otherwise.

Ted, the Consultant

Ted is a sixty-year-old software developer who provides consulting services to start-ups and small businesses throughout the United States. He operates his business though a limited liability company called TSS LLC, of which he is the sole owner. He has no other employees.

Ted's expertise is in the area of database maintenance, and his business has really been growing over the past ten years. He is not ambitious to make his company too large, and he has no desire to take on the responsibility of having full-time employees, but he does have some fairly hefty capital investment needs coming up. Specifically, he wants to spend about $40,000 for new computer equipment and a bigger office.

One day, Ted mentioned those needs to a friend, who suggested that Ted consider adopting a Solo 401(k) and leveraging his own retirement savings to give his business a loan for the capital investments it needs. Ted had $128,000 in his SEP-IRA but not much saved personally, so he was interested in his friend's idea. He would love to save more money and he would love to avoid going deeper into debt to build his business. He decided, as a result, to do some further research by talking to an accountant.

Ted soon learned that if he adopted a Solo 401(k) plan, he would indeed be able to borrow $40,000 tax- and penalty-free, and use those funds for his business. This appealed to Ted. He had been hesitant to apply for a loan from the bank or to use his credit card because he didn't want to add to his debt with high interest rates. A loan feature, Ted's accountant told him, is unique to a Solo 401(k) plan and not available to IRAs. However, not every Solo 401(k) offers a loan feature, Ted's accountant explained, and Ted must make sure that any Solo 401(k) he adopts includes the loan feature in its plan adoption agreement.

The terms of such a loan are surprisingly simple. Ted would need to pay back his Solo 401(k) plan over a five-year period with payments that were at least quarterly at an interest rate of at least Prime as per the *Wall Street Journal*. (When Ted checked the *Journal*, he saw that the Prime rate was 3.25 percent.) Ted then asked whether there were any restrictions as to how he might use such a loan, and Ted's accountant told him that he could use the loan proceeds for any purpose, personal or business. Ted was surprised by this and asked whether that meant he could use some of his loan to pay off some credit card debt. His accountant assured him that the IRS didn't care what he did with the loan proceeds so long as the loan was paid back according to a timely loan repayment schedule, as per the plan documents. The only caution, Ted's accountant added, was that if Ted were ever late on a loan payment, the entire outstanding balance of the loan would automatically be treated as a taxable distribution. However, since Ted was over the age of fifty-nine and a half, a 10 percent early distribution penalty would not apply.

Ted decided that the benefits of a Solo 401(k) plan were well worth his time and effort, so he got a recommendation for a retirement savings expert to get more details about establishing such a plan. The plan provider he contacted told Ted that he was eligible to establish a Solo 401(k) because he was self-employed and had no full-time employees. Ted mentioned that he has an existing SEP-IRA, and the plan provider assured him that he could roll over the funds tax- and penalty-free.

Ted decided to go for it and worked with his plan provider to adopt a Solo 401(k) with a loan feature. Together, they set up the Solo 401(k) plan at a local financial institution, appointing Ted as trustee and plan administrator. Ted was a little reluctant at first to take on the role of plan administrator because he worried that the rules and testing requirements would be complicated and time consuming, but Ted's advisor and bank assured him that ERISA testing rules would not apply to the plan because Ted was the sole owner and employee of the business, and there were no other nonowner employees to cover. In fact, Ted's bank representative said that so long as the asset value of Ted's plan was less than $250,000, there would be no plan testing or annual filing requirements. Ted got a checkbook assigned to his plan and went home.

Five days later, Ted got a rollover check for the total amount of his SEP-IRA funds and deposited that into his new Solo 401(k) account. This completed the very easy process of rolling over his old retirement funds into his new plan. Ted then filled out a Solo 401(k) loan kit and elected to borrow $40,000 and repay it monthly over a five-year period. Ted got a loan payment schedule with all pertinent details from the plan provider company, confirming that he would need to make monthly payments of $723.20 over the next five years. He was excited that the $3,392.01 of interest he would pay over that time would be going back to his plan and actually increase the value of his Solo 401(k) assets. In other words, the $40,000 he was borrowing would become $43,392.01 in five years. It was amazing to Ted that he could leverage up to $50,000 of his 401(k) plan without tax or penalty while actually increasing the value of his assets.

Once the rollover funds deposited into Ted's Solo 401(k) plan became available, Ted used his Solo 401(k) plan checkbook to write a check to himself for $40,000. Ted then went out and bought himself a bigger computer and paid off $10,000 in long-term credit card debt.

Beth, the Doctor

Beth is a thirty-year-old doctor who has just completed her residency at a local hospital. She is lucky enough to secure a job with the university hospital in her town. She's incredibly excited to begin practicing medicine and pleased that she'll be earning $100,000 in her first year.

Beth has a very close relationship with her parents. Her mother is a teacher, and her father is a financial planner. After Beth told her parents about her new job, her father sat her down to explain the opportunity she now has to grow her retirement savings. Beth was not very interested in having the conversation because she felt that she was just getting started in her career while her father was focusing on talking about what life would be like for her when it was over. But, as Beth's father put it, the key to retiring rich is starting young.

Beth's father gave her an example. If her younger brother Joe, who was twenty-five, decided to contribute $5,000 to his retirement savings account for the next ten years, and if Joe is able to earn a 7 percent annual rate of return on his assets, then Joe would have $901,554.63 available to him when he reached the age of seventy. On the other hand, if Beth's ex-boyfriend Mark, who was already thirty-five, finally got his act together and started contributing the same $5,000 for his retirement but did so for the next twenty years, he would only save $662,246.74 by age seventy.

Beth almost couldn't believe her father's math. She had no idea that starting younger and contributing for only ten years could generate so much money for retirement. It seemed almost counterintuitive that someone who put aside twice as much money would have so much less at the end.

That's the power of compounding, her father told her, and he walked her through the numbers again and used different sets of examples to bring the point home. Beth was sold. As a result of her discussion with her father, she began contributing to her hospital's 401(k) plan.

Thirteen years later, Beth left her employment at the hospital to start her own practice. She hired an attorney to form a limited liability company so she could operate her medical practice out of the LLC. Beth was the sole owner and sole full-time employee of the business, though she planned to pay a part-time administrator on a freelance basis once a month and she also expected to engage several medical specialists on a 1099 independent contractor basis.

During her thirteen years of hospital employment, Beth was able to save approximately $107,000 in her 401(k) plan. Her father suggested that she establish a Solo 401(k) plan now. Together, they did some research because Beth was worried about whether having independent contractors and freelancers working for her would violate the terms of a Solo 401(k).

According to the IRS, an employee is not an independent contractor if he or she performs services that can be controlled by an employer (what will be done and how it will be done). This applies even if one is given freedom of action. What matters is whether the employer has the legal right to control the details of how the services are performed. Beth felt comfortable that the workers she wanted to use would not satisfy the definition of an employee and would be treated as an independent contractor for tax purposes. So hiring freelancers and contractors would not be a conflict.

Beth liked what her father was suggesting and elected to adopt a Solo 401(k) plan with her local bank. She then worked with her former employer's plan administrator to complete the direct rollover form so she could roll over her existing 401(k) plan funds into her new Solo 401(k) plan without tax or penalty. Her former employer's plan administrator told her that he would write a rollover check to the name of the Solo 401(k) plan marked FBO (For the Benefit of Her). Ten days later, the check arrived, and she deposited it into her Solo 401(k) plan account.

Beth's private practice became quite successful in the next few years and she decided to hire a full-time assistant. Before doing so, Beth spoke with her CPA about the consequences of hiring a full-time employee with respect to the plan. Beth was told that she would no longer qualify for a Solo 401(k) plan because she would soon have a full-time employee who would become eligible to participate in a retirement plan. Her CPA went on to tell her how she would likely need to amend her plan documents so that they would be covered by ERISA. However, there was a way out, her CPA explained. Beth listened closely.

In 1999, a new twist on the traditional 401(k) plan became available for plan sponsors. This is called the "Safe Harbor 401(k) plan." Under this plan, if employers agree to commit to making a minimum level of contributions to employees (generally 3 percent), then employers adopting the Safe Harbor 401(k) plan do not need to worry about complex ERISA plan testing rules, such as ADP/ACP testing at the end of each year, nor in some cases, the need to make top heavy contributions because Safe Harbor plans have satisfied top heavy requirements since 2002. In general, Beth's CPA assured her that most employers find it easy to make a nonelective contribution of at least 3 percent of each eligible non–highly compensated employee's compensation, regardless of whether the employee actually elects to defer in order to avoid all complex ERISA testing rules.

This sounded quite fair to Beth, and she believed that her new employee would really appreciate the 3 percent match as a way of helping grow her retirement account. Beth was relieved she would not have to cancel her Solo 401(k) plan but merely change it to an ERISA 401(k) plan. Beth's CPA did recommend, however, that Beth consider hiring a third-party record keeper to help administer the plan as well file the annual

IRS Form 5500. Also, as trustee of the plan she would need to purchase a surety bond, but the cost would be very minimal.

Beth was OK with all that but asked how she should decide which investments to make available to her and her employee. Her CPA says that was not his area of expertise and referred her to a certified financial planner who could help her choose between various mutual funds and other financial products as suitable investment products for the 401(k) plan.

Beth then asked whether she could invest in real estate because she had heard that many people with a Solo 401(k) plan did that. Beth's CPA explained that because Beth would have an employee, her plan would no longer be considered a Solo 401(k) and would become subject to ERISA rules. Real estate or other nontraditional investments could pose a liability risk to Beth as the trustee of an ERISA plan. While real estate is permissible for 401(k) plans, it's more suitable for a Solo 401(k) not subject to ERISA—after all, you are not likely to sue yourself over a bad investment. So his advice was that she not put herself in a position where she could be sued by an employee.

Beth appreciated that advice and agreed with it. She then worked with a 401(k) plan document provider company to amend her Solo 401(k) plan into an ERISA 401(k) plan. After that, she went to the financial planner her CPA recommended and set up an investment program for herself and her employee. She established two plan accounts at a financial institution: one for her benefit and one for her employee's benefit. She then contacted her payroll company to inform them that she would be making elective deferrals from her payroll into the 401(k) plan each pay period for her and her employee. Beth went over the exact deduction figures and was told that the funds would automatically be taken from their paychecks and placed in the 401(k) plan account, and then allocated as agreed upon with the financial planner. Beth was really pleased that she would be able to defer a significant amount of income into her 401(k) plan each year as well as help her new employee build up her retirement account with the Safe Harbor match contribution.

Paul and Mark, the Real Estate Developers

Paul is a successful fifty-four-year-old real estate developer who has seen his business grow over the past few years. Paul owns 45 percent of Evergreen Developments Inc., and Paul's son, Mark, thirty-one, owns the remaining 55 percent interest. Evergreen Developments has five full-time employees and is in the business of land developing for single-family-home use. Paul and Mark have now gotten to the point where they feel comfortable taking a sizable salary and feel more confident in their business in light of the fact that they survived the 2008 financial crisis. They decide to become more active with their retirement savings.

Paul and Mark met with their CPA and tax attorney who both suggested that they establish a 401(k) plan for their business so they can begin deferring some of their excess income into the plan and take advantage of available tax deductions while also saving for retirement. Neither Paul nor Mark had any retirement funds and really wanted to establish a 401(k) plan but were reluctant to establish a plan for employees because of the costs involved.

Paul was also concerned about the responsibilities placed on an employer in the case of an ERISA 401(k) plan. He had read recently that an employer with a 401(k) plan must generally make an automatic 3 percent Safe Harbor contribution for each employee based on his or her salary in order to avoid the complex ERISA testing. With Evergreen Developments having three employees in addition to Paul and Mark, and with each employee making more than $60,000 a year, the 401(k) 3-percent match requirement would mean the business would have to make contributions of at least $1,800 a year for each employee. This seemed like a lot of money to Paul, given the company's recent financial difficulties.

Paul and Mark's CPA then suggested that they set up a consulting company. Paul and Mark could be the sole employees of that company and could generate consulting income via the new company, called Paul and Mark Consulting LLC, and then that company could adopt a Solo 401(k) plan for Paul and Mark without including the other three employees of Evergreen Developments. Paul and Mark liked this idea, but their tax attorney nixed it. He said he had heard the same idea many times, but that the IRS was ahead of that game. The IRS has established "controlled group" rules under IRC 414 to prevent business owners from receiving 401(k) plan benefits without offering similar benefits to their employees. The IRS and Department of Labor are concerned that business owners wanting to establish a qualified retirement plan, but not wanting the burden of having to provide benefits to all eligible employees, would create a new separate business that would have no employees other than the owner or executive, and then adopt a Solo 401(k) plan for that company.

In Paul and Mark's case, the tax attorney explained, because the same five or fewer individuals owned at least 80 percent of the stock of Paul and Mark Consulting LLC, the "brother–sister" controlled group rules would be violated and the IRS and Department of Labor would treat Evergreen Developments and Paul and Mark LLC as one company for purposes of determining 401(k) plan eligibility. In other words, those "brother–sister" controlled group rules would prevent Paul and Mark from creating a new company wholly owned by them and adopting a 401(k) plan just for the new company without providing the same 401(k) plan benefits to the three remaining employees at Evergreen Developments. In fact, the tax attorney continued, if Paul and Mark adopted the plan, the three remaining employees would be required to receive the same 401(k) plan benefits offered to them as employees of the new company as if they all worked for the same firm.

Paul and Mark then asked what would happen if they created their own consulting company and generated consulting income that was not related to Evergreen Developments' business activity. The tax attorney chuckled again and said that the IRS had already thought of this as well. Section 414(m) was enacted to prevent such circumvention by expanding the idea of control to separate, but affiliated, entities. An affiliated service group is one type of group of related employers and refers to two or more organizations that have a service relationship and, in some cases, an ownership relationship. The IRS created a category of catch-all types of business that are always considered affiliated service companies. For example, an organization engaged in any one or more of the following fields is a service organization:

- Health
- Law
- Engineering
- Architecture
- Accounting
- Actuarial science
- Performing arts
- Consulting
- Insurance

The tax attorney then explained that because the new company Paul and Mark wanted to establish to circumvent the "controlled group" rules would be a consulting firm and receive income from Evergreen Developments, the affiliated service group rules under Internal Revenue Code 414(m) would prevent Paul and Mark from setting up a new company and then adopting a 401(k) plan just for them without offering benefits to their three employees. Paul and Mark appreciated the advice and decided to adopt a Safe Harbor 401(k) plan for Evergreen Developments, which will be made available to all their employees.

Many Roads to Rome, Some Roadblocks

As you can see from these examples, there are many different reasons for establishing a Solo 401(k) and many benefits to doing so. The Solo 401(k) is ideal for a small business owner, sole proprietor, or self-employed person with no full-time employees. This form of retirement savings plan truly maximizes the amount of money such a person can save for retirement. And the power of such savings, along with the benefit of avoiding unnecessary taxes along the way, enable an individual (especially one who starts putting money aside at a young age) to become wealthy upon retirement.

Moreover, the Solo 401(k) offers such people tremendous flexibility with investments and loans to leverage their own expertise and support their own needs while further building toward their retirement goals.

Life brings many changes, however, and if someone with a Solo 401(k) plan decides to grow their business and add employees, it is easy to transition to an ERISA 401(k) plan and provide Safe Harbor benefit contributions to employees. Unfortunately, some of the investment flexibility of the Solo 401(k) is lost as a result. This is the best course, however, since the IRS and the Department of Labor are vigilant when it comes to protecting the rights of employees to receive the same benefits.

CHAPTER 10

Getting Started

"Three things cannot be long hidden: the sun, the moon, and the truth."

—Buddha

The truth of this book is: you can get rich!

I don't believe in "get rich quick" schemes. If you want to get rich quick, buy a lottery ticket. You won't win, but at least you won't waste a lot of money and effort in the process.

On the other hand, it is remarkably easy to "get rich slow." Building wealth in order to become financially independent in your post-working life is far simpler and more doable than the majority of people realize. If you want to become a millionaire, all you need to do is take a few simple steps, set the course in motion, and go about your life.

The key is to understand that the future is the greatest investment you will ever make. Invest a little of your money in the future, and you will reap significant rewards down the line.

This is not easy. It is remarkably tempting to spend money now. We all have insistent wants and very pressing needs. But if you can defer a few dollars a day and do the right things with that money, that discipline can lead to millions of dollars when you retire.

So how do you get started?

I have found that the people who are the most creative, entrepreneurial, and disciplined in their professional lives face the biggest challenges in saving for retirement. The self-employed architect, the store owner, the engineering consultant, the doctor in private practice, the contract plumber, the website developer, the landscape designer, the real estate agent—such people strive incredibly hard, take calculated risks every day, and achieve more satisfaction and fulfillment through their work than most of the people I know who are employed by corporations or businesses. Yet the independent, creative risk takers confront bigger obstacles when it comes to saving for retirement, such as:

- **Salary:** Few self-employed people have a predictable income. As a result, they find it difficult to save in a consistent way. The ups and downs of income mean they are either paying off debts or putting aside a cushion for the next lean time.
- **Expenses:** For self-employed people, there's a cost-of-doing-business factor that employed people do not need to worry about. Equipment, office space, training, credentials, resources, marketing, and so on—so often extra cash goes to these sorts of needs. When you work for someone else, they usually pay the freight—that's part of the deal.
- **Retirement Plan:** When you are employed by a company or business, chances are you spend a few minutes in your first week on the job with HR or the office accountant to get enrolled in a 401(k) plan. You make a decision about how much of your salary you will defer and where it will go. From that point forward, your retirement contribution will be deducted automatically before your salary hits your bank account, and if you're lucky, your employer will chip in, too. Someone has done the hard work for you, given you a push, and helped build your momentum along the way.

I'm not sure how clearly the government understands the plight of the independent self-employed entrepreneur, but the government does seem to get that such people need extra help when it comes to saving for retirement. The beauty of the Solo 401(k) is that it doesn't just level the playing field, it actually gives you a significant advantage in the game.

As a self-employed person, your income will probably always have ups and downs. The beauty of risk is that it comes with reward. Self-employed people like that empowerment. But a Solo 401(k) allows you to save more money than almost any retirement savings vehicle available to an employed person. So even if you can't have consistency every year, you can save even more on your good years—a lot more. For 2017, you can put aside as much as $54,000 per year tax-free, or $60,000 if you are over age fifty. And you can make your contributions in pretax, after-tax, or Roth dollars as suits your needs so long as the plan documents allow for it.

A self-employed person will always have capital and other expenses that chip away at gross income. But a Solo 401(k) allows you to borrow up to $50,000 tax- and penalty-free to pay for capital and other business or life expenses. And you not only pay back that loan at the lowest interest rate possible, but you add that interest payment to your own retirement savings plan: the definition of a win-win.

A self-employed person does get the support of a company to easily set up a 401(k). But a Solo 401(k) plan is incredibly easy to establish and administer as well. There's no annual tax filing or reporting required if your assets are under $250,000. There's no cumbersome testing to administer. Set costs and annual fees are very low. You can use your local financial institution to hold the account. You have "checkbook control."

And while an employed person may get matching contributions from his employer, a Solo 401(k) gives self-employed people tremendous freedom to invest their plan assets into stocks, mutual funds, real estate, precious metals, and more. They can shelter assets from creditors inside and outside bankruptcy. They can even use nonrecourse leverage for buying real estate without tax, and even receive an opinion letter from the IRS confirming the validity and offering IRS audit protection.

The Solo 401(k) is the most tax advantageous, investor-friendly, low-cost, and easy-to-operate retirement wealth builder available. So why isn't the Solo 401(k) plan more widely known and discussed? It ought to be. I suspect it's less well recognized because it offers you a more unique and tailored approach with more freedom and independence. This means that accountants and financial advisors have to color a little outside the lines to get you set up, and they risk losing your operating costs and investment dollars by letting you in on the secret. It's better for them financially to keep you out of the know and under their control.

However, for the self-employed person, there's just no comparison. The SIMPLE and SEP-IRAs are not as flexible, easy, and powerful as the Solo 401(k). A CPA, tax professional, or retirement expert who has your best interests in mind will let you know that.

Let's say your name is Joe or Diane. You're thirty years old and have no money saved for retirement, so you decide to establish a Solo 401(k) plan. You're not rich by any means. You can only put aside about $67 a week for fifty-two weeks of the year. As a result, you're able, however, to invest $3,500 in your future each year for the next forty years until you retire at age seventy. Let's assume that you can generate a modest annual rate of return of 9 percent and the prevailing tax rate over the course of your working life is 25 percent. By the time you reach retirement, you will have $1,289,022 available in your retirement savings account.

In contrast, if you invested that same $3,500 a year on your own, outside of a tax-deferred retirement savings account, and still earned 9 percent annual rate of return, you would only end up with $699,475. Not bad. But not as much. Your Solo 401(k) plan enables you to build an additional $589,547 of wealth for retirement.

You might be in the same situation as Joe or Diane. And $67 a week might seem incredibly tight for your budget. But I bet it's doable, somehow, someway. And look at what it gets you: over a million for retirement!

Now let's say you get started a little later than that but are making a better income and can put aside $10,000 per year from age forty. And let's say you're more conservative in your investments and average only 7 percent return per year. By age seventy, you'll have over $1 million in retirement savings. That same money, invested through a taxable account, would garner you only $730,000.

The numbers don't lie. Getting rich is an attainable goal. You can start at any age, but starting young is the smartest decision you could ever make. Whether you put away $5,000 or $50,000 per year, you will be a millionaire when you retire.

So what's stopping you?

If you've already established a Solo 401(k) plan, my hat goes off to you. If you haven't, there is no better time than right now. The Solo 401(k) plan is incredibly easy to set up and can help make you rich by retirement. At the same time, it offers you the ability to invest in what you know and understand. You can invest in tangible assets like real estate that are under your control. You can supercharge your returns by using nonrecourse leverage without tax, and make high annual tax-deductible, after-tax, or Roth contributions (up to $54,000, or $60,000 if over the age of fifty, in 2017). You can borrow up to $50,000 for any purpose. In the process, you gain estate planning opportunities and valuable asset and creditor protection.

As Dawson Trotman, a famous evangelist, once said, "The greatest amount of wasted time is the time not getting started."

If you haven't set up a Solo 401(k) plan yet, what's next?

You've read the book.

You understand the advantages of the Solo 401(k).

You know what's possible and what's not permitted.

Are you eligible, or do you plan to be?

Good.

Now go to a retirement savings expert, CPA, or tax accountant, and tell them your plans. If they have your best interests at heart and you meet the Solo 401(k) eligibility requirements, they will support you.

Establish your Solo 401(k) plan.

Start putting aside your money.

Figure out how you can grow that money best.

And go about your life while your retirement wealth builds.

Appendix A

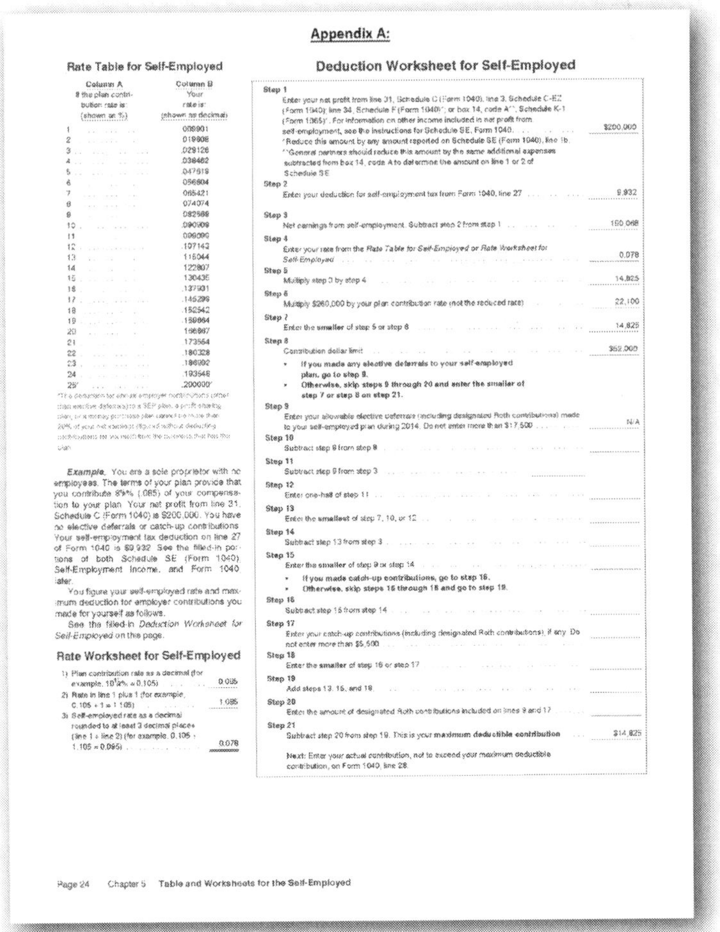

Appendix A:

Rate Table for Self-Employed

Column A If the plan contribution rate is: (shown as %)	Column B Your rate is: (shown as decimal)
1	.009901
2	.019608
3	.029126
4	.038462
5	.047619
6	.056604
7	.065421
8	.074074
9	.082569
10	.090909
11	.099099
12	.107143
13	.115044
14	.122807
15	.130435
16	.137931
17	.145299
18	.152542
19	.159664
20	.166667
21	.173554
22	.180328
23	.186992
24	.193548
25*	.200000*

*The deduction for annual employer contributions (other than elective deferrals) to a SEP plan, a profit-sharing plan, or a money purchase plan cannot be more than 20% of your net earnings (figured without deducting contributions for yourself) from the business that has the plan.

Example. You are a sole proprietor with no employees. The terms of your plan provide that you contribute 8½% (.085) of your compensation to your plan. Your net profit from line 31, Schedule C (Form 1040) is $200,000. You have no elective deferrals or catch-up contributions. Your self-employment tax deduction on line 27 of Form 1040 is $9,932. See the filled-in portions of both Schedule SE (Form 1040), Self-Employment Income, and Form 1040 later.

You figure your self-employed rate and maximum deduction for employer contributions you made for yourself as follows.

See the filled-in *Deduction Worksheet for Self-Employed* on this page.

Rate Worksheet for Self-Employed

1) Plan contribution rate as a decimal (for example, 10½% = 0.105)	0.085
2) Rate in line 1 plus 1 (for example, 0.105 + 1 = 1.105)	1.085
3) Self-employed rate as a decimal rounded to at least 3 decimal places (line 1 ÷ line 2) (for example, 0.105 ÷ 1.105 = 0.095)	0.078

Deduction Worksheet for Self-Employed

Step 1
Enter your net profit from line 31, Schedule C (Form 1040); line 3, Schedule C-EZ (Form 1040); line 34, Schedule F (Form 1040)*; or box 14, code A**, Schedule K-1 (Form 1065)*. For information on other income included in net profit from self-employment, see the instructions for Schedule SE, Form 1040. ... $200,000
*Reduce this amount by any amount reported on Schedule SE (Form 1040), line 1b.
**General partners should reduce this amount by the same additional expenses subtracted from box 14, code A to determine the amount on line 1 or 2 of Schedule SE.

Step 2
Enter your deduction for self-employment tax from Form 1040, line 27 ... 9,932

Step 3
Net earnings from self-employment. Subtract step 2 from step 1 ... 190,068

Step 4
Enter your rate from the *Rate Table for Self-Employed* or *Rate Worksheet for Self-Employed* ... 0.078

Step 5
Multiply step 3 by step 4 ... 14,825

Step 6
Multiply $260,000 by your plan contribution rate (not the reduced rate) ... 22,100

Step 7
Enter the **smaller** of step 5 or step 6 ... 14,825

Step 8
Contribution dollar limit ... $52,000

- **If you made any elective deferrals to your self-employed plan, go to step 9.**
- **Otherwise, skip steps 9 through 20 and enter the smaller of step 7 or step 8 on step 21.**

Step 9
Enter your allowable elective deferrals (including designated Roth contributions) made to your self-employed plan during 2014. Do not enter more than $17,500 ... N/A

Step 10
Subtract step 9 from step 8 ...

Step 11
Subtract step 9 from step 3 ...

Step 12
Enter one-half of step 11 ...

Step 13
Enter the **smallest** of step 7, 10, or 12 ...

Step 14
Subtract step 13 from step 3 ...

Step 15
Enter the **smaller** of step 9 or step 14 ...

- **If you made catch-up contributions, go to step 16.**
- **Otherwise, skip steps 16 through 18 and go to step 19.**

Step 16
Subtract step 15 from step 14 ...

Step 17
Enter your catch-up contributions (including designated Roth contributions), if any. Do not enter more than $5,500 ...

Step 18
Enter the **smaller** of step 16 or step 17 ...

Step 19
Add steps 13, 15, and 18 ...

Step 20
Enter the amount of designated Roth contributions included on lines 9 and 17 ...

Step 21
Subtract step 20 from step 19. This is your **maximum deductible contribution** ... $14,825

Next: Enter your actual contribution, not to exceed your maximum deductible contribution, on Form 1040, line 28.

Page 24 Chapter 5 Table and Worksheets for the Self-Employed

Appendix B

Appendix B

Form **5500-EZ**

Department of the Treasury
Internal Revenue Service

Annual Return of One-Participant (Owners and Their Spouses) Retirement Plan

This form is required to be filed under section 6058(a) of the Internal Revenue Code.
Certain foreign retirement plans are also required to file this form (see instructions).
► **Complete all entries in accordance with the instructions to the Form 5500-EZ.**
► **Information about Form 5500-EZ and its instructions is at *www.irs.gov/form5500ez*.**

OMB No. 1545-0956

2014

This Form is Open to Public Inspection.

Part I **Annual Return Identification Information**

For the calendar plan year 2014 or fiscal plan year beginning (MM/DD/YYYY) **and ending**

A This return is: (1) ☐ the first return filed for the plan; (2) ☐ an amended return; (3) ☐ the final return filed for the plan; (4) ☐ a short plan year return (less than 12 months).

B If filing under an extension of time, check this box (see instructions) ► ☐

C If this return is for a foreign plan, check this box (see instructions) ► ☐

Part II **Basic Plan Information** — enter all requested information.

1a Name of plan	**1b** Three-digit plan number (PN) ►
	1c Date plan first became effective (MM/DD/YYYY)
2a Employer's name	**2b** Employer Identification Number (EIN) (Do not enter your Social Security Number)
Trade name of business (if different from name of employer)	**2c** Employer's telephone number
In care of name	**2d** Business code (see instructions)
Mailing address (room, apt., suite no. and street, or P.O. Box)	
City or town, state or province, country, and ZIP or foreign postal code (if foreign, see instructions)	
3a Plan administrator's name (if same as employer, enter "Same")	**3b** Administrator's EIN
In care of name	**3c** Administrator's telephone number
Mailing address (room, apt., suite no. and street, or P.O. Box)	
City or town, state or province, country, and ZIP or foreign postal code (if foreign, see instructions)	
4a Name of trust (optional)	**4b** Trust's EIN (optional)

5 If the name and/or EIN of the employer has changed since the last return filed for this plan, enter the name, EIN, and plan number for the last return in the appropriate space provided:	**5b**	EIN
a Employer's name	**5c**	PN
6a Total number of participants at the beginning of the plan year	**6a**	
b Total number of participants at the end of the plan year	**6b**	

Part III **Financial Information**

		(1) Beginning of year	(2) End of year
7a Total plan assets	**7a**		
b Total plan liabilities	**7b**		
c Net plan assets (subtract line **7b** from **7a**)	**7c**		

For Privacy Act and Paperwork Reduction Act Notice, see the instructions for Form 5500-EZ. Cat. No. 63263R Form **5500-EZ** (2014)

Form 5500-EZ (2014) Page 2

Part III *(Continued)*

			Amount
8	Contributions received or receivable from:		
a	Employers	8a	
b	Participants	8b	
c	Others (including rollovers)	8c	

Part IV **Plan Characteristics**

9 Enter the applicable two-character feature codes from the List of Plan Characteristics Codes in the instructions:

Part V **Compliance and Funding Questions**

			Yes	No	Amount
10	During the plan year, did the plan have any participant loans? If "Yes," enter amount as of year end	10			
11	Is this a defined benefit plan that is subject to minimum funding requirements? If "Yes," complete Schedule SB (Form 5500) and line 11a below. (See instructions.)	11			
a	Enter the unpaid minimum required contribution for current year from Schedule SB (Form 5500), line 39			11a	
12	Is this a defined contribution plan subject to the minimum funding requirements of section 412 of the Code? If "Yes," complete lines 12a or 12b, 12c, 12d, and 12e below, as applicable:	12			
a	If a waiver of the minimum funding standard for a prior year is being amortized in this plan year, enter the month, day, and year (MM/DD/YYYY) of the letter ruling granting the waiver (see instructions)			12a	
b	Enter the minimum required contribution for this plan year			12b	
c	Enter the amount contributed by the employer to the plan for this plan year			12c	
d	Subtract the amount in line 12c from the amount in line 12b. Enter the result (enter a minus sign to the left of a negative amount)			12d	

			Yes	No	N/A
e	Will the minimum funding amount reported on line 12d be met by the funding deadline?	12e			

Caution. A penalty for the late or incomplete filing of this return will be assessed unless reasonable cause is established.

Under penalties of perjury, I declare that I have examined this return including, if applicable, any related Schedule MB (Form 5500) or Schedule SB (Form 5500) signed by an enrolled actuary, and to the best of my knowledge and belief, it is true, correct, and complete.

Sign Here

Signature of employer or plan administrator | Date | Type or print name of individual signing as employer or plan administrator

Preparer's name (including firm name, if applicable) and address, including room or suite number (optional) | Preparer's telephone number (optional)

Form **5500-EZ** (2014)

Appendix C

Appendix C:

In- Plan Roth Conversion

9898 ☐ VOID ☐ CORRECTED

PAYER'S name, street address, city or town, state or province, country, and ZIP or foreign postal code

Your 401K Plan Name
Street Address
City, State & Zip Code

1 Gross distribution
$ Conversion Amount

2a Taxable amount
$ Conversion Amount

OMB No. 1545-0119
2015
Form 1099-R

Distributions From Pensions, Annuities, Retirement or Profit-Sharing Plans, IRAs, Insurance Contracts, etc.

2b Taxable amount not determined ☐ Total distribution ☐

Copy A For Internal Revenue Service Center

PAYER'S federal identification number
401K Trust EIN

RECIPIENT'S identification number
Your SSN

3 Capital gain (included in box 2a)
$

4 Federal income tax withheld
$ See Below

File with Form 1096.

RECIPIENT'S name
Your Name

5 Employee contributions /Designated Roth contributions or insurance premiums
$

6 Net unrealized appreciation in employer's securities
$

For Privacy Act and Paperwork Reduction Act Notice, see the 2015 General Instructions for Certain Information Returns.

Street address (including apt. no.)
Your Street Address

7 Distribution code(s)
See Below

IRA/SEP/SIMPLE ☐

8 Other
$ %

City or town, state or province, country, and ZIP or foreign postal code
Your City, State & Zip Code

9a Your percentage of total distribution %

9b Total employee contributions
$

10 Amount allocable to IRR within 5 years
$

11 1st year of desig. Roth contrib.

12 State tax withheld
$
$

13 State/Payer's state no.

14 State distribution
$
$

Account number (see instructions)

15 Local tax withheld
$
$

16 Name of locality

17 Local distribution
$
$

Form 1099-R Cat. No. 14436Q www.irs.gov/form1099r Department of the Treasury - Internal Revenue Service

Do Not Cut or Separate Forms on This Page — Do Not Cut or Separate Forms on This Page

When submitting the Form 1099-R you will also need to complete the Form 1096 (Annual Summary and Transmittal of U.S. Information Returns).

In Box 4, you may elect out of federal income tax withholding at the time of conversion. The Roth conversion amount is subject to federal and in some instances state and local income tax. Please consult your tax professional for more details

In Box 7, use code "2" if you are under 59½ years old or "7" if you are 59½ years old or older.

This is an instructional sample to help guide you in filling out a IRS Form 1099-R for your particular situation.

Please remember that you will need to obtain a certified IRS Form to complete and file with the IRS by February 28, 2015.

Appendix D

Appendix D

SEC
OFFICE *of* INVESTOR
EDUCATION *and* ADVOCACY

Investor Alert: Self-Directed IRAs and the Risk of Fraud

The SEC's Office of Investor Education and Advocacy (OIEA) and the North American Securities Administrators Association (NASAA) are issuing this Investor Alert to warn investors of the potential risks associated with investing through self-directed Individual Retirement Accounts (self-directed IRAs). NASAA has noted a recent increase in reports or complaints of fraudulent investment schemes that utilized a self-directed IRA as a key feature. State securities regulators have investigated numerous cases where a self-directed IRA was used in an attempt to lend credibility to a fraudulent scheme. Similarly, the SEC has brought numerous cases in which promoters of fraudulent schemes steered investors to self-directed IRAs. While self-directed IRAs can be a safe way to invest retirement funds, investors should be mindful of potential fraudulent schemes when considering a self-directed IRA. Investors should understand that the custodians and trustees of self-directed IRAs may have limited duties to investors, and that the custodians and trustees for these accounts will generally *not* evaluate the quality or legitimacy of an investment and its promoters. As with every investment, investors should undertake their own evaluation of the merits of a proposal, and should check with regulators about the background and history of an investment and its promoters before making a decision.

I. Investing through Self-Directed IRAs

An Individual Retirement Account (IRA) is a form of retirement account that provides investors with certain tax benefits for retirement savings. Some common examples of IRAs used by investors include the traditional IRA, Roth IRA, Simplified Employee Pension (SEP) IRA, and Savings Incentive Match Plan for Employees (SIMPLE) IRA. All IRA accounts are held for investors by custodians or trustees. These may include banks, trust companies, or any other entity approved by the Internal Revenue Service (IRS) to act as a trustee or custodian.

A self-directed IRA is an IRA held by a trustee or custodian that permits investment in a broader set of assets than is permitted by most IRA custodians. Most IRA custodians are banks and broker-dealers that limit the holdings in IRA accounts to firm-approved stocks, bonds, mutual funds and CDs. Custodians and trustees for self-directed IRAs, however, may allow investors to invest retirement funds in other types of assets such as real estate, promissory notes, tax lien certificates, and private placement securities. While self-directed IRAs may offer investors access to an array of private investment opportunities that are not available through other IRA providers, investments in these kinds of assets may have unique risks that investors should consider. Those risks can include a lack of disclosure and liquidity -- as well as the risk of fraud.

Investor Assistance (800) 732-0330 www.investor.gov

1

II. Self-Directed IRAs and the Risk of Fraud

According to a 2011 report by the Investment Company Institute, U.S. investors held approximately $4.7 trillion in IRAs. Estimates from various sources approximate that investors hold 2 percent, or $94 billion, of IRA retirement funds in self-directed IRAs. The large amount of money held in self-directed IRAs makes them attractive targets for fraud promoters. Fraud promoters also may target other types of retirement accounts by attempting to lure investors into transferring money from those accounts to new self-directed IRAs in order to participate in the fraud promoter's scheme.

In particular, fraud promoters who want to engage in Ponzi schemes or other fraudulent conduct may exploit self-directed IRAs because they permit investors to hold unregistered securities and the custodians or trustees of these accounts likely have not investigated the securities or the background of the promoter. There are a number of ways that fraud promoters may use these weaknesses and misperceptions to perpetrate a fraud on unsuspecting investors. For example:

- Misrepresentations Regarding Custodial Responsibilities – Fraud promoters can misrepresent the responsibilities of self-directed IRA custodians to deceive investors into believing that their investments are legitimate or protected against losses. Fraud promoters often explicitly state or suggest that self-directed IRA custodians investigate and validate any investment in a self-directed IRA. Self-directed IRA custodians are responsible only for holding and administering the assets in a self-directed IRA. Self-directed IRA custodians generally do not evaluate the quality or legitimacy of any investment in the self-directed IRA or its promoters. Furthermore, most custodial agreements between a self-directed IRA custodian and an investor explicitly state that the self-directed IRA custodian has no responsibility for investment performance.

- Exploitation of Tax-Deferred Account Characteristics – Self-directed IRAs are tax-deferred retirement accounts that carry a financial penalty for prematurely withdrawing money before a certain age. This financial penalty may induce self-directed IRA investors to keep funds in a fraudulent scheme longer than those investors who invest through other means. Also, the prospect of an early withdrawal penalty could encourage an investor to become passive with a lesser degree of oversight than a managed account might receive, allowing a fraud promoter to perpetrate his fraud longer.

- Lack of Information for Alternative Investments – Self-directed IRAs usually allow investors to hold alternative investments such as real estate, mortgages, tax liens, precious metals, and private placement securities. Unlike publicly-traded securities, financial and other information necessary to make a prudent investment decision may not be as readily available for these alternative investments. Even when financial information for these alternative investments is available, it may not be audited. Furthermore, self-directed IRA custodians usually do not investigate the accuracy of this financial information. This lack of available information for alternative investments makes them a popular tool for fraud promoters' schemes.

III. Ways to Avoid Fraud with Self-Directed IRAs

Verify information in self-directed IRA account statements. Alternative investments may be illiquid and difficult to value. As a result, self-directed IRA custodians often list the value of the investment as the original purchase price, the original purchase price plus returns reported by the promoter, or a price provided by the promoter. *Investors should be aware that none of these valuations necessarily reflect the price at which the investment could be sold, if at all.*

Investor Assistance (800) 732-0330 www.investor.gov

2

Avoid unsolicited investment offers. Investors should be very careful when they receive an unsolicited investment offer. Whether from a total stranger or from a friend, trusted co-worker, or even family member, investors should ask themselves, "Why would anyone tell me about a really great investment opportunity?" *Investors also should be especially wary of an unsolicited investment offer that promotes the use of a self-directed IRA.* As noted above, fraud promoters may attempt to lure investors into transferring money from traditional IRAs and other retirement accounts into new self-directed IRAs in order to participate in the fraud promoter's scheme.

Ask questions. Always ask if the person offering the investment is licensed and if the investment is registered, then check out the answers with an unbiased source, such as the SEC or your state securities regulator. The SEC has a short publication called "Ask Questions" that discusses many of the other questions investors should ask of anyone who wants them to make an investment. Please take a look at it before making any investment decision.

Be mindful of "guaranteed" returns. Every investment carries some degree of risk, and the level of risk typically correlates with the return an investor can expect to receive. Low risk generally means low yields, and high yields typically involve higher risk. Fraud promoters often spend a lot of time trying to convince investors that extremely high returns are "guaranteed" or "can't miss." Don't believe it. High returns represent potential rewards for investors who are willing and financially able to take big risks.

Ask a professional. For complex investment opportunities, particularly those which involve the opening or creation of a new account outside a traditional financial institution or well-recognized broker, investors should consider getting a second opinion from a licensed unbiased investment professional or an attorney.

IV. Recent Cases Involving Self-Directed IRAs

Some recent examples of SEC and state enforcement cases that involve funds from self-directed IRAs invested in fraudulent schemes include:

SEC v. United American Ventures

The SEC filed charges alleging that two companies and four individuals misrepresented and concealed numerous material facts in connection with the offer and sale of $10 million in bonds to approximately 100 individual investors in various states. In particular, the SEC alleged that the defendants promised guaranteed returns in purported investments in medical technologies and raised money by convincing investors to invest through self-directed IRAs and steering them to custodians who offered the self-directed IRAs. Approximately $3.5 million of the funds invested in the bonds came from self-directed IRAs.

SEC v. Stinson

The SEC filed charges alleging that an individual perpetrated an offering fraud and Ponzi scheme in which at least $16 million was raised from more than 140 investors. In particular, the SEC alleged that the defendant promised "safe and risk free" returns in purported investments in real estate and commercial mortgage loans. The defendant raised money by targeting, among others, investors in self-directed IRAs. Approximately $9.2 million of the funds invested in the fraudulent scheme came from self-directed IRAs.

SEC v. Durmaz

The SEC filed charges alleging that a company and its partners perpetrated a Ponzi scheme in which at least $20 million was raised from more than 120 investors. In particular, the SEC alleged that the defendants promised safe, guaranteed returns in purported investments in foreign bonds and raised money by convincing investors to invest in self-directed IRAs and steering them to custodians who offered the self-directed IRAs. $20 million of the funds invested in the fraudulent scheme came from self-directed IRAs.

Investor Assistance (800) 732-0330 *www.investor.gov*

3

State v. Smith (24C02-1102-FB-00044) and State v. Snelling (24C02-1102-FB-00046) (Indiana)

The Indiana state securities regulators pursued an action alleging that Jerry Smith and Jasen Snelling bilked investors out of more than $4.5 million in a nearly decade-long Ponzi scheme where Mr. Smith and Mr. Snelling told investors they were talented day traders and promised up to 20% returns. Mr. Smith and Mr. Snelling, through various companies, encouraged investors to roll over their traditional IRA accounts into self-directed IRAs at a trust company. Mr. Smith and Mr. Snelling would immediately take the funds from those accounts and use them for personal living expenses, but investors continued to receive statements from the trust company, as well as bills for custodial fees, even after their money was taken out of the accounts. Mr. Smith and Mr. Snelling are charged with more than fifty counts of violations of the Indiana Uniform Securities Act.

In re: Stephen Edward Gwin, et al. (Missouri)

The Missouri Securities Division issued final orders against Stephen Gwin in two separate cases where Mr. Gwin, a federal felon, and others misled senior citizens into investing in unregistered securities, and diverting investment proceeds through self-directed IRAs at trust companies into accounts that Mr. Gwin controlled. Mr. Gwin promoted his million dollar scam through free lunch investment seminars. Mr. Gwin and his co-respondents were found liable and ordered to pay various civil penalties.

Texas v. Warr Investment Group, LLC, et al. (Texas)

The Texas State Securities Board has filed a petition alleging that James Elton Warr through Warr Investment Group LLC and other entities encouraged investors to transfer their funds to a self-directed IRA that was not independent, but instead was secretly controlled by his daughter. According to the petition the Warr entities defrauded the public through their illegal and deceptive sales of securities in real estate investment programs. Mr. Warr claimed that investors would receive a guaranteed 8% annual return and that the real estate investments were a safe and lucrative alternative to more traditional investments such as certificates of deposit and stocks. Mr. Warr and his entities raised at least $970,000 from 30 investors. A Texas court granted the Texas State Securities Board request to freeze Mr. Warr's assets and appoint a receiver to take control of Warr Investment Group LLC and its related entities.

V. Recourse for Fraud Victims

If you have lost money in a fraudulent investment or scheme involving a self-directed IRA or a third-party custodian or trustee, or have information about one of these scams, you should contact:

- The SEC Complaint Center.
- Your state's securities administrator. You can find links and addresses for your state regulator by visiting the North American Securities Administrators Association's website.

You also can check the SEC's Investor Claims Funds webpage for information concerning the appointment of a receiver or claims administrator in any SEC enforcement action.

Investor Assistance (800) 732-0330 *www.investor.gov*

4

Additional Information

For additional educational information for investors, see the SEC's Office of Investor Education and Advocacy's homepage, the SEC's Investor.gov website or NASAA's investor education webpage. For additional information related to avoiding fraud, also see:

- Questions You Should Ask About Your Investments
- How to Avoid Fraud

For additional information regarding IRAs, please see the Internal Revenue Service's IRA Online Resource Guide.

The Office of Investor Education and Advocacy has provided this information as a service to investors. It is neither a legal interpretation nor a statement of SEC policy. If you have questions concerning the meaning or application of a particular law or rule, please consult with an attorney who specializes in securities law.

Appendix E

Appendix E

Form **990-T** | **Exempt Organization Business Income Tax Return (and proxy tax under section 6033(e))** | OMB No. 1545-0687 | **2014**

Department of the Treasury
Internal Revenue Service

For calendar year 2014 or other tax year beginning ________, 2014, and ending ________, 20____.

▶ Information about Form 990-T and its instructions is available at *www.irs.gov/form990t*.

▶ Do not enter SSN numbers on this form as it may be made public if your organization is a 501(c)(3).

Open to Public Inspection for 501(c)(3) Organizations Only

A ☐ Check box if address changed

B Exempt under section
☐ 501( )( )
☐ 408(e) ☐ 220(e)
☐ 408A ☐ 530(a)
☐ 529(a)

C Book value of all assets at end of year

Print or Type:
Name of organization (☐ Check box if name changed and see instructions.)
Number, street, and room or suite no. If a P.O. box, see instructions.
City or town, state or province, country, and ZIP or foreign postal code

D Employer identification number (Employees' trust, see instructions.)

E Unrelated business activity codes (See instructions.)

F Group exemption number (See instructions.) ▶

G Check organization type ▶ ☐ 501(c) corporation ☐ 501(c) trust ☐ 401(a) trust ☐ Other trust

H Describe the organization's primary unrelated business activity. ▶

I During the tax year, was the corporation a subsidiary in an affiliated group or a parent-subsidiary controlled group? ▶ ☐ Yes ☐ No
If "Yes," enter the name and identifying number of the parent corporation. ▶

J The books are in care of ▶ Telephone number ▶

Part I Unrelated Trade or Business Income

		Line	(A) Income	(B) Expenses	(C) Net
1a	Gross receipts or sales				
b	Less returns and allowances / c Balance ▶	1c			
2	Cost of goods sold (Schedule A, line 7)	2			
3	Gross profit. Subtract line 2 from line 1c	3			
4a	Capital gain net income (attach Schedule D)	4a			
b	Net gain (loss) (Form 4797, Part II, line 17) (attach Form 4797)	4b			
c	Capital loss deduction for trusts	4c			
5	Income (loss) from partnerships and S corporations (attach statement)	5			
6	Rent income (Schedule C)	6			
7	Unrelated debt-financed income (Schedule E)	7			
8	Interest, annuities, royalties, and rents from controlled organizations (Schedule F)	8			
9	Investment income of a section 501(c)(7), (9), or (17) organization (Schedule G)	9			
10	Exploited exempt activity income (Schedule I)	10			
11	Advertising income (Schedule J)	11			
12	Other income (See instructions; attach schedule)	12			
13	**Total.** Combine lines 3 through 12	13			

Part II Deductions Not Taken Elsewhere (See instructions for limitations on deductions.) (Except for contributions, deductions must be directly connected with the unrelated business income.)

				Line	
14	Compensation of officers, directors, and trustees (Schedule K)			14	
15	Salaries and wages			15	
16	Repairs and maintenance			16	
17	Bad debts			17	
18	Interest (attach schedule)			18	
19	Taxes and licenses			19	
20	Charitable contributions (See instructions for limitation rules)			20	
21	Depreciation (attach Form 4562)	21			
22	Less depreciation claimed on Schedule A and elsewhere on return	22a		22b	
23	Depletion			23	
24	Contributions to deferred compensation plans			24	
25	Employee benefit programs			25	
26	Excess exempt expenses (Schedule I)			26	
27	Excess readership costs (Schedule J)			27	
28	Other deductions (attach schedule)			28	
29	**Total deductions.** Add lines 14 through 28			29	
30	Unrelated business taxable income before net operating loss deduction. Subtract line 29 from line 13			30	
31	Net operating loss deduction (limited to the amount on line 30)			31	
32	Unrelated business taxable income before specific deduction. Subtract line 31 from line 30			32	
33	Specific deduction (Generally $1,000, but see line 33 instructions for exceptions)			33	
34	**Unrelated business taxable income.** Subtract line 33 from line 32. If line 33 is greater than line 32, enter the smaller of zero or line 32			34	

For Paperwork Reduction Act Notice, see instructions. Cat. No. 11291J Form **990-T** (2014)

Form 990-T (2014) Page **2**

Part III Tax Computation

35	**Organizations Taxable as Corporations.** See instructions for tax computation. Controlled group members (sections 1561 and 1563) check here ▶ ☐ **See instructions** and:		
a	Enter your share of the $50,000, $25,000, and $9,925,000 taxable income brackets (in that order): **(1)** $ **(2)** $ **(3)** $		
b	Enter organization's share of: **(1)** Additional 5% tax (not more than $11,750) $		
	(2) Additional 3% tax (not more than $100,000) $		
c	Income tax on the amount on line 34 ▶	35c	
36	**Trusts Taxable at Trust Rates.** See instructions for tax computation. Income tax on the amount on line 34 from: ☐ Tax rate schedule or ☐ Schedule D (Form 1041) ▶	36	
37	**Proxy tax.** See instructions ▶	37	
38	Alternative minimum tax	38	
39	**Total.** Add lines 37 and 38 to line 35c or 36, whichever applies	39	

Part IV Tax and Payments

40a	Foreign tax credit (corporations attach Form 1118; trusts attach Form 1116)	40a			
b	Other credits (see instructions)	40b			
c	General business credit. Attach Form 3800 (see instructions)	40c			
d	Credit for prior year minimum tax (attach Form 8801 or 8827)	40d			
e	**Total credits.** Add lines 40a through 40d			40e	
41	Subtract line 40e from line 39			41	
42	Other taxes. Check if from: ☐ Form 4255 ☐ Form 8611 ☐ Form 8697 ☐ Form 8866 ☐ Other (attach schedule)			42	
43	**Total tax.** Add lines 41 and 42			43	
44a	Payments: A 2013 overpayment credited to 2014	44a			
b	2014 estimated tax payments	44b			
c	Tax deposited with Form 8868	44c			
d	Foreign organizations: Tax paid or withheld at source (see instructions)	44d			
e	Backup withholding (see instructions)	44e			
f	Credit for small employer health insurance premiums (Attach Form 8941)	44f			
g	Other credits and payments: ☐ Form 2439 ____ ☐ Form 4136 ____ ☐ Other ____ Total ▶	44g			
45	**Total payments.** Add lines 44a through 44g			45	
46	Estimated tax penalty (see instructions). Check if Form 2220 is attached ▶ ☐			46	
47	**Tax due.** If line 45 is less than the total of lines 43 and 46, enter amount owed ▶			47	
48	**Overpayment.** If line 45 is larger than the total of lines 43 and 46, enter amount overpaid ▶			48	
49	Enter the amount of line 48 you want: **Credited to 2015 estimated tax** ▶ Refunded ▶			49	

Part V Statements Regarding Certain Activities and Other Information (see instructions)

		Yes	No
1	At any time during the 2014 calendar year, did the organization have an interest in or a signature or other authority over a financial account (bank, securities, or other) in a foreign country? If YES, the organization may have to file FinCEN Form 114, Report of Foreign Bank and Financial Accounts. If YES, enter the name of the foreign country here ▶		
2	During the tax year, did the organization receive a distribution from, or was it the grantor of, or transferor to, a foreign trust? If YES, see instructions for other forms the organization may have to file.		
3	Enter the amount of tax-exempt interest received or accrued during the tax year ▶ $		

Schedule A—Cost of Goods Sold. Enter method of inventory valuation ▶

1	Inventory at beginning of year	1		6	Inventory at end of year	6	
2	Purchases	2		7	**Cost of goods sold.** Subtract line 6 from line 5. Enter here and in Part I, line 2	7	
3	Cost of labor	3					
4a	Additional section 263A costs (attach schedule)	4a		8	Do the rules of section 263A (with respect to property produced or acquired for resale) apply to the organization?	Yes	No
b	Other costs (attach schedule)	4b					
5	**Total.** Add lines 1 through 4b	5					

Sign Here

Under penalties of perjury, I declare that I have examined this return, including accompanying schedules and statements, and to the best of my knowledge and belief, it is true, correct, and complete. Declaration of preparer (other than taxpayer) is based on all information of which preparer has any knowledge.

▶ Signature of officer | Date | ▶ Title

May the IRS discuss this return with the preparer shown below (see instructions)? ☐Yes ☐No

Paid Preparer Use Only

Print/Type preparer's name	Preparer's signature	Date	Check ☐ if self-employed	PTIN
Firm's name ▶			Firm's EIN ▶	
Firm's address ▶			Phone no.	

Form **990-T** (2014)

Form 990-T (2014) Page **3**

Schedule C—Rent Income (From Real Property and Personal Property Leased With Real Property) (see instructions)

1. Description of property
(1)
(2)
(3)
(4)

	2. Rent received or accrued		3(a) Deductions directly connected with the income in columns 2(a) and 2(b) (attach schedule)
	(a) From personal property (if the percentage of rent for personal property is more than 10% but not more than 50%)	(b) From real and personal property (if the percentage of rent for personal property exceeds 50% or if the rent is based on profit or income)	
(1)			
(2)			
(3)			
(4)			
	Total	Total	(b) Total deductions. Enter here and on page 1, Part I, line 6, column (B) ▶

(c) Total income. Add totals of columns 2(a) and 2(b). Enter here and on page 1, Part I, line 6, column (A) ▶

Schedule E—Unrelated Debt-Financed Income (see instructions)

	1. Description of debt-financed property	2. Gross income from or allocable to debt-financed property	3. Deductions directly connected with or allocable to debt-financed property: (a) Straight line depreciation (attach schedule)	(b) Other deductions (attach schedule)
(1)				
(2)				
(3)				
(4)				

	4. Amount of average acquisition debt on or allocable to debt-financed property (attach schedule)	5. Average adjusted basis of or allocable to debt-financed property (attach schedule)	6. Column 4 divided by column 5	7. Gross income reportable (column 2 × column 6)	8. Allocable deductions (column 6 × total of columns 3(a) and 3(b))
(1)			%		
(2)			%		
(3)			%		
(4)			%		
				Enter here and on page 1, Part I, line 7, column (A).	Enter here and on page 1, Part I, line 7, column (B).
Totals ▶					

Total dividends-received deductions included in column 8 ▶

Schedule F—Interest, Annuities, Royalties, and Rents From Controlled Organizations (see instructions)

Exempt Controlled Organizations

	1. Name of controlled organization	2. Employer identification number	3. Net unrelated income (loss) (see instructions)	4. Total of specified payments made	5. Part of column 4 that is included in the controlling organization's gross income	6. Deductions directly connected with income in column 5
(1)						
(2)						
(3)						
(4)						

Nonexempt Controlled Organizations

	7. Taxable Income	8. Net unrelated income (loss) (see instructions)	9. Total of specified payments made	10. Part of column 9 that is included in the controlling organization's gross income	11. Deductions directly connected with income in column 10
(1)					
(2)					
(3)					
(4)					
				Add columns 5 and 10. Enter here and on page 1, Part I, line 8, column (A).	Add columns 6 and 11. Enter here and on page 1, Part I, line 8, column (B).
Totals ▶					

Form **990-T** (2014)

Form 990-T (2014) Page **4**

Schedule G—Investment Income of a Section 501(c)(7), (9), or (17) Organization (see instructions)

1. Description of income	2. Amount of income	3. Deductions directly connected (attach schedule)	4. Set-asides (attach schedule)	5. Total deductions and set-asides (col. 3 plus col. 4)
(1)				
(2)				
(3)				
(4)				
Totals ▶	Enter here and on page 1, Part I, line 9, column (A).			Enter here and on page 1, Part I, line 9, column (B).

Schedule I—Exploited Exempt Activity Income, Other Than Advertising Income (see instructions)

1. Description of exploited activity	2. Gross unrelated business income from trade or business	3. Expenses directly connected with production of unrelated business income	4. Net income (loss) from unrelated trade or business (column 2 minus column 3). If a gain, compute cols. 5 through 7.	5. Gross income from activity that is not unrelated business income	6. Expenses attributable to column 5	7. Excess exempt expenses (column 6 minus column 5, but not more than column 4).
(1)						
(2)						
(3)						
(4)						
Totals ▶	Enter here and on page 1, Part I, line 10, col. (A).	Enter here and on page 1, Part I, line 10, col. (B).				Enter here and on page 1, Part II, line 26.

Schedule J—Advertising Income (see instructions)

Part I Income From Periodicals Reported on a Consolidated Basis

1. Name of periodical	2. Gross advertising income	3. Direct advertising costs	4. Advertising gain or (loss) (col. 2 minus col. 3). If a gain, compute cols. 5 through 7.	5. Circulation income	6. Readership costs	7. Excess readership costs (column 6 minus column 5, but not more than column 4)
(1)						
(2)						
(3)						
(4)						
Totals (carry to Part II, line (5)) ▶						

Part II Income From Periodicals Reported on a Separate Basis (For each periodical listed in Part II, fill in columns 2 through 7 on a line-by-line basis.)

1. Name of periodical	2. Gross advertising income	3. Direct advertising costs	4. Advertising gain or (loss) (col. 2 minus col. 3). If a gain, compute cols. 5 through 7.	5. Circulation income	6. Readership costs	7. Excess readership costs (column 6 minus column 5, but not more than column 4).
(1)						
(2)						
(3)						
(4)						
Totals from Part I ▶						
Totals, Part II (lines 1-5) ▶	Enter here and on page 1, Part I, line 11, col. (A).	Enter here and on page 1, Part I, line 11, col. (B).				Enter here and on page 1, Part II, line 27.

Schedule K—Compensation of Officers, Directors, and Trustees (see instructions)

1. Name	2. Title	3. Percent of time devoted to business	4. Compensation attributable to unrelated business
(1)		%	
(2)		%	
(3)		%	
(4)		%	
Total. Enter here and on page 1, Part II, line 14 ▶			

Form **990-T** (2014)

Appendix F

Appendix F:

IRS FORM 5500-EZ

HOW TO REPORT THE FAIR MARKET VALUE OF ASSETS HELD BY YOUR SOLO 401K PLAN TO THE IRS

The Internal Revenue Service ("IRS") Form 5500-EZ is an annual information return that is required to be filed by every "One-Participant Plan" (owners and their spouses), also known as a Solo 401(k) Plan, with plan asset value in excess of $250,000 as of December 31 of the previous tax year. The purpose of filing and reporting the fair market value ("FMV") of your solo 401(k) plan's assets is to inform the IRS of assets over $250,000.00 annually held in a Solo 401(k) Plan. You must file the Form 5500-EZ if a plan meets the requirements alone or combined with any other qualified retirement plan owned greater than 80% by the business owner or a related party (one controlled group) exceeding $250,000.00.

You do not have to file the form 5500-EZ for a plan year for a one-participant plan if the total of the plan's assets and the assets of all other one-participant plans maintained by the employer at the end of the plan year does not exceed $250,000.00, unless the current year is the final plan year of the plan.

FILING TIPS:

- The Form 5500-EZ is due every **July 31st** of the next plan year. Ex: for a plan that was established in 2015, the IRS Form 5500-EZ is due by July 31st, 2016. If the filling date falls on a Saturday, Sunday, or legal holiday it may be filed on the next day that is not.

- The Form 5500-EZ must be filed as a **hard copy** and sent directly to the IRS at the following address:

  Department of the Treasury

  Internal Revenue Service

  Ogden, UT 84201-0020

- To file the Form 5500-EZ using a private delivery service, you must use the approved IRS Designated providers (PDS) as follows:

- **DHL Express (DHL): Same Day Service.**

Federal Express (FedEx): Priority Overnight, Standard Overnight, FedEx 2 Day, FedEx International Priority and FedEx International First.
United Parcel Service (UPS): UPS Next Day Air, UPS Net Day Air Saver, UPS 2nd Day Air A.M., UPS Worldwide Express Plus, and UPS Worldwide Express.

The Private delivery services should use the following address:

Internal Revenue Service
1973 Rulon White Blvd.
Ogden, UT 84404

- The Form 5500-EZ **cannot** be e-filed electronically.
- The Plan Administrator or employer (owner) must use the official printed paper Form 5500-EZ obtained from the IRS, and use blue or black ink for a wet signature. **NO ELECTRONIC SIGNATURE ALLOWED**. Print, **sign** and **date** before mailing.
- **Do not** use a felt tip pen or other inks that bleed through, the other side should be blank.
- **Do not** use arrows or make notes on the Form 5500-EZ and only enter information in the specific fields provided. Abbreviate if necessary.
- **Do not** include schedules or attachments. However, you should retain them for your records.

PENALTIES:

The Internal Revenue Code imposes a penalty of **$25 a day (up to $15,000)**.

COMPLETING THE IRS FORM 5500-EZ

Attached please find a sample IRS Form 5500-EZ, which has been completed based on the responses to the questions below. The attached form should serve as a guide to assist you in successfully completing the IRS Form 5500-EZ.

PART I - Annual Return identification Information:

Enter the beginning date of the plan and then the ending date.

A) Check **(1)** the first return filed for the plan;

B) Typically, do not check this box unless filed Form 5558 for an extension of time.

C) Typically, do not check this box unless this plan is maintained outside the United States.

PART II – Basic Plan Information:

1a) Enter the name of the plan as it appears on the EIN letter from the IRS: **ABC CONSULTING 401K TRUST**.

1b) Enter the numbers **001** for this year and every year's future fillings use the same number. Note – if this plan will be amending an existing solo 401(k) Plan, you will need to include the appropriate 3 digit code (i.e. 002), which can be found in the plan Adoption Agreement.

1c) Enter **01-01-2015** as of the date the plan became effective.

2a) Enter the name of the Adopting Employer:

ABC Consulting LLC.

dba or c/o if applicable.

1234 Ginger Street
(P.O. Box ONLY if USPS does no does not deliver).
Family, FL 55555.

2b) Enter the Adopting Employer EIN **XX-XXXXXXX** no SS#. If plan is under a Sole Proprietor, **YOU MUST OBTAIN AN EIN FROM THE IRS** by completing the online application:

Apply for an EIN

Alternatively, you can acquire an EIN by preparing and faxing the Form SS-4 to the IRS at 1-800-829-3676 then call 1-800-829-4933 to receive your EIN by phone. The EIN is issued immediately once the application information is validated.

2c) Enter the Adopting Employer telephone number: **888-888-8888**.

2d) Enter the 6 digit applicable code **XXXXXX** that best describes the nature of the plan sponsors business from the list of principal business activity codes included at the end of these instructions.

3a) Enter the Plan Administrator information **OPTIONAL**. If preparer is the same as above, enter the same information.

3b) Enter and repeat the same EIN **XX-XXXXXXX** number as listed in **2b**.

3c) Enter the Plan Administrator telephone number: **888-888-8888**.

4a) Enter the name of the Trust: **ABC CONSULTING 401K TRUST**.

4b) Enter the EIN number as it appears on the EIN letter from the IRS: **XX-XXXXXXX**.

5a), 5b) and 5c) is not required if no changes were made to the plan.

6a) Enter the total number of participants at the beginning of the year. If solo 401K plan: Ex: 1 participant. Note – if the plan will include the spouse of a participant or a second business owner, then the appropriate number would need to be included (i.e. 2).

6b) Enter the total number of participants at the end of the plan year. If solo 401K plan: Ex: 1 participant. Note – if the plan will include the spouse of a participant or a second business owner, then the appropriate number would need to be included (i.e. 2).

PART III – Financial Information:

7a(1) Enter the "Total Plan Assets" or the same amount in 7a(2) from last year; if filed Form 5500-EZ previously. Otherwise, this figure includes "Total Plan Assets" as: rollovers, unrealized gains and losses such as appreciation/depreciation in assets. It also includes specific assets held by the plan at any time during the plan year (for example, partnership/joint venture interests, employer real property, real estate (other than employer real property), employer securities, loans (participants and non-participant loans), and tangible personal property). **Please do not include contributions**.

7a(2) Enter end of year "Total Plan Assets" as listed above. **Please do not include contributions**.

7b(1) Enter "Total plan liabilities" to include but are not limited to benefit claims payable, operating payables, acquisition indebtedness (i.e. nonrecourse loan) and other liabilities. Do not include the value of future distributions what will be made to participants.

7b(2) Enter end of year "Total plan liabilities" as listed above.

7c(1) Enter "Net plan assets" the sum of by subtracting 7b(1) from 7a(1).

7c(2) Enter end of the year "Net plan assets" sum of by subtracting 7b(2) from 7a (2).

8a) and 8b) Enter total cash contributions received and/or receivable from employer and participants during the plan year.

8c) Enter all contributions including rollovers received from other plans valued on the date of contribution.

PART IV – Plan Characteristics:

9) Enter the applicable two-character feature Codes. In most cased, the following codes would be used: **2E, 2J, 3B, 3D. Note, if your plan assets are held in a brokerage account, then you would want to include 2R**.

PART V – Compliance and Funding Questions:

10) Check **YES** if any of the participants entered into a loan from the plan and the amount or **NO** if not applicable.

11) Check **NO**.

11a) Enter **N/A** for amount.

DO NOT complete any information for 12a) , 12b) , 12c) , 12d) and 12e). This pertains to a defined benefit plan.

For additional instructions on completing the IRS Form please contact the IRS Help Line at **1-877-829-5500** or consult with your tax professional or CPA.

Appendix G

Appendix G

IRS IRA Required Minimum Distribution Worksheet

Use this worksheet to figure this year's required withdraw for your traditional IRA UNLESS your spouse[1] is the sole beneficiary of your IRA and he or she is more than 10 years younger than you.

Deadline for receiving required minimum distribution:

- Year you turn age 70 ½ - by April 1 of the following year
- All subsequent years - by December 31 of that year

1. **IRA balance[2] on December 31 of the previous year.** $________
2. **Distribution period from the table below for your age on your birthday this year.** ________
3. **Line 1 divided by number entered on line 2. This is your required minimum distribution for this year from this IRA.** $________
4. **Repeat steps 1 through 3 for each of your IRAs.**

Table III (Uniform Lifetime)

Age	Distribution Period	Age	Distribution Period	Age	Distribution Period	Age	Distribution Period
70	27.4	82	17.1	94	9.1	106	4.2
71	26.5	83	16.3	95	8.6	107	3.9
72	25.6	84	15.5	96	8.1	108	3.7
73	24.7	85	14.8	97	7.6	109	3.4
74	23.8	86	14.1	98	7.1	110	3.1
75	22.9	87	13.4	99	6.7	111	2.9
76	22.0	88	12.7	100	6.3	112	2.6
77	21.2	89	12.0	101	5.9	113	2.4
78	20.3	90	11.4	102	5.5	114	2.1
79	19.5	91	10.8	103	5.2	115 and over	1.9
80	18.7	92	10.2	104	4.9		
81	17.9	93	9.6	105	4.5		

Once you determine a separate required minimum distribution from each of your traditional IRAs, you can total these minimum amounts and take them from any one or more of your traditional IRAs.

For additional information, see:

- Publication 590-B, *Distributions from Individual Retirement Arrangements (IRAs)*
- Retirement Topics – Required Minimum Distributions

[1] Generally, your marital status is determined as of January 1 of each year. If your spouse is the beneficiary of your IRA on January 1, he or she remains a beneficiary only for purposes of calculating the required minimum distribution for that IRA even if you get divorced or your spouse dies during the year.

[2] You must increase your IRA balance by any outstanding rollover and recharacterized Roth IRA conversions that were not in any traditional IRA on December 31 of the previous year.

Appendix H

Appendix H

(Single Life Expectancy)
(For Use by Beneficiaries)
As Indicated in IRS Publication 590-B

Age	Life Expectancy	Age	Life Expectancy
0	82.4	56	28.7
1	81.6	57	27.9
2	80.6	58	27.0
3	79.7	59	26.1
4	78.7	60	25.2
5	77.7	61	24.4
6	76.7	62	23.5
7	75.8	63	22.7
8	74.8	64	21.8
9	73.8	65	21.0
10	72.8	66	20.2
11	71.8	67	19.4
12	70.8	68	18.6
13	69.9	69	17.8
14	68.9	70	17.0
15	67.9	71	16.3
16	66.9	72	15.5
17	66.0	73	14.8
18	65.0	74	14.1
19	64.0	75	13.4
20	63.0	76	12.7
21	62.1	77	12.1
22	61.1	78	11.4
23	60.1	79	10.8
24	59.1	80	10.2
25	58.2	81	9.7
26	57.2	82	9.1
27	56.2	83	8.6
28	55.3	84	8.1
29	54.3	85	7.6
30	53.3	86	7.1
31	52.4	87	6.7
32	51.4	88	6.3
33	50.4	89	5.9
34	49.4	90	5.5
35	48.5	91	5.2
36	47.5	92	4.9
37	46.5	93	4.6
38	45.6	94	4.3
39	44.6	95	4.1
40	43.6	96	3.8
41	42.7	97	3.6
42	41.7	98	3.4
43	40.7	99	3.1
44	39.8	100	2.9
45	38.8	101	2.7
46	37.9	102	2.5
47	37.0	103	2.3
48	36.0	104	2.1
49	35.1	105	1.9
50	34.2	106	1.7
51	33.3	107	1.5
52	32.3	108	1.4
53	31.4	109	1.2
54	30.5	110	1.1
55	29.6	111 and over	1.0

Appendix I

Appendix I:

Required Minimum Distribution

9898 ☐ VOID ☐ CORRECTED

PAYER'S name, street address, city or town, state or province, country, and ZIP or foreign postal code

Your 401K Plan Name
Street Address
City, State & Zip Code

1 Gross distribution
$ Distribution Amount

2a Taxable amount
$ Distribution Amount

OMB No. 1545-0119

2015

Form 1099-R

Distributions From Pensions, Annuities, Retirement or Profit-Sharing Plans, IRAs, Insurance Contracts, etc.

2b Taxable amount not determined ☐ Total distribution ☐

Copy A For Internal Revenue Service Center

File with Form 1096.

PAYER'S federal identification number: 401K Trust EIN

RECIPIENT'S identification number: Your SSN

3 Capital gain (included in box 2a) $

4 Federal income tax withheld $ See Below

RECIPIENT'S name: Your Name

5 Employee contributions /Designated Roth contributions or insurance premiums $

6 Net unrealized appreciation in employer's securities $

For Privacy Act and Paperwork Reduction Act Notice, see the **2015 General Instructions for Certain Information Returns.**

Street address (including apt. no.): Your Street Address

7 Distribution code(s): See Below IRA/ SEP/ SIMPLE ☐

8 Other $ %

City or town, state or province, country, and ZIP or foreign postal code: Your City, State & Zip Code

9a Your percentage of total distribution %

9b Total employee contributions $

10 Amount allocable to IRR within 5 years $

11 1st year of desig. Roth contrib.

12 State tax withheld $ $

13 State/Payer's state no.

14 State distribution $ $

Account number (see instructions)

15 Local tax withheld $ $

16 Name of locality

17 Local distribution $ $

Form 1099-R Cat. No. 14436Q www.irs.gov/form1099 Department of the Treasury - Internal Revenue Service

Do Not Cut or Separate Forms on This Page — Do Not Cut or Separate Forms on This Page

When submitting the Form 1099-R you will also need to complete the Form 1096 (Annual Summary and Transmittal of U.S. Information Returns).

In Box 4, withholding is 10% of your minimum distribution. Any amount above the required minimum distribution is subject to 20% withholding.

In Box 7, use code "1" if you are under 59½ years old or "7" if you are 59½ years old or older.

This is an instructional sample to help guide you in filling out a IRS Form 1099-R for your particular situation.

Please remember that you will need to obtain a certified IRS Form to complete and file with the IRS by February 28, 2015.

Appendix J

Traditional Distribution

9898 ☐ VOID ☐ CORRECTED

PAYER'S name, street address, city or town, state or province, country, and ZIP or foreign postal code

Your 401K Plan Name
Street Address
City, State & Zip Code

1 Gross distribution
$ Distribution Amount

2a Taxable amount
$ Distribution Amount

OMB No. 1545-0119
2015
Form 1099-R

Distributions From Pensions, Annuities, Retirement or Profit-Sharing Plans, IRAs, Insurance Contracts, etc.

2b Taxable amount not determined ☐ Total distribution ☐

Copy A For Internal Revenue Service Center

File with Form 1096.

PAYER'S federal identification number
401K Trust EIN

RECIPIENT'S identification number
Your SSN

3 Capital gain (included in box 2a)
$

4 Federal income tax withheld
$ See Below

RECIPIENT'S name
Your Name

5 Employee contributions /Designated Roth contributions or insurance premiums
$

6 Net unrealized appreciation in employer's securities
$

For Privacy Act and Paperwork Reduction Act Notice, see the **2015 General Instructions for Certain Information Returns.**

Street address (including apt. no.)
Your Street Address

7 Distribution code(s)
See Below

IRA/ SEP/ SIMPLE ☐

8 Other
$ %

City or town, state or province, country, and ZIP or foreign postal code
Your City, State & Zip Code

9a Your percentage of total distribution %

9b Total employee contributions
$

10 Amount allocable to IRR within 5 years
$

11 1st year of desig. Roth contrib.

12 State tax withheld
$
$

13 State/Payer's state no.

14 State distribution
$
$

Account number (see instructions)

15 Local tax withheld
$
$

16 Name of locality

17 Local distribution
$
$

Form 1099-R Cat. No. 14436Q www.irs.gov/form1099r Department of the Treasury - Internal Revenue Service

Do Not Cut or Separate Forms on This Page — Do Not Cut or Separate Forms on This Page

When submitting the Form 1099-R you will also need to complete the Form 1096 (Annual Summary and Transmittal of U.S. Information Returns).

In Box 4, withholding is 20% of your total distribution.

In Box 7, use code "1" if you are under 59½ years old or "7" if you are 59½ years old or older.

This is an instructional sample to help guide you in filing out a IRS Form 1099-R for your particular situation.
Please remember that you will need to obtain a certified IRS Form to complete
and file with the IRS by February 28, 2015.

45496984R00194

Made in the USA
San Bernardino, CA
09 February 2017